TWENTIETH-C

Twentieth-Century Gothic

Lucie Armitt

UNIVERSITY OF WALES PRESS
CARDIFF
2011

www.uwp.co.uk

British Library CIP Data
A catalogue record for this book is available from the British Library.

ISBN   978-0-7083-2007-5 (hardback)
        978-0-7083-2043-3 (paperback)
e-ISBN 978-0-7083-2362-5

Typeset by Eira Fenn Gaunt at the University of Wales Press
Printed on demand by CPI Group (UK) Ltd, Croydon, CR0 4YY

CONTENTS

SERIES EDITORS' FOREWORD

The History of the Gothic series consists of four volumes: *Gothic Literature 1764–1824, Gothic Literature 1825–1914, Twentieth-Century Gothic* and *American Gothic.* The series provides a comprehensive introduction to the history of Gothic Literature and to a variety of critical and theoretical approaches. Volumes in the series also raise questions about how the Gothic canon has been received and seek to critically challenge, rather than simply reaffirm, commonplace perceptions of the Gothic tradition. Whilst intended as an introduction to the history of the Gothic they thus also provide a rigorous analysis of how that history has been developed and suggest ways in which it can be critically renegotiated.

The series will be of interest to students of all levels who are new to the Gothic and to scholars and teachers of the history of Gothic Literature. The series will also be of interest to students and scholars working more broadly within the areas of literary studies, cultural studies, and critical theory.

Andrew Smith, University of Glamorgan
Benjamin F. Fisher, University of Mississippi

Acknowledgements

More years ago than I care to remember, Nickianne Moody lent me two books, Joseph Grixti, *Terrors of Uncertainty* (London: Routledge, 1989), and James B. Twitchell, *Dreadful Pleasures* (New York: Oxford University Press, 1985). I enjoyed them so much I never got around to returning them; this is both to thank Nickianne for her generosity in setting me off on a path that ultimately resulted in this book and to offer a grovelling apology. Another important milestone in this journey was a kind invitation by Anna Powell, back in 1994, to speak at her day conference on the Gothic at Manchester Metropolitan University. It was to prove not only a day that marked my entry into the arena of Gothic criticism but one that sealed my personal happiness. I am more grateful to Anna than she knows.

Many thanks are due to Andrew Smith for inviting me to contribute this volume to the series. Professor David Punter has been a long-term mentor and support and I wish to acknowledge the importance of that here, along with my gratitude. I also wish to express my gratitude to colleagues at the University of Salford, especially Gaynor Bagnall, for her friendship in desperate and not so desperate times, and the irrepressible and inspirational Jane Kilby. Many thanks are due to colleagues in the Gender Reading Group at Salford, with whom I have shared a number of joyful and informative debates, and to Mike Freeman and Matt Mason for their technical support. I especially acknowledge the input of my students on 'Twenty-First-Century Women's Fiction' at the University of Salford, particularly the class of 2008, in dialogue with whom I shaped my reading of 'The Thing in the Forest' (see chapter 1). Specifically in relation to the intertexual connection between the ending of that story and 'Little Red Riding Hood', I would single out Lee Beales for particular acknowledgement.

Some of the work included in this volume has appeared previously in earlier or partial form. A section of the material on *Fingersmith* in chapter 4 is already published in 'Dark Departures: Contemporary Women's Writing after the Gothic' in Benjamin A. Brabon and Stéphanie Genz (eds), *Postfeminist Gothic: Critical Interventions in Contemporary Culture* (Basingstoke: Palgrave Macmillan, 2007), pp. 16–29. Some of the material on *The Little Stranger* appearing here in chapter 6, was published as 'Garden Paths and Blind Spots' in *New Welsh Review*, 85 (2009). I am grateful to Stéphanie and Ben and to Kathryn Gray, Editor of *New Welsh Review*, for their kind permission to reproduce that material here. Co-writing (with Sarah Gamble) 'Haunted Geometries', published in *Textual Practice* in 2006, helped inform my subsequent understanding of architecture (especially the work of Escher and Piranesi) within a contemporary Gothic frame and has enabled the more recent developments of those ideas included here in chapter 2. I am grateful to Sarah for her collegial friendship, not to mention the kind donation of her copy of Steve Szilagyi's *Photographing Fairies*. Additionally, invited papers at University College London, the universities of Oxford, Hull, Edge Hill and Bolton, and at the Salford Film Seminar have enabled me to air some of these ideas with my peers. I here gratefully acknowledge the input of all who attended and participated in the resulting discussions and especially thank Nadine Muller, Matthew Gandy and Johan Anderssen, Ann Heilmann, Stéphanie Genz and Ben Brabon, David Rudd, Peter Buse and Andy Willis for their kind invitations.

All academic works of literary criticism rely on the close discussion of primary material and I am especially grateful to the following for permission to quote from these works: 'The Thing in the Forest', in *Little Black Book of Stories* by A. S. Byatt, published by Chatto & Windus. Reprinted by permission of The Random House Group Ltd., copyright © 2003 A. S. Byatt. Reproduced by permission of the author c/o Rogers, Coleridge & White Ltd., 20 Powis Mews, London W11 1JN; *The Name of the Rose*, by Umberto Eco, translated by William Weaver, published by Secker and Warburg, reprinted by permission of The Random House Group Ltd; *The Seventh Horse and Other Tales*, by Leonora Carrington, published by Virago Press, an imprint of Little, Brown Book Group; *The Wasp Factory*, by Iain Banks, published by Abacus, an imprint of Little, Brown Book Group; 'The Angel' and *Dr Haggard's Disease*, by Patrick McGrath, Gregory and Company Authors' Agents, 3 Barb Mews, London W6 7PA;

Fingersmith © Sarah Waters 2002, *The Night Watch* © Sarah Waters 2006, *The Little Stranger* © Sarah Waters 2009. Reproduced by kind permission of Virago, an imprint of Little, Brown Book Group; 'The Birds', by Daphne Du Maurier, reproduced with permission of Curtis Brown Group Ltd London on behalf of the Chichester Partnership, copyright © Daphne du Maurier 1952; *The Hellbound Heart*, by Clive Barker, copyright © 1991 by Clive Barker, reprinted by permission of HarperCollins publishers. Sustained efforts have been made to trace copyright holders for all primary material discussed in this book, but it has not been possible to trace them in all cases. The author apologises for any resulting omission and requests that the copyright holder contact the publisher in any such case.

As ever, my wholehearted gratitude and devotion go to my children, Bethany and Rowan, for tolerance and understanding well beyond their years, and to Scott for coming to my paper at MMU all those years ago. The whole book is in dearest memory of my Mum, Jean Armitt, who died during its final stages.

1886   Robert Louis Stevenson publishes *The Strange Case of Dr Jekyll and Mr Hyde*, his first really successful book. Its influence is perhaps greater than any other on the twentieth-century Gothic.

1891   Oscar Wilde publishes *The Picture of Dorian Gray*, a narrative which continues to exert an influence over Gothic narratives throughout the twentieth century, particularly, though not exclusively, those connected with homosocial and homosexual male characters.

1892   Charlotte Perkins Gilman publishes *The Yellow Wallpaper*, a story originally published as a ghost story but adopted by many, during the Second Wave feminist movement of the 1970s and 1980s, as a 'textbook' narrative for the politicisation of female hysteria. Its impact on ghost narratives remains evident, nevertheless, especially on those by female writers.

1897   Bram Stoker publishes *Dracula*, a narrative twentieth-century critics will associate with fears of contagion relating to the *fin de siècle* syphilis outbreak across Britain and Europe.

1898   Henry James, in *The Turn of the Screw*, introduces the concept of the 'unspeakable' in relation to the corruption and untimely death of children. Its influence continues to be felt throughout the twentieth century, especially in the later decades, as social paranoia regarding paedophilia and children's safety reach epidemic proportions.

1902   Sir Arthur Conan Doyle publishes *The Hound of the Baskervilles*, the best known of the Sherlock Holmes stories, made into a classic movie, starring Basil Rathbone, in 1939.

1904 J. M. Barrie writes *Peter Pan* for the theatre. The first run had 145 performances and its popularity continued throughout the twentieth century, reputedly having peaked during the First World War among young men about to be conscripted.

1908 Henry James writes 'The Jolly Corner', published in *The Altar of the Dead and Other Tales* in 1909.

1914–18 The First World War, an event that continues to haunt Gothic narratives throughout the century. Both Conan Doyle and Kipling lose sons to this war.

1915 Rudyard Kipling first publishes 'Swept and Garnished'; he loses his son, John (aged 17), in the same year.

1917–20 Elsie Wright and Frances Griffiths take photographs purportedly of fairies in the Yorkshire village of Cottingley, these being the inspiration for Steve Szilagyi's novel *Photographing Fairies* (1995), Nick Willing's film adaptation of the same name (1997) and a further, more child-oriented film, *Fairy Tale: A True Story* (1997). How the girls accomplished the technical trickery required has never been fully understood, but Elsie finally confessed that they were fakes to the *British Journal of Photography* in 1983.

1919 Sigmund Freud publishes his landmark essay, 'The Uncanny', one that continues to frame our understanding not only of the uncanny, but also of the twentieth-century Gothic.

1919 Wiene directs the classic silent movie *The Cabinet of Dr Caligari*, reputed to have cost 18,000 dollars (*Halliwell's Film Video and DVD Guide*, 2005).

1921 Murnau directs another classic monster movie, *Nosferatu*, based on Stoker's *Dracula*.

1923 M. R. (Montague Rhodes) James writes 'The Haunted Dolls' House' for the library of Her Majesty the Queen's Doll's House (M. R. James, 'Preface' to *Ghost Stories of M. R. James* (1931; Harmondsworth: Penguin, 1994)).

1924 E. M. Forster publishes *A Passage to India*, a novel in which the uncanny aspects of the Marabar Caves are explored as a means of exposing the differences between British Imperialism and colonised India during the early decades of the twentieth century.

1937–40   During this period Leonora Carrington writes 'The Skeleton's Holiday', 'As They Rode Along the Edge', 'The Sisters' and 'The Débutante'. Her work remained in comparative obscurity until much later in the century, 'The Débutante' being anthologised by Angela Carter in her collection of stories *Wayward Girls and Wicked Women* (London:Virago, 1986) and the other three in Carrington's own collection, *The Seventh Horse and Other Tales* (London: Virago, 1988).

1938   Publication of Daphne Du Maurier's *Rebecca*, a narrative that shapes our subsequent understanding of the female Gothic, and which was made into a classic film by Alfred Hitchcock in 1941. Elements of Du Maurier's Manderley can be identified in Sarah Waters's depiction of Hundreds Hall in *The Little Stranger* (2009).

1939–45   The Second World War, an event that manifests itself in twentieth-century Gothic narratives in the form of burnt-out buildings and (in the case of A. S. Byatt's 'The Thing in the Forest') the fears of evacuated children.

1945   Elizabeth Bowen writes 'The Demon Lover', one of several Gothic narratives exploring the uncanny aspects of London in the Blitz.

1952   Daphne Du Maurier publishes her story 'The Birds' in a collection titled *The Apple Tree* (Victor Gollancz). Such is the popularity of the movie that this story collection initially published as *The Apple Tree* has now been republished under the title *The Birds and Other Stories* (Virago, 2004).

1963   Alfred Hitchcock directs his classic version of *The Birds*, claiming 'We're throwing away everything but the title and the notion of birds attacking human beings.'

1979   Angela Carter publishes *The Bloody Chamber*, a collection of stories that has proved highly influential on our understanding of the relationship between the fairy tale and Gothic literature and that instigated an appetite for the work of writers such as Leonora Carrington.

1980   Umberto Eco writes *Il nome della rosa*, translated into English by William Weaver as *The Name of the Rose* in 1983.

	The novel was made into a major film (dir. Jean-Jacques Annaud) in 1986.
1983	The *British Journal of Photography* manages to obtain a confession from Elsie Wright that the photographs she and Frances Griffiths took sixty years before had not been genuine.
1984	Iain Banks writes his debut novel, *The Wasp Factory*, beginning a career that will see a re-energising of Scottish Gothic in the contemporary period.
1986	Clive Barker publishes *The Hellbound Heart*, adapted by the author for cinema the following year and released under the title *Hellraiser*.
1988	Patrick McGrath publishes his story 'The Angel' in the collection *Blood and Water*. 'The Angel' is a pathological tale exploring 'the undead', using the theme of male homosexuality and 'sickness'. Several novels by McGrath follow in quick succession: *The Grotesque* (1989), *Spider* (1990) and *Dr Haggard's Disease* (1993).
1995	Steve Szilagyi publishes *Photographing Fairies*, based on the Cottingley photographs. It is made into a film (dir. Nick Willing) in 1997.
1996	Graham Joyce publishes *The Tooth Fairy*, a novel detailing childhood trauma linked to issues of sexual abuse, sodomy and child murder.
1997	*Fairy Tale: A True Story* (dir. Charles Sturridge) is released, also based on the story of the Cottingley photographs.
1998	Sarah Waters publishes her debut novel, *Tipping the Velvet*. Though of limited application to the Gothic, its immediate successors, *Affinity* (1999) and *Fingersmith* (2002), establish Waters as a significant writer of the lesbian Gothic.
2000	*What Lies Beneath* (dir. Robert Zemeckis) is released. Though easily dismissed as a simple Hollywood 'box-office' movie, the film employs elemental imagery in its depiction of female characters and takes as its centrepiece the designer bathroom as a metaphorical conduit for the ways in which women become 'wasted' by male success.
2001	(11 September) The terrorist attacks on the World Trade Center, New York, set in train a new understanding of

the contemporary Gothic based around the 'War on Terror'.

2001 *The Others* (dir. Alejandro Amenábar) is released, a film re-inforcing the level of our fascination with child murder and the ongoing influence of James's *The Turn of the Screw.*

2003 A. S. Byatt publishes 'The Thing in the Forest', in *The Little Black Book of Stories*, a story set during the Second World War in which two evacuated children murder a third, younger, girl. The story tackles issues of re-memorying and how one narrates the unspoken.

2006 Sarah Waters publishes *The Night Watch*, a London-centred narrative set during the Second World War, featuring a group of lesbians whose lives become emancipated by their access to gainful employment in public service roles during wartime.

2007 *Jekyll* (screenwriter, Steve Moffat) is serialised in six episodes on the BBC. The drama follows the demise of Dr Jackman, who learns he is descended from the original (Victorian) Mr Hyde.

2009 Sarah Waters publishes *The Little Stranger*, a ghost story exploring the means by which the lesbian is erased in the years immediately following the Second World War, as women are propelled back into the home and encouraged to marry and have children.

ILLUSTRATIONS

Dedicated to the memory of
Jean Armitt (1928–2008)

Introduction

ဢ

It is no longer necessary to justify why one would want to write a book on the Gothic, as Eve Kosofsky Sedgwick does in 1980:

> While there is very little difficulty in identifying or setting a date to the Gothic novel proper, most Gothic novels are not worth reading ... I want to make it easier for the reader of 'respectable' nineteenth-century novels to write 'Gothic' in the margin next to certain especially interesting passages[1]

Kosofsky Sedgwick's book is a revised edition of her Yale Ph.D. thesis (1976), but that moment of revision is itself timely. The following year Julia Briggs published her book *Night Visitors: The Rise and Fall of the English Ghost Story*, the book of her Oxford University B.Litt. dissertation, about which it has been said 'she was denied a doctorate because of its non-mainstream subject matter'.[2] The shift in 'respectability' seems to have come three years later, when David Punter brought out his original one-volume edition of *The Literature of Terror*, a book setting much of the agenda in Gothic criticism for a decade or more subsequently, impelling a rising tide of fascination in the Gothic which may not yet have reached its apex.[3]

Gothic, then, is a mode of writing for which there is limitless appetite (a quality it shares with its best-loved monsters) and yet, despite this success and its reflection in the popularity of undergraduate-level modules on Gothic film and fiction, it also faces an element of crisis, which Chris Baldick and Robert Mighall voice thus: 'Gothic Criticism has abandoned any credible historical grasp upon its object', running the risk of becoming 'condemned to repeat what it has failed to understand'.[4] Unlike the origins of Gothic, which clustered around a specific, but small, group of writers, thinkers and painters (Horace Walpole (1717–97), Edmund Burke (1729–97), Clara Reeve (1729–1807), Henry Fuseli (1741–1825), (Mrs) Ann Radcliffe (1764–1823) and Matthew Lewis (1775–1818)), all engaging with similar cultural and literary questions in work spanning broadly the years 1750–1820, twentieth-century reignition of interest in the contemporary Gothic has us reeling in terms of how best to tame this amorphous and ever-expanding 'monster'.

Allan Lloyd-Smith, in *American Gothic Fiction*, provides a succinct shortlist of traditional Gothic features:

> extreme situations, anxiety, darkness, threat, paranoia; exaggerated villains and innocent victims; subterfuge and plots; ancient houses, castles, monasteries, dungeons, crypts and passages; wild scenery, craggy mountains or winding maze-like tracts; stage machinery, hidden trap-doors, secret passageways; speaking portraits, ghosts, doubles, and other supernatural-seeming beings; monstrous and grotesque creatures; pain, terror, horror, and sadism.[5]

Nevertheless, if one were to identify elements that specifically characterise twentieth-century Gothic, one would have to signal, in the early part of the century, the manner in which the real-life horror of two world wars takes over from the imagined horrors of the supernatural and/or superstition; those tortured individuals who, in the nineteenth century, refused to play dead, began to do so on a mass(ive) scale during and after the First World War, as spirit photographers, theosophists, spiritualists and clairvoyants pandered to the devastation felt by parents grieving for their lost sons. This climate of melancholia re-energised performances of plays such as J. M. Barrie's *Peter Pan* (1904), which, though masquerading as an appealing combination of fairy fantasy and children's play, is actually a text about children and death, and its popularity soared during these early decades, not least among young men.

Such is the length of shadow cast by world events that tropes of haunting frame much of the twentieth-century literature of warfare and can be found in works as different in time of publication and authorial politics as Rudyard Kipling's story 'Swept and Garnished' (1915) and Pat Barker's novel *The Ghost Road* (1995). However, as the memories of two world wars begin to recede in the later decades of the twentieth century one also finds another darkness beginning to evolve for, as I will argue in chapter 1, we reinvent Gothic horror most absolutely and 'feel' it most acutely in relation to the threats we believe face our children. That we continue to invest these fears with Gothic significance is clear in the monster narratives the media constructs around 'the paedophile', 'the child abductor', 'the child murderer', 'the child abuser', all of whom populate our diurnal and nocturnal fears. So, twentieth-century haunting differs from that of nineteenth-century ghost stories, and takes on a more psychological (perhaps also a more metaphorical) dimension.

As we trace the Gothic through a literary landscape dominated by postmodernism and post-structuralism in the 1970s and 1980s, and as we watch the thrill of literary theory take hold, we see ghosts and the spectral providing surprisingly fertile ground for a range of theoretical positions and their conceits, from Jacques Derrida's re-reading of Karl Marx to Lynne Pearce's theory of the feminist reader.[6] Though a certain degree of ambivalence accompanies this temptation to exploit the full imaginative potential of the Gothic, one welcomes, simultaneously, the broadening of the applicability of a mode of literature that pre-dates the scientific advances that radically redefined our relationship to both the supernatural and to death. Furthermore, such arguing over terminological territory is as old as twentieth-century Gothic criticism itself, hence the subject of Alfred Longueil's article, 'The word "Gothic" in eighteenth-century criticism', first published in 1923, which opens with the conversational gambit, 'Critical terms ... have their ups and downs. So it has been with the adjective "gothic".' Longueil is almost apologetic when he adds, in a footnote:

> I have attempted to follow the term 'Gothic' only as a critical adjective
> in letters, ignoring its application as a racial, a linguistic, a typographical
> word. Its use in English from at least 1641 as a term in architecture I

have not tried to chronicle, because it is there part of a different and highly specialized vocabulary which has for the most part little to do with literature.[7]

Longueil, of course, pre-dates the type of literary theoretical play that has enabled objects as apparently diverse as buildings (storeys) and books (stories) to shelter under this same umbrella term: thus, what Longueil identifies as difference within apparent similarity (the sharing of a label) becomes genuine similarity within apparent difference (that architecture and narrative do both tell stories about culture) later in the century. Despite Longueil's reservations, Gothic's disciplinary home in architecture enables a very close relationship between space and the 'fabric' of buildings in twentieth-century texts, and this is examined in greater detail in chapter 2. First, however, we consider three historical monuments and their continuing relevance to the twentieth-century Gothic: Horace Walpole's Strawberry Hill, Alton Towers and Warwick Castle.

The Gothic attraction and / of the counterfeit

Founded in 1698, Strawberry Hill was originally 'a modest house, built by the coachman of the Earl of Bradford'.[8] Over the ensuing sixteen years Walpole transformed it into a Gothic centrepiece based in part on 'a print of Aston-house in Warwickshire, in Dugdale's history of that county'.[9] Dugdale's book is an authoritative compendium documenting the size, lifestyle, significant buildings and traditions of the various settlements of Warwickshire at the time, from the smallest village to its county town and cities such as Coventry. Through the medium of print, therefore, Dugdale comes as close as one could to the visual 'mapping' of a county or, to use a phrase Dianne S. Ames develops in relation to Gothic projects such as this, a rendering of 'as if' architecture in print.[10] That Walpole may have gone to Dugdale for a model on which to base Strawberry Hill suggests, in itself, a tendency towards aggrandisement. At the same time, a playful counter-balancing trend towards diminution accompanies it, as Walpole's delight in his villa is revealed to be that of a child and his plaything:

It will look, I fear, a little like arrogance in a private Man to give a printed Description of his Villa and Collection, in which almost every thing is diminutive. It is not, however, intended for public sale, and originally was meant only to assist those who should visit the place . . . The general disuse of Gothic architecture, and the decay and alterations so frequently made in churches, give prints a chance of being the sole preservatives of that style.[11]

Note, here, the role played by imitation in print, almost 'as if' the catalogue itself takes on architectural existence, met by Ames's observations regarding the papery elements of the house's decor: 'Strawberry Hill is, in part, literally paper – papier mâché. The battlements and several ceilings are made of this material . . . The house may thereby be viewed as an extension, almost a transfer print, of Walpole's archeological pen-and-paper drawings copied from Dugdale.'[12] This foundational relationship to imitation (or diminution) alters our aesthetic response to originality. Jerrold E. Hogle's own reading of the Gothic situates the mode centrally within a consideration of the relationship between fakery and the cultural potency of the Gothic, or, as he puts it, 'the ghost of the counterfeit'.[13]

As we will see increasingly in this book, Gothic sells, and the phonier it is the better. Hence, from Strawberry Hill as 'ghost of the counterfeit' only a very small step is needed to take us to what is possibly *the* icon of contemporary entertainment architecture and Gothic Revival architecture rolled into one, Alton Towers. Now best known as 'one of Europe's most popular tourist attractions', offering, as Michael J. Fisher puts it, 'a significant slice of England's architectural and social history set in the midst of "white-knuckle" rides and a fantasy-world not entirely at variance with its nineteenth-century origins as a pleasure-park designed to challenge the imagination',[14] it is also, of course, a historic country house and one whose history bears a striking resemblance to Strawberry Hill's. As Fisher observes, over a couple of decades Alton Towers metamorphoses from a reasonably modest seventeenth-century hunting lodge, called Alton (or sometimes Alveton) Lodge, into the summer residence of the fifteenth Earl of Shrewsbury. On the way its name changes from Abbey House (1811) to Alton Abbey, and finally to

Alton Towers in 1832, the final phases of this transformation taking place under the watchful guidance of the famous Gothic revivalist architect, Augustus Pugin (1812–52). Though Fisher says of Pugin that, for him, 'the true Gothic style was not an option, but an historical, moral and religious necessity', his own book's subtitle, 'A Gothic Wonderland', implies 'purity' to be under pressure: Gothic is always 'retro', always 'fake', always a copy without an illusion. As Hogle observes:

> [S]ince it employs symbols from earlier times largely emptied of many older meanings, [Gothic] quite readily becomes a symbolic space into which the fears and horrors generated by early modern cultural changes can be 'thrown off' or 'thrown under' as though they exist more in the now obscure and distant past than in the threatening present.[15]

Alton Towers is, in that sense, ripe for exploitation from the start and, following the demise of the aristocratic links with the family in the 1920s, pure commercialism ensues. Intriguingly, however, what late twentieth-century Gothic culture demonstrates (and in this respect Derrida's reading of Marx may prove prescient again) is that raw capitalism, far from threatening to reduce the impact of the Gothic, frequently results in its greater potency. Hence, and surely contrary to expectations, Fisher argues that it is only once Alton Towers is purchased in 1990 by Tussauds (now known as the Merlin Entertainments Group) that it starts to regain its importance, not just as a commercial venture, but as a Gothic landmark:

> the Towers chapel was cleared and its magnificent Pugin ceiling restored . . . the Octagon and Talbot Gallery were cleared of rubble and debris, and a section of the House Conservatory was restored, all in preparation for a new theme-park attraction which, although outside the historic buildings, is accessed via the Armoury, Picture Gallery and Octagon.[16]

The attraction Fisher is referring to here is 'Hex – The Legend of the Towers', not exactly a 'ride' (although it concludes with a ride), but a more sustained uncanny experience framed in terms of an intriguing combination of the ancient and the new, tall tales and technology. As Fisher remarks, in order to experience the attraction, the 'rider' is required to enter the building itself. No sooner has one stepped through the doorway than a billboard informs the visitor restoration work is in progress, thereby framing the attraction entirely in architectural terms which speak of 'authenticity', 'origins' and a journey back in time. At the same time, equally important is the use of manufactured atmospherics. The attraction is based around a local legend of the beggar woman's curse, claimed to derive from an encounter with the Earl of Shrewsbury when she halted his carriage one night. In response to his refusal to accede to her demands for money she issued a curse: for every branch of the ancient oak tree that fell, one member of his family would perish. That night, a lightning storm blew up and severed a limb of the tree, following which a family death ensued. Henceforth, the severed branch was sealed in the family vault and the rest of the tree chained up to prevent recurrences.

How 'atmospherics' are conveyed is crucial to the twentieth-century Gothic and epitomised by Hex. Here, the nuisance factor of queuing, well known to all theme-park devotees, becomes part of the 'ride'. No sooner is one encased by the stone architecture than one is immediately presented with several television monitors, spanning the estimated length of the queue. It is here that one is told the story of the curse, but the storyteller, bizarrely, is a middle-aged man (the manager of the restoration project), dressed in everyday work clothes and wearing a construction worker's hard hat. The chronotope is clearly that of the contemporary construction industry, while the narrative is pure nineteenth-century Gothic. The architecture of the interior is used to reinforce the sense of journeying ever further into the interior, as a designated number of guests are permitted access beyond each set of double doors and then required to wait in semi-darkness as the next portion of the legend is unveiled. The inner sanctum of the attraction is entry into the formerly sealed vault, where one finds a replica (presumably) of the felled branch, chained in the centre of the room and surrounded by pews resembling a set of choir stalls. The attraction culminates with a ride in which the stalls begin to swing, gaining an ever steeper gradient with each rocking motion, until the entire structure starts to revolve through 360 degrees, as if the walls themselves were crashing down around one's ears.

Alton Towers brands many of its attractions with supernatural themes: witness 'Forbidden Valley', 'Gloomy Wood', 'Haunted Hollow' and 'Duel – The Haunted House Strikes Back!', not to mention 'Spooks R Us', a stall selling 'Spooky tricks & treats for all ages'. In August 2008, Alton Towers was advertising a 'Scarefest' to take place during the Hallowe'en holidays later that year, using as an advertising hoarding a 'souped-up' funeral hearse decked out with pumpkin accessories. Theme-park attractions aside, however, there seems to be comparatively little in the way of 'ghostly' narratives attached to the actual house, a point evinced, perhaps, by its most uncanny associated tale concerning a curse rather than a phantom. So, despite the fact that Pugin himself spent entire summers alone there during the late 1840s, while the sixteenth earl and his family 'summered' in Italy, when the following account, as recounted by Fisher, is as chilling as it got, Alton Towers is not especially 'spooky':

> On an October night in 1849 he was staying in a room in a remote part of the Towers, with a strong gale blowing outside. As if that were not enough, Pugin heard the sound of bells tolling every few minutes as though for a funeral. So strong was the wind as it blew through the openings in the chapel tower that it had set the bells tolling.[17]

In this respect Alton Towers is well worth contrasting with another tourist attraction run by the Merlin Entertainments Group, Warwick Castle. Originally built in the fourteenth century and mentioned extensively in Dugdale, Warwick Castle is now branded 'Britain's Greatest Mediæval Experience' and, rather than offering up the more transparently synthetic experience of 'Hex', Warwick Castle boasts an 'authentic' Ghost Tower, reputedly haunted by the Castle's former owner, Sir Fulke Greville.[18] Rather like the fifteenth and sixteenth Earls of Shrewsbury at Alton Towers and Horace Walpole at Strawberry Hill, Greville is seen to be the owner responsible for the significant moment of restoration in relation to Warwick Castle, namely from a 'semi-derelict castle into a stately residence. Work was sufficiently advanced for James I to be received in 1617'.[19] The advantage Warwick Castle has over both Alton Towers and Strawberry Hill is that it is (at least in part) 'authentically' medieval – a feature which, Longueil might remind us, in earlier periods such as the Renaissance would render it 'barbarous'.[20] Like much of the castle, the so-called Ghost Tower pre-dates its existence *as* a Ghost Tower,

Fig. 1 'Halloween Hearse', Alton Towers, August 2008. Photograph by the author. Included with kind permission of Merlin Entertainments Group.

being of fourteenth-century origin; like Alton Towers's 'Hex', its reinvention is pure storytelling.

Paradoxically, however, just as 'Hex' parades a kind of 'mock-Gothic' experience, the legend of the Ghost Tower at Warwick Castle is similarly 'theme park' in orientation. Again, one queues up to buy separate tickets for the Ghost Tower, queues in a one-way system to enter and exit the Ghost Tower and encounters, inside the Ghost Tower, people dressed up in 'authentic' costume acting out the 'original' ghost story of a vengeful servant and a betraying master. Late twentieth-century Gothic never allows 'authenticity' to stand in the way of commercial enterprise, reinforced at Warwick Castle by its use as a staged backdrop for non-historical entertainments (on the evening of the day I visited, Simply Red were booked to perform). As Lloyd-Smith observes, 'we need to remember that the Gothic is fantasy and amusement, games and fancy dress, entertainment that engages with its [public] on many levels from trauma to laughter'.[21]

Gothic culture and the marketplace

Such contemporary landmarks raise one of the compelling features especially pertinent to twentieth-century rather than any previous period of Gothic history, namely that it gathers momentum in tandem with the burgeoning 'new' academic discipline of Cultural Studies. Mark Edmundson's excellent study of American Gothic culture opens with the following observation about late twentieth-century America:

> Gothic is alive not just in Stephen King's novels and Quentin Tarantino's films, but in media renderings of the O. J. Simpson case, in our political discourse, in our modes of therapy, on TV news, on talk shows like *Oprah*, in our discussion of AIDS and of the environment. American culture at large has become suffused with Gothic assumptions, with Gothic characters and plots.[22]

Gothic, then, has become a means of reading culture, not just a cultural phenomenon to read. Take, for instance, one of our most recent blights on the entertainment landscape, 'celebrity culture'. Framed by twin illusions, firstly, that conspicuous wealth equates with personal happiness and, secondly, that the more one is 'sold' as a fashion icon the more one is loved, we recall the cautionary note Mary Daly strikes over the word 'glamour' in *Gyn/Ecology*: 'Originally it was believed that witches possessed the power of glamour, and according to the authors of the Malleus Maleficarum, witches in their glamour could cause the male "member" to disappear.'[23] Hence, elements of the 2008 television 'docu-pulp' series 'Katie and Peter', a public relations documentary based around the lives of the formerly married couple, Peter André and Katie Price (aka Jordan), unfolded as an increasingly disturbing pseudo-Gothic narrative, complete with mansion, as Katie's compulsive drive for more and more surgical enhancements – driven by the glamour industry, of course – showed her, in one episode, reduced to a frightened (and frightening) state of debilitating sickness. What is just as well documented in British culture is the manner in which celebrity culture (spawned and fed upon by the tabloid media) constructs ordinary people as 'super-' (super-models, super-heroes), firstly to encourage our identification with them ('that could be me, if only I . . .'), then to desecrate those same icons, using an ugly, deliberately cultivated, body of public envy.

Such consumerist visions of the Gothic find a natural antecedent in Franco Moretti's reading of Bram Stoker's *Dracula*: 'Stoker does not want a thinking reader, but a frightened one', Moretti argues, claiming that the relationship between readers and texts changes from Shelley's *Frankenstein* in 1818 to *Dracula* in 1897. Stressing the presentness of Stoker's narrative stance, as opposed to Shelley's retrospective set of embedded narrative boxes, Moretti claims that Stoker's reader is dragged along with the characters, rather than standing back and evaluating their plots. The result, he claims, is that readers cleave more absolutely to the very ideology by which they are undone. Returning to 'Katie and Peter', in an aside to the camera, André directly addresses the implied (female) viewer of the series, imploring her to by all means admire and follow Katie's business acumen, but not her desire for surgery, yet Jordan's face continues to adorn glossy magazines aimed at female readers. The allure of cosmetic surgery remains one combining terror and delight, promise and horror. Moretti continues: 'Professing to save the individual, it in fact annuls him' (or, in this case, 'her'). In Moretti's cautionary summing up we hear especially pertinent words for cosmetic surgery: 'whoever breaks its bonds is done for . . . The more [it] frightens, the more it edifies. The more it humiliates, *the more it uplifts*.'[24]

However, it is not just popular culture that has its Gothic elements; so, too, does the political establishment. As Mark Edmundson observes,

> Gothic thrives in a world where those in authority – the supposed exemplars of the good – are under suspicion. The mind of terror Gothic senses hypocrisy in high places. But it is also fascinated by heights, by power, position, fame. It requires contact with glamour to keep its spirits up, yet mistreats the fascination on which it compulsively feeds. It seeks absolute stability and assurance from leaders,

and then rebels when the leaders are revealed as fallible and not fully in charge, or (worse yet) when they really do succeed in establishing complete control. A deep ambivalence about authority lies near the heart of our culture of Gothic.[25]

As British society's interest in the political process wanes, it is perhaps understandable that media gurus turn to the Gothic to breathe new life into politics. Nevertheless, the outcome of the contest defining victor and victim may prove as resistant to control as the best of Gothic monsters. In 1997, when the British Conservative Party produced an election poster depicting the then Leader of the Opposition, Tony Blair, as a devil with red eyes and a lascivious grin, it backfired spectacularly, effectively playing its role in 'ushering' Blair into his premiership. Edmundson cautions us against over-simplification in our mapping of sociopolitics onto a Gothic template, beginning with a rhetorical question posed to the reader:

> Isn't there a very good reason for the proliferation of Gothic in the American 1990s? Isn't it the simple truth that our culture has become more Gothic or . . . that the explosion of violence, mayhem, and craziness that the nation has witnessed over the past few years can reasonably be represented by recourse to the Gothic idiom?
> No, not really. Since 1991 . . . America has actually been becoming a more secure place to live.[26]

There is, of course, a horrible irony attendant in the fact that Edmundson's book is published in 1997, four years before the 9/11 terrorist attacks on the World Trade Center, and it is undoubtedly true that Edmundson could not have written that same paragraph afterwards: nevertheless, he has a point. The extent of the proliferation of our fascination with the Gothic is thankfully not matched by an attendant increase in real-life cultural horror on 'Main Street' (to quote the title of Edmundson's book). Instead, we cannot leave the Gothic alone, because it deals in what will not leave us alone. It is everywhere and yet nowhere, because therein lies the source of the paranoia upon which it feeds.

Chapter 1 of this book examines precisely such paranoia as it impacts on what we seem to find the most threatening of all fears, those involving haunted children and childhood. As our culture becomes increasingly anxious about child safety (at the same time that society genuinely *is* one of child safety), we will begin by establishing the Gothic manifestations of this anxiety in the contemporary media, in the so-called 'misery' genre and as it is handed down to us in the Gothic fairy tale. It is Henry James's *The Turn of the Screw* and the 2001 film *The Others* which provide the impetus for this discussion, which then moves on to a sustained unravelling of A. S. Byatt's 'The Thing in the Forest', read in conjunction with Graham Joyce's *The Tooth Fairy*. These are texts in which children are both victims and assailants, and as the chapter moves on to a discussion of Steve Szilagyi's *Photographing Fairies* (based on the Cottingley photographs of 1917–20) and two of its cinematic adaptations, Nick Willing's *Photographing Fairies* and *FairyTale: A True Story* (dir. Charles Sturridge) we examine the child in relation to adult mourning and grief. Two world wars frame our understanding of loss (both through death and of innocence) in this chapter, and accordingly child's play becomes tainted with nostalgia. The chapter therefore concludes with a discussion of the doll's house, linking *FairyTale: A True Story* with M. R. James's 'The Haunted Dolls' House'.

Chapter 2 takes us to the role played by architecture in twentieth-century Gothic. The haunted house is, of course, the Gothic centre-piece par excellence, but after the demise of the aristocratic seat during the nineteenth century, the Gothic 'goes to town' in the bombed-out spaces of the Blitz. Beginning with a discussion of Rudyard Kipling's 'Swept and Garnished' as haunted domestic interior, the role of the disruption of architectural and ornamental pattern and order is more fully developed in a discussion of Umberto Eco's *The Name of the Rose*. Moving from medieval monasteries to contemporary suburbia, we interrogate the outer respectability of the suburban terrace as a mask for sexual horror through a reading of Clive Barker's *The Hellbound Heart*, before effecting a direct intertextual comparison, in a remote rural setting, with Iain Banks's *The Wasp Factory*. London Gothic is the focus of the middle section of this chapter, more specifically during the Blitz, as the relationship between abandoned housing and the city streets is discussed in relation to Elizabeth Bowen's 'The Demon Lover' and Sarah Waters's

The Night Watch. The chapter concludes with an interrogation of American suburban respectability and horrors 'buried alive' through a detailed reading of the Hollywood film, *What Lies Beneath.*

In chapter 3 we turn to questions of monstrosity linked to the human and the inhuman. This is an area traditionally linked to the horror end of the Gothic, and we begin with a section on bestial monsters, using Sir Arthur Conan Doyle's *The Hound of the Baskervilles* before looking at a sustained reading of the beast stories of Leonora Carrington. Moving from beasts to vampires we return to Barker's *The Hellbound Heart,* in this chapter through a consideration of at what stage the formerly human mutates, through monstrosity, to produce purely inhuman horror. The final section offers a detailed comparative reading of Du Maurier's story 'The Birds' and Hitchcock's cinematic adaptation/re-reading of it before concluding with a brief reading of the recent British television drama *Jekyll* as depiction of the adolescent monster.

Chapter 4 turns to the question of Queer Gothic, opening up where the previous chapter ended, with *Jekyll,* this time in terms of camp humour and its relationship to anxieties about closeted sexuality, before moving on to a consideration of Henry James's story 'The Jolly Corner', another story in which open and shut doors encode the protagonist's relationship to a sexuality best understood in terms of what it cannot speak. A sustained section on the writing of Sarah Waters follows, looking at the fictional exploration of the concept of the 'apparitional lesbian' across all her novels, but especially *Fingersmith*. The chapter concludes with a reading of the work of Patrick McGrath in relation to cultural homophobia and paranoia in the wake of the HIV/AIDS crisis, with particular attention to his third novel, *Dr Haggard's Disease,* and an early story, 'The Angel'. It is surely in relation to perceived sexual deviance that the Gothic has offered up the most liberating possibilities for writers and readers. Following a survey of criticism in chapter 5, the conclusion turns briefly to Waters's most recent novel, *The Little Stranger* (2009), bringing the book full circle to where it began: with the theme of haunted childhood. It is to this we now turn as we contemplate the question of whether our anxieties about child safety are constructing the society in which we live as one haunted by the spectre of childhood imprisonment.

1

Gothic Pathologies: Haunted Children

છ

What it was least possible to get rid of was the cruel idea that, whatever I had seen, Miles and Flora saw more – things terrible and unguessable that sprang from dreadful passages of intercourse in the past.[1]

Henry James's *The Turn of the Screw* (1898), from which this epigraph is taken, anticipates and uncannily shadows our anxieties as they are woven into twentieth-century childhood. One might argue that one of the key ways in which twentieth-century Gothic literature differentiates itself from its predecessors is in its treatment of the theme of the haunted child. That *The Turn of the Screw* continues to have a cultural resonance is in part shown by the success of *The Others* (2001, writer/director Alejandro Amenábar), a film set in Jersey in 1945, commonly read as having a direct intertextual connection with James's novella. In *The Others*, the father is away fighting in the Second World War – a war his wife, Grace, repeatedly describes as 'someone else's', Jersey already being occupied by the Nazis. While he is away, Grace remains behind in their country mansion, accompanied by their two children, Anne and Nicholas. The entire narrative plays with the boundaries between the living and the dead. The film opens as three servants arrive on the doorstep, apparently in answer to a job advertisement, but soon Grace discovers the advert was never placed. For much of the narrative the viewer is aware that the three servants are ghosts: what is far less clear, until the end, is that so are Grace and the children.

As is typically the case in traditional narratives concerning pre-pubescent girls, haunting and the supernatural, Anne is given a particularly privileged role as 'seer'. She witnesses what she calls 'intruders' entering and walking through the house, characters remaining invisible to us for much of the film, reinforcing our assumptions that they are spectral. However, it turns out we are viewing this film from beyond the grave, and hence are positioned as dead, too. Only later do we discover the 'intruders' comprise a living family, the catalyst for the arrival of the servants being that this family has employed a medium to exorcise the point-of-view protagonists. During the seance which brings both sides into contact, an 'interior' story surfaces: Grace has murdered her children and shot herself in the head, being unable to tolerate her husband's death. Surrounding this narrative of child murder is therefore the wider horror that takes the father to war: the servants have enlisted, just like him, in a fight against alien occupation. Hence it is Victor, the son of the living family, who embodies most poignantly the consequences of this conflict. As the family flees the house he looks back wistfully, espying the ghostly trio staring from the window. Victor's 'knowing' sorrow reinforces the irony of his naming: despite bearing the nomenclature of military success, he is already 'marked' by death, and hence represents the doomed youth of western Europe.

That military might and masculine duty frame the otherwise domesticated plot of *The Others* is wholly appropriate. Berthold Schoene-Harwood reads *The Turn of the Screw* as a critique of the 'deformative impact patriarchal gender norms exert', especially within a context of 'political anxieties in late nineteenth-century Britain', whereby 'Bly could be construed as an abbreviation of "Blighty", a term popular amongst British servicemen abroad and originally derived from the Hindi word *Bilayati* meaning "foreign land" or "England"'.[2] Eric Haralson similarly identifies in *The Turn of the Screw* 'a fable of jeopardized masculine emergence . . . [in relation to] Miles, as a "little gentleman" . . . [and] the heavy cost that British society was ready to pay in order to keep its young gentlemen away from the "wrong path altogether"'.[3] Thus are we reminded of the 'murky circumstances surrounding Miles's expulsion from school' and Michael Bakewell's portrait of Charles Dodgson, 'who recalled the prevalence of what he tactfully called "annoyance[s] at night" while at Rugby in the 1840s'. Questions of dubious innocence and likely guilt resonate throughout the disquiet of James's text. As Haralson cautions, citing Bakewell, 'James does not foreclose the other possibility: that Miles was no "muff" at all, but rather one of the aggressors'.[4] At the same time, uppermost among our readerly fears are those linked to the dangers so acutely posed by the adult characters in the text: the abandoning father, the ghostly (perhaps demonic) Quint and Jessel, not to mention the suffocating governess. All in all, as I argue elsewhere, 'a twenty-first century reader has little doubt in labelling James's story a tale of paedophilia, articulated in a culture with no clear definition of the term'.[5]

The Turn of the Screw, then, confronts its readers with the unsayable ('the love that dare not speak its name', perhaps, to follow Haralson), ravelled up in a Gothic frame which enables the horrible to become articulated as the underside of 'respectable' upper-class society, coupled with the powers adults in general hold over theirs and others' (*Others*'?) children. James's historical positioning at the meeting point of two centuries is significant: the Victorian period is one in which childhood is often perceived to have been 'established' and, indeed, reified for the first time as a concept tied to vulnerability and innocence. As the twentieth century progresses, childhood advances towards a phase of increasing freedom and social protection, only to retreat, towards the end of the century, into one of fear and a stifling lack of freedom to roam.

Child murder and the media storm

A series of late twentieth- and twenty-first-century child victims meet the gaze of our mind's eye as they stare out at us through our memories of newspaper articles and television footage, from the Moors murders of 1963–4 (Ian Brady and Myra Hindley entering the annals of twentieth-century history as counterparts to Quint and Jessel, perhaps), to the more recent murders of Jessica Chapman and Holly Wells in 2002. Add to these the mysterious disappearance of Madeleine McCann in May 2007 and what we recognise – beyond the instantaneous sense of shared grief and societal mourning – is a longer-term fascination among the wider public that can only be diagnosed as pathological. Browsing the shelves of a local bookshop recently, I was unexpectedly confronted by a free-standing Harper-Collins publicity display housing solely the following titles: Torey Hayden, *One Child* (1980; HarperElement, 2004), Torey Hayden, *Ghost Girl: The True Story of a Child in Desperate Peril* (HarperElement, 1991), Jane Elliott and Andrew Crofts, *The Little Prisoner: How a Childhood was Stolen and a Trust Betrayed* (HarperElement, 2005), Judy Westwater and Wanda Carter, *Street Kid: One Child's Desperate Fight for Survival* (HarperElement, 2006), Anya Peters, *Abandoned: The True Story of a Little Girl who Didn't Belong* (HarperElement, 2007), Toni Maguire, *Don't Tell Mummy: A True Story of the Ultimate Betrayal* (HarperElement, 2007), David Thomas, *Tell Me Why, Mummy: A Little Boy's Struggle to Survive* (HarperElement, 2007) and Toni Maguire, *When Daddy Comes Home* (HarperElement, 2007). Three words recur: 'True', 'Survival' and 'Betrayal', collectively carrying resonances of the child's game, 'Truth, Dare or Promise'; some of these books also carry strap-lines such as '*Sunday Times Bestseller*' or '*Sunday Times Bestselling Author*' (in one case the novel is sponsored by the *Sun* newspaper). Is there no sense of cultural shame inherent in our determination to devour our children through the 'popular' media? Can we who read books not identify a sense of disturbance at the word 'best' being used to boast about the appeal of selling (not to mention sponsoring) child misery? In an age in which conventional fear of the dead is lessening, in which super-stition is reducing and in which we no longer believe in ghosts, demons or vampires, paedophiles have become their 'natural' descend-ants: worse, they appear to inspire in us an insatiable appetite for 'more'.

Nor is this manifestation of cultural morbidity the only way in which our collective response to dead or 'disappeared' children carries Gothic resonances. Following the abduction and subsequent murder of Sarah Payne in 2000, her mother Sara became involved in cam-paigning for new legislation, colloquially titled 'Sarah's Law', one which would enable people to have access to information con-cerning convicted sex offenders living locally.[6] The key debates surrounding the possible full implementation of 'Sarah's Law' oscil-late around a traditional Gothic anxiety concerning visible and invisible dangers. In 'The 'Uncanny', Sigmund Freud cites but then questions

Schelling's observation that 'everything is *unheimlich* [uncanny] that ought to have remained secret and hidden but has come to light'.[7] This is precisely the difficulty here: would we feel safer were we to discover that the person living across the road is a convicted sex offender, or would that not give us nightmares? Other groups express reservations equally linked to invisibility, fearing that such legislation 'would drive child sex offenders underground'.[8] Freud has a phrase for this, too: 'It may be true that the uncanny . . . is something which is secretly familiar . . . which has undergone repression and then returned'.[9] At the same time, the very term 'underground' belongs to the Gothic, with its graveyards, crypts and demons rising after dark. This is the fuel upon which the 'popular' press feeds and it is one of the reasons why, in Graham Joyce's novel *The Tooth Fairy*, discussed later, we find his protagonist, Sam, identifying newspaper journalists as 'ghouls. . . They looked like ordinary people . . . but Sam knew that beneath the human disguise these ghouls leaked luminous gray slime from ear and nostril'.[10]

Yet, and in the face of an all-pervasive media hysteria implying the contrary, official statistics tell us that our children are no more at risk from 'stranger danger' than they have ever been – except, perhaps, insofar as the media's fuelling of parental fear consigns children who (to play with Freud's definition) ought to 'be out in the light' to becoming suffocated, as effectively as Miles is hugged to death by his governess. Ironically, this becomes a bizarre extension of the Victorian maxim 'children should be seen and never heard', for now they should not be seen (at least unaccompanied) either. In May 2004, the *Observer* newspaper ran a story on this very subject:

> Children choose to stay indoors watching TV and playing computer games because they are terrified of the world outside, fresh research reveals. In a high-profile launch this week, Education Secretary Charles Clarke will announce the findings which disclose that young children carry a daily expectation of being kidnapped by a stranger, sexually abused by a paedophile or becoming a victim of terrorism . . . The survey of more than 1,000 children aged 10 and 11 reveals that the choice to remain indoors is being made because of an increasingly un-realistic assessment by children and their parents of the risks of the outside world.[11]

What is it that makes us believe child abuse, death and abduction to be the defining fear of our own age, despite us knowing that infanticide, child neglect and child poverty were key themes in Dickens's writing and Hogarth's etchings ('Gin Lane' (1750) was reputedly 'produced as part of a campaign to restrict the sale of gin'[12] – colloquially known as 'Mother's Ruin', of course), and that Wordsworth wrote of them in *Lyrical Ballads* (1798–1800), in poems such as 'The Two April Mornings' and 'We Are Seven'? Indeed, in the poem 'Lucy Gray' (1800), from the same collection, we have a similar scenario to that reported about Madeleine McCann, in the disappearance that speaks of neither a life nor a death: 'They followed from the snowy bank / The footmarks, one by one, / Into the middle of the plank, / And further there were none.' As in all such cases, we cleave to hopes and tales of the child continuing her life elsewhere: 'Yet some maintain that to this day / She is a living child: / That you may see sweet Lucy Gray / Upon the lonesome wild.'

Fairy stories and 'burial alive': A. S. Byatt and Graham Joyce

It is not just ghost stories, but fairy stories which have traditionally documented the terrifying ordeal childhood can be. The development of a genre specifically labelled the 'Gothic Fairy Tale' perhaps originates with Angela Carter's *The Bloody Chamber* (1979), a collection of stories in which she takes existing well-known fairy tales, such as 'Bluebeard', 'Little Red Riding Hood', 'Beauty and the Beast' or 'Sleeping Beauty', retitles them in many cases ('Little Red Riding Hood' becomes 'The Company of Wolves', 'Beauty and the Beast' becomes 'The Courtship of Mr Lyon', 'Sleeping Beauty' becomes 'The Lady of the House of Love' and 'Bluebeard' the titular 'The Bloody Chamber'), and radically retells them, while maintaining and sustaining the presence of the original frame. This is a process Carter herself describes, in a 1983 essay, as 'putting new wine into old bottles',[13] and what it ensures is the salvaging of the fairy tale, formerly sanitised as a consolationist mode of storytelling shored up by surprisingly influential thinkers such as Bettelheim, who both oversimplifies and underestimates the alluring danger of fairy tales and, along with it, the excitement child (like adult) readers find in them.[14]

It seems strange, in a century so concerned to keep its children close at hand, that in 1939 and 1940 we should have sent our children away en masse in the name of 'Operation Pied Piper', as wartime child evacuation was officially called: '[L]abelled like pieces of luggage . . . [m]ost were unaware of where they were going, what they would be doing and all were wholly ignorant of when they would be coming back.'[15] A. S. Byatt uses the Gothic implications of this government policy as the backdrop to her short story, 'The Thing in the Forest' (2003), in which two young girls, Penny and Primrose, befriend each other on the journey out and decide to go exploring on arrival at their mystery location. What the story narrates is their subsequent encounter with a 'monster'. Like Carter, Byatt uses the fairy tale to bring out its Gothic foundations, but her intertextual approach differs in straying further from the path of the original. The 'other' text in this case is 'Hansel and Gretel' (though, as we shall see, she throws in a dose of 'Little Red Riding Hood' for good measure) and, though she sticks with two children, unlike in the Brothers Grimm's version these are two girls.

In 'Hansel and Gretel', danger is cloaked in the most seductive guise possible for a child: 'the bird spread his wings and flew before them, and they followed him until they came to a little house . . . [when] they saw that the house was built of bread, and roofed with cakes; and the window was of transparent sugar'.[16] What Penny and Primrose recount seeing is very different:

> Did they hear it first or smell it first? . . . A crunching, a crackling, a crushing, a heavy thumping, combined with threshing and thrashing . . .
>
> . . . Its face – which was triangular – appeared like a rubbery or fleshy mask . . . Its colour was the colour of flayed flesh, pitted with wormholes, and its expression was . . . pure misery. Its most defined feature was a vast mouth, pulled down and down at the corners, tight with a kind of pain . . . It had blind, opaque white eyes, fringed with fleshy lashes . . . Its face was close to the ground. . . The flesh on [the] forearms was glistening and mottled, every colour, from the green of mould to the red-brown of raw liver, to the dirty white of dry rot.
>
> The rest of its very large body . . . had a tubular shape, as a turd has a tubular shape . . . It had feeble stubs and stumps of very slender legs . . . The little girls observed, with horrified fascination, that when it

met a sharp stone, or a narrow tree-trunk, it allowed itself to be sliced through. . . They thought it could not see, or certainly could not see clearly . . . [as it left] behind it a trail of bloody slime and dead foliage, sucked to dry skeletons.[17]

However focused we are as readers, our powers of concentration struggle to take in the sheer excess of detail Byatt supplies here (though I have quoted at apparent length, the original extends to three pages). What we also notice is the shifting nature of the description, which seems to build in the act of its own telling, much like a 'tall tale' told by (two) children. For instance, in the phrase 'threshing and thrashing' one imagines one of the two coming up with 'threshing', before the second quickly adds 'and thrashing'; this is surely a retrospectively concocted account, presumably told to an adult. In this respect one might argue that the monster *is* the story, in all its trailing, ill-fitting detail: the question is, 'Why do these girls go to such elaborate lengths to cover their tracks?'

Here we return to the seductive nature of the house of sweets, encountered by Hansel and Gretel. As all sensible child readers know, such sugary sweetness is too good to be true; unless, that is, it comes in the form of a much younger girl, Alys, 'barely out of nappies' (p. 11) who determines to latch on to Penny and the equally sweet-named Primrose. Alas, Alys is 'extraordinarily pretty, pink and white, with large pale blue eyes, and sparse little golden curls all over her head and neck, through which her pink skin could be seen' (pp. 11–12). What also characterises Alys is her persistence:

> She had made several attempts to attach herself to Penny and Primrose. They did not want her . . . She said now:
> 'I'm coming too, into the forest.'
> 'No, you aren't,' said Primrose.
> 'You're too little, you must stay here,' said Penny.
> 'You'll get lost,' said Primrose.
> 'You won't get lost. I'll come with you,' said the little creature, with an engaging smile, made for loving parents and grandparents.
> 'We don't want you, you see,' said Primrose.
> 'It's for your own good,' said Penny.
> Alys went on smiling hopefully, the smile becoming more of a mask.
> (p. 12)

Notice, here, how a number of the elements we have formerly seen the two girls attach to 'the monster' are reworked aspects of Alys's appearance. Her 'large pale blue eyes', once applied to the monster, become 'blind, opaque white eyes'. The smile that is the most resonant feature of that face prior to entry into the forest becomes, in the girls' account, 'a vast mouth, pulled down and down at the corners, tight with a kind of pain'. The pretty pink skin becomes 'mottled, every colour, from the green of mould to the red-brown of raw liver, to the dirty white of dry rot', and even the fact that Alys is 'barely out of nappies' may have some bearing on the later reference to the monstrous body having become turd-like in shape.

Taken at face value, Penny and Primrose's adventure depicts them as children who have had a 'brush' with danger, but who emerge physically unscathed, if utterly transformed – just like Hansel and Gretel. The small child, on the other hand, seems to have disappeared: gone, it seems, but not forgotten. Many years later, Penny returns to the scene, apparently on a leisurely, if not a nostalgic pretext. Intending to set off in the opposite direction to that taken with Primrose as a child, Penny nevertheless discovers that 'her path was deflected by fieldforms and the lie of the land into a snaking sickle-shape'. (p. 40) Inevitably, she finds herself approaching the site from which she was apparently retreating and, as she does so, she 'snuff[s] the air for the remembered rottenness' (p. 40) and we notice Byatt's eccentric use of the verb 'snuff', rather than 'sniff' here, conveying an inescapable connection between memory and death. So the passage continues:

> She heard her own heartbeat . . . There were things caught in the thorns, flimsy colourless shreds of damp wool or fur . . . She found things she remembered, threadworms of knitting wool, unravelled dishcloth cotton . . . odd sausage-shaped tubes of membrane . . . It had been here, but how long ago? . . . She found a mock tortoiseshell hairslide, and a shoe-button with a metal shank . . . She found – spread around, half-hidden by roots, stained green but glinting white – a collection of small bones, finger-bones, tiny toes, a rib, and finally what might be a brain-pan and brow. (pp. 40–42)

This passage confirms a suspicion that builds with the story: Penny and Primrose are child murderers who exploited the anonymity inherent in the evacuation process to torture and kill a smaller and more vulnerable child (inescapable echoes of the James Bulger case resound in the reader's mind as this '(P)penny' drops).[18] This would be Gothic enough, but Byatt adds another twist about the dangers of storytelling. As 'luck' would have it, a type of alibi is provided for the girls in the existence of a local legend of the Loathly Worm, a presence that turns a crime scene into a horror story. As adults, not only Penny but Primrose returns one 'autumn day in 1984' (p. 23), a coincidence that can only be credible if we assume this to be a significant anniversary of the murder – forty years, perhaps. Again, the description of their encounter gestures towards their shared guilt:

> They *prowled* around the room, each alone with herself . . . They coincided because both of them, at the same moment, half saw an image in a medieval-looking illustrated book . . . It showed a knight, on foot, in a forest, lifting his sword to slay something . . . It was not possible to see what was being slain. This was because, both in the tangled vegetation of the image, and in the way the book was displayed in the case, the enemy, or victim, was in shadows. (pp. 23–4; my emphasis)

As well as the legend, the women share a more personal connection with damaged storytelling. Penny was, we learn, a 'reading child' (p. 43) and later uses stories to negotiate the world of children, cloaking herself in the role of the 'child psychologist' who specialises in 'the abused, the displaced, the disturbed' (p. 21). Primrose, on the other hand, connects storytelling with maternal rejection, for, as a girl, she had a mother who 'didn't tell stories and didn't open gates into imaginary worlds' (p. 34). Fortunately for her, however (in the same way that we are encouraged to find the mother's death 'fortunate' for Hansel and Gretel at the end of the original fairy story), 'Both their mothers had died that spring, within a week of each other . . .' (p. 23). In this way is Primrose at last free to 'tell all'.

As we leave Byatt's story, Primrose has established a role for herself as a children's storyteller and arranges a grouping of chairs in a shopping centre, itself decked out like a setting for a fairy encounter: 'They were in front of a dimpling fountain, with lights shining up through the greenish water, making golden rings round the polished pebbles and wishing-coins that lay there' (p. 50). As the small children's trusting mothers leave them behind with instructions to 'be good and quiet and listen to the nice lady' (p. 50) (one can again hear the echoes of the parting words of so many parents of evacuated children), our attention is drawn to a child wearing a coat with a 'scarlet hood'. As Primrose 'smile[s] her best, most comfortable smile, and adjust[s] her golden locks' (p. 50), it is as if she has dressed herself as Alys in order to conceal her prowling, wolfish heart.

Byatt's 'moral' in this tale, perhaps, is that childhood innocence is a collective myth to which we cling: the monster the girls claim to have seen is an outward projection of what lurks in their psyches; at the same time, Byatt hints that these children carry maternal scars even before the encounter with Alys. Freud, indeed, hints at a pathological fear potentially innate to *all* childhood, namely that our fears of burial alive (though in Byatt's story it is the 'truth' that is buried alive, not the child) may result from repressed memories of intra uterine existence.[19]

A more metaphorical understanding of the term 'live burial', however, would take us to the controversial phenomenon of recovered memory, a form of testimony in which, as Mark Edmundson observes, individuals are encouraged to recast their own life stories as narratives in which they star as the central protagonist of a Gothic-style family saga: 'The hero-villain, the father-molester, haunts the inner life of the child, who cannot remember the incident . . . The therapist plays the role of rescuer (another Gothic archetype) . . . freeing the patient from the grip of the past.'[20] This is a contested area particularly applicable to issues of child abuse, especially when (as in 'The Thing in the Forest'), the narrative is retrospectively narrated by an adult. As Janice Haaken observes, 'For women, particularly, the process of remembering . . . means creating representations of the past out of a shadowy historical landscape . . . As wife, mother, daughter, the woman is the one who is left and returned to',[21] a dynamic that fits the abandonment of evacuation, the haunting potency of the dead child and the returning guilt of the child murderer equally well.

Yet, that such stories of child abuse and child abusing are not wholly the property of girls and women is made clear in Graham Joyce's own novelistic account of young children 'burying alive' their sexual terrors, *The Tooth Fairy* (1996). Where Byatt focuses upon the relationship between two young girls and their murder of Alys, Joyce focuses upon the childhood relationship between three young boys, Sam, Terry and Clive, who also become haunted by traumas attached to their believed collaboration in the murder of a child in a forest: Tooley, the scout-camp bully. From the start, Joyce's narrative equates childhood with death and mutilation; playing together at the nearby pond, Terry has two toes bitten off by a pike, which itself takes on the qualities of a 'phantom, a spirit from another world'.[22] This is another narrative blending Gothic horror with fairy-tale mythology and, as in all fairy tales, the key motif at the centre of everything is the family.

Terry, we learn, lives in a 'rust bucket Bluebird caravan in an untidy garden behind a cottage', which he shares with his parents and 'his twin brothers, who were not yet nine months old' (p. 10). In that reference to lower-class existence, we find a masculine equivalent of Aschenputtel or Cinderella, 'who was obliged to do heavy work from morning to night, get up early in the morning, draw water, make the fires, cook, and wash'.[23] Certainly, Joyce provides us with one of the key openings to fairy-tale stardom, the 'rags to riches' success story, but the apparent class-markers are almost immediately complicated by unexplained factors that accrue around Terry's father, Chris:

> Whatever status Mr Morris had dropped by living in a caravan he reclaimed by owning a sports car ... It seemed to the boys something of an injustice that both Clive's and Sam's fathers worked in a car factory and didn't possess a car, yet Terry's father, whose work was a mystery to everyone, was the proud owner of a spoke-wheeled, soft-top MG glinting in the yard alongside the rusting caravan. (p. 11)

Not only does Terry fail to ascend to 'higher' things (at the end of the text he is left behind as Sam and Clive prepare to go to university), he also is 'marked' from the start. His is a story of utter family mutilation, begun when Chris Morris decides to shoot himself and his family, a death which Terry escapes only through the intervention of the eponymous tooth fairy.

The tooth fairy emerges into the narrative in the familiar manner in which we encounter it in children's popular folk-legend, namely as a benign creature who creeps into bedrooms at night to remove the ejected milk-tooth from under the young child's pillow, replacing it with a coin; except that, at the end of the twentieth century, even this reading of a strange being creeping into children's bedrooms propels us into a latent sense of anxiety. We can no longer entertain such fantasies easily and, in the early stages of the novel, it is this mixture of magic and fears of sexual predators that Joyce's novel exploits to the full. Far from being a sugary souvenir from Victorian England, this tooth fairy is far more in keeping with traditional Celtic folk-lore, which saw fairies as typically 'treacherous and dangerous . . . demons, deformed and malignant'.[24] Lewd in temperament, sacri-legious in attitude, the tooth fairy could also be seen as a contemporary gargoyle, as its appearance on the roof of the church during Christmas midnight Mass attests:

> the Tooth Fairy had the side of her face pressed flat against the sky-light, her sooty curls tumbling over her head. Her mouth was open and her filed teeth reflected the light from inside the church. Meanwhile her fingers, with their extraordinary corkscrewing nails, cantered over the glass like the fall of a horse's hooves. (p. 144)

Such ambivalence dogs Sam throughout his daily life, even when shopping with his mother: 'A gargoyle leered at them from the gothic arch overhead. Its teeth were sharpened to points' (p. 43). Later, as Sam stands in Chris Morris's garage following the fateful shootings, he does so 'motionless as a gargoyle' (p. 57). Unlike traditional gargoyles, however, whose evil is purely ornamental (if also superstitious), the dangers of the tooth fairy are utterly visceral. Sam's first experience of this is the cast which the tooth fairy inflicts on his eye, a punishment once again reflecting the violence of traditional fairy lore, in which humans were blinded for being able to see fairies: 'Spitting or striking is usually the means adopted . . . sometimes the eye is torn from its socket.' At the same time, it also re-enacts the popular legend of the boys' home city of Coventry, wherein Peeping Tom is blinded for spy-ing on Lady Godiva as she rides her horse naked through the streets. This is a legend Edwin Sidney Hartland considers part of a tradition of stories concerning 'Magical Ointment', the means by which humans are blinded by fairies, and a series of stories hingeing 'upon

human curiosity and disobedience'.[25] According to Hartland's tran-
scription of the version of the tale laid down by Roger of Wendover
at the beginning of the thirteenth century, 'one low churl, compact
of thankless earth, / The fatal byword of all years to come, / Boring a
little auger-hole in fear, / Peep'd – but his eyes, before they had their
will, / Were shrivell'd into darkness in his head, And dropt before him'.[26]

For a contemporary reader this theme inevitably returns us to
Freud's reading of 'The Sand Man' in his essay on 'The Uncanny',
and his argument that fears linked to eye injuries are manifestations
of the castration complex. Much as in the case of Peeping Tom,
Freud equates such fears with a sense of perceived guilt for one's
actions: 'The self-blinding of the mythical criminal, Oedipus, was
simply a mitigated form of the punishment of castration – the only
punishment that was adequate for him by the *lex talionis*'.[27] In that
sense a squint becomes a means of marking the self as culpable, or
imprinting upon the body that which one will not speak aloud, a
problem Sam clearly carries with him after the death of Terry's family.
Furthermore, despite (or perhaps because of) the cast in his eye, it
is what Sam sees that others cannot that 'tells': 'Sam saw a familiar
shadow whispering to Morris . . . work[ing] its pink tongue close
to Morris's ear, back and forth, back and forth' (p. 50).

The myth of Oedipus is perhaps the ultimate riddle of cause and
effect, but the question here is whether blinding is a punishment for
transgression, or whether it marks out Sam as one who will potentially *invite* transgression, for the key crime Sam commits but of
which he cannot speak is the afore-mentioned murder of Tooley in the
woods, an incident which does not occur for another eleven chapters
in narrative chronology or, in terms of fictional chronology, another
five years after Terry's family's death. Irrespective of how we interpret
Sam's relation to innocence and guilt, as the novel progresses the
encounters between Sam and the tooth fairy take on obvious sexual
dimensions, reinforced by the fairy's manifestation in the young boy's
bedroom (combined with its exhortations that he must not inform
his parents about its presence):

> The Tooth Fairy exuded a sweet, unpleasant, mushroom-like odor. Sam
> couldn't take his eyes from the creature's erect cock. Straining from
> the swart bush of black curls, it was unpleasantly white and marbled with

prominent veins. Sam was mesmerized into wanting to touch it and yet simultaneously repulsed by the terrifying organ. (p. 62)

What makes this explicit description especially disturbing is our growing realisation that the tooth fairy takes on shape and form partly in relation to Sam's own neuroses, a connection that is first made just prior to this description of the fairy, as Sam stands in the garage:

> Something quivered in the crate. Objects shivered and tumbled aside. Some black, unpleasantly warm, hairy thing brushed against [Sam's] hand, sweeping along his arm . . .
> Even as it moved, the black thing seemed to take its shape and form from the box of objects itself. Black trailing wires resolved them-selves into hair. Interlocking cogs became a face. Pieces of wood, cardboard and metal accreted to the thing as it shook itself free of the other objects in the box, until spitting and snarling, still gripping his wrist in a handcuff of wire, it was the Tooth Fairy. (p. 58)

According to Todorov, fantastic narratives must sustain a degree of hesitancy on the part of the reader as to whether the narrative being read is of a supernatural or a psychological nature: 'In a world which is indeed our world, the one we know, a world without devils, sylph-ides, or vampires, there occurs an event which cannot be explained.'[28] It is not only in relation to Sam that the problematic boundaries between realist and anti-realist narrative modes are explored: as *The Tooth Fairy* progresses, the relationship between hallucination and the supernatural becomes more confused. Supporting the suggestion that the tooth fairy is an outward projection of childhood trauma is the fact that the gender of the fairy shifts in relation to aspects of Sam's own sexual and behavioural development. Shoring up the suggestion that the tooth fairy is an actual supernatural presence, as the narrative progresses characters other than Sam become not only affected but apparently contacted by the fairy: '*It's spilling over, he thought, it's spilling over*' (p. 193; original italics). Question marks continually accrue around the border territory between reality and dreams, from Sam's 'off the cuff' remark to his girlfriend Alice that, 'You can't tell the difference between fantasy and reality' (p. 197) through to a more sustained interrogation of this relationship, often through the mechanism of dreams.

As in Byatt's story, on more than one occasion the wood in which Tooley's body is believed to be buried becomes a space in which normality is suspended. Hence, in chapter 23, an unusual instance of 'purple prose' accompanies Sam's entrance: 'It was a moment in closed time, a dream of ecstatic paralysis, a phase of Creation in which the trees waited impatiently to take on color, sound, texture. Sam felt like an intruder offered a glimpse of the miraculous' (p. 155). The fact that something is 'wrong' in the writing here is mirrored, two chapters later, by a dream not signalled to us as a dream at all: 'Some days after that Sam found himself in the woods, on his way to see Alice' (p. 173). Fear and mistrust accompany Sam's every step until he finds Alice has, all along, been a 'honey-trap' in league with Tooley, himself returned from the dead. As Tooley and his gang strip Sam and bind him to a tree, Alice supplies them with cigarettes: 'Understanding what they were about to do, Sam pissed himself with fright. Together they advanced on him, lighted cigarettes held like darts and leveled at his face, chest and genitals' (p. 175). A mixture of fear and betrayal are shared between Sam and the reader before Sam wakes to discover that he has simply been having a differ-ent type of wet dream: 'He woke up, still hyperventilating ... He'd had the dream several times before, and he knew he would have it again. Then in shame he realised he'd pissed the bed in his sleep' (p. 175).

Photographing Fairies: *framing the dead*

Like Joyce's novel and Byatt's story, Steve Szilagyi's novel *Photo-graphing Fairies* (1995) explores the conventional interface between childhood innocence and the fairy realm in a manner that reconceives the relationship between the supernatural, sex and death. Once again this novel engages with a contemporary legend, this time born out of early twentieth-century technological illusion. Between 1917 and 1920, two young girls, Frances Griffiths and Elsie Wright, claimed to have taken photographs of fairies living in a 'beck', or small stream, by their house, in the Yorkshire village of Cottingley.

Fig. 2 'Alice and the Fairies' © 1917. Reproduced by kind permission of the Science and Society Picture Library, National Museum of Science and Industry.

For many decades, although the photographs were 'known' to be fakes, it proved impossible for experts to discover the means by which they had been produced. Only when the *British Journal of Photography* finally extracted a confession from Elsie in 1983 was the fakery 'proven' (or at least admitted).

In this alluring but escapist staging of pre-adolescent femininity, the supernatural, technical trickery and British pastoral idealism, packaged as both a fiction (the names Alice and Iris replacing Elsie and Frances) and a 'fact' (that fairies are real), we find an apparent antidote to the horrors of the First World War, a time when, Anthony Vidler argues, 'The site of the uncanny ... more properly extended to the no man's land between the trenches, or the fields of ruins left after bombardment'.[29] At the same time, in all the various adaptations exploring the Cottingley legend we see that the Gothic darkness of death and perversity is never far removed from child's play.

Fig. 3 'Fairy Offering Flowers to Iris' © 1920. Reproduced by kind permission of the Science and Society Picture Library, National Museum of Science and Industry.

Szilagyi's novel is framed by his narrator, Charles Castle, telling the story retrospectively from the confined space of a condemned cell on the eve of his execution. Of what he is believed to be guilty we do not discover for another two hundred pages, divided into twenty-nine chapters, each of which (ironically, considering Frances and Elsie's reluctance to 'tell all') takes the form of a type of confessional, reinforced by every chapter carrying the heading 'How I ...'. As the narrator's reminiscences become progressively darker we find fairies and death forming the natural accompaniments for unnatural desire. The narrative opens with Castle, a photographer, becoming embroiled in a case linked to fairy photographs after a bluff police-officer brings him a set of prints to verify. Castle, a born sceptic, dismisses the claim until he subjects the images to closer scrutiny in his darkroom, at which point he discovers that 'what had previously appeared to be nothing more than a murky pattern of grays . . .

contained a human figure . . . hidden in the shadowy pattern the way objects are hidden in those illustrations for children'.[30]

It is while pursuing the riddle of the fairy photographs that Castle travels to Burkinwell (Szilagyi's fictional version of Cottingley) in search of Clara and Anna (the fictional versions of Frances and Elsie). En route he befriends a young woman on the train, who turns out to be the wife of an athletic and well-respected man of the cloth, bearing the strange name Reverend Drain. As Castle and Mrs Linda Drain become closer, the village starts to gossip about inappropriate intimacy, an intimacy that reaches its climax beneath the floor of the church, in a mysterious room of unspecified former function and accessible only from behind the altar. Castle turns this subterranean closet into a makeshift darkroom and then Linda persuades Castle to let her help him develop the images. What makes this stranger is Castle's decision that he will oil himself from head to toe and strip naked to develop them, apparently to prevent contamination of the images from dust particles. Linda joins him, stoking their shared desires:

> I recall great waves of perfect sensation (working in the dark wonderfully sharpens the senses); kisses were more profound than any I had ever felt . . . We lost ourselves in each other. Such sliding, rolling, perfect disembodied pleasure I have never known . . . We are born, we suffer, and we die. But it may all be worthwhile, if only for moments such as those I enjoyed with Linda Drain in the basement of that church. (p. 281)

Despite the erotic use to which Castle and Linda Drain put the room, it is a space to which superstition easily attaches itself. Castle cannot resist taunting Dennis, the church handyman, a forty-year-old man with learning difficulties, telling him ghost stories:

> Maybe it's an old tomb. Or an ancient dungeon. Or a torture chamber. Think of how many lost souls may have died in agony between those very walls! Why, the stones may reverberate to eternity with their ghostly cries of men hung from chains, torn on the rack, or lashed with a cat-o'nine-tails . . .
>
> The graveyard comes right up to the side of the church. That means, when I'm down in my darkroom, only a few feet of stone and earth stand between me and a hundred buried corpses. Imagine what spirits could seep through as I stand there in total darkness. (pp. 198–9)

Like Penny and Primrose in Byatt's story, Castle has a pre-history where ghost stories are concerned. Though we encounter him as an adult, the child is very much to the fore in Castle's psyche:

> I've been [scaring myself] since I was a little boy . . .
>
> I recall the approach of midnight when I was a child. Lying in my bed, in my little room . . . I would stiffen as the Old North Church chimed the quarter hours after eleven; the hands of its black-faced clock inexorably crawling toward 'the witching hour' . . .
>
> My terrors would last for a full hour . . . Lying awake, I would stare at the door, expecting it at any minute to creak slowly open and admit the shrouded, scythe-bearing figure I had seen in magazine illustrations labeled 'Death' . . . (pp. 204–5)

Castle, then, is susceptible to ghosts and it is this, as much as his photographic trade, that makes him a magnet for the exploration of child and adult relationships in *Photographing Fairies*. Indeed, despite Castle's final promise that, beyond the grave he 'will not communicate with anyone by Ouija board, table rapping, or mediumistic trance' (p. 315), one cannot but argue that the adult Castle, too, is attracted to darkness:

> I was immersed in darkness. But that darkness was not complete. Luminous creatures, loosed from the pool of dreams, patrolled the deep, black trenches of my oblivion . . . Gradually suffusing the murk with shades of gold, peach, and amber, [a] light drew me forward, luring me from the caverns of sleep with the promise of a new beginning, on a new ground: not the permanently scarred, corpse-strewn Cemetery Ridge of a life lived so far . . . (p. 163)

This passage falls midway through the book, as Castle is re-emerging from unconsciousness, having been beaten up by Paolo and Shorty, two thugs masquerading as porters, whom he first meets at his departure station as he catches the train to Burkinwell. His ill-advised decision to employ their services proves the fatal flaw that sets in train the sequence of events resulting in his murder conviction. Though his first sight, on waking, is that of 'an exquisite blond [*sic*] child, carrying an armload of linens' (p. 165), she is swiftly replaced by Linda, whose libertine tendencies are once again reflected in her chastisement of her husband for his disapproval of Castle, whose plight he assumes to derive from licentious encounters at the gypsy camp: 'He doesn't have to tell us anything . . . Mr Castle's private affairs are his own business' (p. 169).

Linda Drain combines both the vamp and (reinforced by her married name) elements of the vampire. For her, Castle's active libido and tangential relationship to 'respectable' life are attractive features, matched in her own, and her appetites fill Castle with 'a terrible longing' inspired by her 'eyes, face, lips, hands, waist, and curving lips [read hips?]' (p. 237). On one of the first occasions when Castle meets her in the church, she is 'lying on a stack of pillows piled in front of the altar . . . an illustrated magazine on her lap and a box of chocolates at her side. A shoe dangled from one foot' (pp. 123–4). Throughout this novel, one of its most Gothic aspects derives from the very adult sexuality surrounding the childhood sensuality that enables the communion with fairies to occur. The children's father, Brian Templeton, has syphilis; Walsmear is shown to have had an adulterous relationship with Templeton's wife and Castle has a highly developed libido himself, as his sexual dalliances with the full-bodied Esmirelda at the Starry Night pub demonstrate. Later we learn that Walsmear has transferred his affections from Templeton's wife to Esmirelda, following the former's death, news that is greeted with a ribald toast by her former paramours at the inn. As Castle eavesdrops on this spectacle, he is hypocritical enough to contemplate that 'The men seemed to be from the whole range of social classes. My God, I thought. What diseases might I have caught?' (p. 273). Most shocking of all, however, in this amoral novel, are the nocturnal passions of the Reverend Drain, who – despite appearances to the contrary – is revealed to be far from chaste. Creeping, naked, into the garden of the child photographers at dead of night, he slides on his back under a bush, concealed by the foliage and drooping blossoms:

> His hands stroked his torso, then moved down toward his groin. There, they hovered, and he seemed to be gathering some invisible substance in the air. He did not touch his member, but as he made his gathering movement around it, it achieved a condition of straining engorgement. I turned away, sick with disgust . . . But his hands – they were strangely inactive. I couldn't help thinking that Drain was not

actually doing anything to himself; but that he was, in fact, having something done to him. It was eerie. I didn't like it. (pp. 213–14)

As the Reverend's pleasure builds, Castle, who witnesses at first hand, realises Drain is lying on the spot where the children play fairies, and immediately assumes Drain to have paedophiliac tendencies: 'You bastard, I thought; and as he reached his jetting goal, I hurled the stone at his head' (p. 214). In fact, Drain's erotic charge is provoked (and drained) by the fairies, not the children, but this does not prevent, at its periphery, the possibility of uncomfortable desires in relation to young girls, for whom the fairies might stand in as decoy.

Though Castle continually expresses his lack of connection with the world of children, informing us, at the end of chapter 4 that, 'being unmarried, thirty-two, and without a close female companion, I couldn't see any children entering my life soon' (p. 39) and again, in chapter 17, that 'I don't usually get along well with children (I had no brothers or sisters myself) . . . [yet] the Templeton girls had no trouble bringing me on to their level and making a suitable play-mate out of me' (p. 175), we recognise, not least in the aforementioned recounting of his fear of ghosts, the child in Castle that is awakened by the girls' relationship with the 'beyond'. This occurs even before he meets them in person, as he stares, transfixed, at the fairy photographs: 'Damned how they affected me! . . . They seemed to burst right out of those common, uninteresting snapshots and right into my heart' (p. 23). Castle's relationship with the fairies is not the same as Drain's, therefore. When he enjoys his own sensual encounter with them it is far more child-like (perhaps even innocent) in form:

Being touched by the fairies was an experience that was so far unlike anything that I had felt before, my mental workings had trouble finding their accustomed channels . . . This splendid zephyr seemed to whisk away the accumulated experience of my adult life like so much dust, baring what lay beneath: that delightful childhood state where fascinations succeed one another without stopping, where curiosity aches and is satisfied and renewed with every glance. (p. 249)

In part it is Castle's ability to both embrace the erotic pleasures of adult sexuality and maintain sufficient innocence to engage with the fairies at play that heightens his awareness of the inevitable death confronting childhood innocence. At one point he opines, 'I knew of the stream of filth running beneath the surface of respectable life' (p. 213), an observation immediately drawing our attention to the (D)drains. Hence, immediately following his delight in the photographic images of Clara and Anna, he realises 'those girls were going to die ... someday their bright, fresh, freckled faces would wither and disintegrate. Just as those cheap photographs would someday turn brown and curl up at the edges' (p. 23).

At this early point in the twentieth century, photography sustains a close association with the supernatural, one not entirely eradicated as the century progresses. As J. Sconce observes at its end, 'the electronically mediated worlds of telecommunications often evoke the supernatural by creating virtual beings that appear to have no physical form'.[31] Though Jo Collins and John Jervis observe that 'it is doubtless the camera that carried [the] sense of technology as uncanny into the heart of nineteenth-century culture',[32] the direct economic legacy of that uncanny presence in the twentieth results in the monstrous proliferation of that aspect of commercial photography which claimed to be able to capture the image of dead spirits on camera, a 'profession' that was especially lucrative during the First World War. In relation to this desire to see what cannot be seen, the issue of how one views the fairies in Templeton's garden becomes central. Castle tells us that, in spying on the fairies, 'I had to both look and to *not* look: to stare hard out of the corner of my eye, to swoop in with the full pupil, then look away and swoop in again at the last possible moment' (p. 245). In the darkroom, under the church, a similar sensation haunts him: 'I kept seeing things ... out of the corner of my eye. Flickering shadows. I would quickly turn. Nothing' (p. 200). In pulling together, here, apparitions prompted by superstition and apparitions prompted by scientific procedure, we realise that just as images imprint themselves upon photographic paper with the aid of chemicals, so the fairies are only to be seen once the viewer has ingested a hallucinogenic plant from the garden. At this point questions of drug-induced hallucination enter the text and, certainly, the manner in which Castle comes round from his enchantment appears to be a form of 'cold turkey':

As my body dropped into the attitude of slumber, I had the impression that at the same time it was being lifted off the ground . . . and the velocity of my transportation seemed to accelerate . . . As I went faster and faster, my heart began to race, my stomach seized up, and all my muscles grew disobedient in their dread. Then, when it seemed like I had reached a truly awful rate of speed, I crashed. It was like slamming into a wall. There was a horrible, sickening second of unconsciousness. Then I awoke. (p. 251)

Early on in the text, Castle warns Sir Arthur Conan Doyle (or, at least, his fictional version in the text) of the mistake of assuming that a fairy 'in nature' would mirror the form it takes on a Victorian nursery frieze:

Look, this fairy here is wearing a gown. Now where did she get it? Are there fairy dress shops? Are there fairy mills where they weave the fabric? And who works in the mills and dress shops? Is there a fairy class system? Are there fairy unions and fairy strikes? (p. 65)

According to Nicola Bown, far from manufacturing industry flourishing in fairyland, 'It is a little-known fact that the industrial revolution caused the extinction of the fairies'. She continues her discussion of this phenomenon through an evaluation of competing scales:

The scene of industry is one in which natural laws have been cast aside, in which human operatives are dwarfed by the vast magnificence of the machinery, rendered obscure by the fiery glow of the furnaces and runnels of liquid metal, or made ant-like in their multitude, and in which the inhuman speed and power of the steam engine is cast as positively demonic.[33]

Here we have it again, the ease with which discussions of the artificial in juxtaposition with the natural consume the debate about the unnatural and the supernatural in relation to children, the discussion of which, it seems, always returns us to this issue of the 'demonic' as an alternative to the saccharine-sweet filter we often overlay upon our cultural readings of children. James R. Kincaid returns us to manufacture: 'what we think of as "the child" has been assembled in reference to desire [and] built up in erotic manufactories . . . we have been labouring ever since, for at least two centuries, both to deny that horrible and lovely product and to maintain it.'[34]

In general terms, Szilagyi does not keep too close an eye on the traditions of fairy lore rather than fairy friezes (for instance, his fairies happily meet Castle's gaze). However, this is a feature that proves in keeping with the nursery style of the original Cottingley images and, for our purposes, it is this that enables the novel to function primarily as a study of haunted innocence, rather than 'pure' super-naturalism. Hence, the coupling scene, in which engorged and aggressive male fairies (or 'elves', as Castle calls them) take their partners to a 'little death' that has the appearance of a real one:

> I now saw before me a grotesque little man . . . not much larger than
> ten inches. But his neck was almost nonexistent, and his head was
> nearly as wide as his shoulders . . . The only parts of his body that lacked
> hairs were his outsized hands and feet and, oddly, his large, knobbly
> genitalia. (pp. 252–3)

Both in their appearance and their voracious sexual appetite, these creatures simultaneously resemble and threaten our view of adult masculinity. As Castle stares at this 'little man' (the length and engorged head of which pose another resemblance to the human phallus), he is shocked to discover that this 'elf' not only meets his gaze, but issues a challenge in the form of 'bar[ing] his little teeth under his beard' (p. 253). Again, metaphors of paedophilia come to mind through these grotesque monsters preying upon innocence under our noses and, not surprisingly, Castle's concern once more is for Anna and Clara: 'This sight, as natural as it might be for the fairies, was nothing for a human child to witness. These were, after all, not mating dragonflies, but creatures cast from a mold similar to that of the human beings around them' (p. 255). The girls, however, have quite another strategy in mind. Grabbing the entwined fairy couples on the pretext that the males are 'hurting' the females, the girls free the females before expertly assassinating the males:

> Clara reached up and took [the male's] large head between her thumb
> and the first three fingers of her free hand. Then she gave it a sharp

little twist, quickly and neatly breaking the elf's neck. Opening her hand, she let the lifeless body flop to the ground, and immediately reached for another. (p. 255)

This is, effectively, a novel about the relationship between the licit and the illicit in all its forms (sexual, criminal, liturgical and medical), which uses the relationship between the supernatural and the natural to frame questions of desire as they accrue around the world of child's play and as they affect children and adults alike. Hence, Castle's 'brush with the law' frames the entire narrative, both in the sense that we follow him from his meeting with Constable Walsmear to his final view of the gallows and in the sense that the entire narrative is bound by the walls of the condemned cell; and, though Castle is no 'innocent', he is innocent of the charge for which he will die: the murder of the Reverend Drain, acted out in Templeton's garden. In a final violent struggle between Castle, Paolo and Shorty, interrupted by the arrival of the Reverend Drain on one of his nocturnal pleasure visits, Shorty crushes Drain's skull with a piece of lead piping (the plumbing connection adding one of two further layers of irony to the demise of Drain, for where does Castle then find sanctuary, but in a brick sewer pipe). The two thugs convince themselves that Drain and Castle have been planning a homosexual tryst, 'evidence' that spurs them on to their attack.

At its most suggestive, one might argue Castle's role resembles that of Poe's narrator in 'The Pit and the Pendulum' (1843), in that his 'confessional' style could also be read as a logician's attempt to evade the inevitable. Poe's protagonist, incarcerated under the Spanish Inquisition, discovers in the darkness a trap and contraptions designed for his execution which, in their ingenuity, in other contexts one might associate with toy-making. Ironically, it is our narrator's fascination with rules and measurements that saves him, for he avoids the pit by stumbling as he paces out the dimensions of his cell, finding that, although '[his] chin rested upon the floor of the prison ... [his] lips and the upper portion of [his] head ... touched nothing'.[35] Having survived that challenge he wakes to find himself bound and prone, facing a bladed pendulum which descends, incrementally, with every swing. This he evades by calculating the arc of the blade in tandem with the dimensions of the descent. Having effected the calculation, he employs logic in enlisting the help of a swarm of rats, coating his bindings in rancid meat in order to encourage the rats to gnaw them off. Freed from that fate at the final swing of the blade, he finds the walls of his cell begin to glow with heat and, like the blade, advance upon him. Szilagyi will let Castle die in his cell, but Poe is more merciful, saving his prisoner on the brink of impending doom as the French army burst in.

Poe's story is effectively one of burial alive and takes much of its Gothicism from darkness combined with demonic architecture and fittings belonging to medieval church iconography; hence, the 'seven tall candles upon the table' which 'seemed white slender angels' to our protagonist before metamorphosing into 'meaningless spectres, with heads of flame, and I saw from them there would be no help'.[36] By contrast, the church of St Anastansias in *Photographing Fairies*, 'was like a great stone shed with Gothic ornaments attached, the way decorations are stuck to a wedding cake' (p. 196). It is this aspect of what one might call 'Strawberry Hill playfulness' which characterises much of Szilagyi's novel and which ensures that, though we pity Castle, we never greatly fear for him as we do for Poe's narrator: in *Photographing Fairies*, *kitsch* ultimately wins out over *kirche*.

The Cottingley fairies continue to hold a kitsch fascination for us in the present day, from an episode of the BBC television programme *Antiques Roadshow*, broadcast on 4 January 2009 from Belfast, which featured the original photographs brought for valuation by descendants of Elsie and Frances, through to Nick Willing's erotically charged cinematic adaptation of *Photographing Fairies* (1997), awarded a '15' certificate by the British Board of Film Censors, an aspect that is perfectly in keeping with Szilagyi's original narrative. Again, this film employs the photographs in order to focus upon death and adult melancholia, Nick Willing and Chris Harrald adding a prelude to the narrative, in which Castle marries and honeymoons in Switzerland in 1912. While walking in the Alps, a crevasse opens in the snowfield and his new bride plummets to her death. From this point Castle addresses his grief by dedicating himself stolidly to exploding any myths of the occult or the afterlife. Though he takes photographs which will be sold as family portraits containing the dead sons lost in the War, the parents are fully aware that these are artificially composed from a photograph taken of his assistant in army uniform, a photograph of the face of the dead man having been inserted in place of the assistant's face, and the whole image rephotographed. Castle's later encounters with the fairies therefore open up a door into that forbidden space of desire where resides his dead wife.

Death and the doll's house: FairyTale: A True Story *and* M. R. James

It is to a third adaptation of the Cottingley legend, *Fairy Tale: A True Story* (1997), this time aimed directly at children and carrying a 'U' (Universal) certificate, that we now turn. This film returns us, through its title, to the litany attached to the child misery narratives discussed above (Truth, Survival and Betrayal) and shares the fascination with death and melancholia explored by both Szilagyi and Willing. However, and perhaps because of the necessary absence of explicit sexual content, *FairyTale: A True Story* is much more centrally engaged with the ghostly elements of child's play and their connection with traditional fairy lore, the centrepiece for which in this film is the doll's house.

The doll's house is the work of the late Joseph Wright, a child who has recently died of consumption, aided by his sister Elsie (in this film both girls retain the same name as their real-life counterparts). Standing in as a souvenir of his loss, post-death the toy takes on the status of a miniature mausoleum: 'Don't touch it!' Elsie exclaims, as it takes Frances's interest. The reason for its construction are the fairies who inhabit the local beck, for whom Joseph believed he was providing both a shelter and an offering. The fairies are said to have abandoned the beck following Joseph's death, and there is more than a suggestion (certainly a belief held by his mother, who forbids Elsie from playing in the beck again) that it might have been the fairies' resentment at his trespassing on their territory, rather than gratitude for the gift, that played a role in his demise. So we recall the vindictiveness of the traditional fairy, as discussed earlier in relation to Joyce's novel.

Where Castle plays the sceptic in Szilagyi's novel, in *FairyTale: A True Story* two other characters fill this function: Harry Houdini, the American escapologist (1874–1926), whose role is to draw attention to two differing forms of 'impossibility', the staged illusion versus the supernatural, and a newspaper journalist from the *Bradford Telegraph and Argus*, to whom the true Gothic aspects of this film attach themselves. One evening Frances, Elsie and her mother are invited to London by Sir Arthur Conan Doyle, while Elsie's father competes in and wins a local chess competition. Knowing the house to be empty, the journalist breaks in and enters Joseph's room, seeking out evidence of fakery in relation to the photographs. Here he finds Joseph's drawings and proceeds to manipulate the figures to see if he can 'prove' the images are staged. At this point the window opens and the wind scatters Joseph's papers, pelting the journalist in the face (the similarity to flying fairies is obvious). The Gothic storm inside the room shortly dies down as the casement is lowered and an apparition can be seen: Joseph, at his desk. He stands, candle in hand, and approaches the journalist, who backs away. As we watch, Joseph passes through the man's body – itself a nice reminder of the possibilities afforded by celluloid trickery – and out of the door behind. The journalist, who enters the house thinking he is going to prove the non-existence of fairies and leaves with proof of the existence of ghosts, throws himself out of the window. What is most affecting for the viewer on the level of mourning is that it is only the journalist who ever sees the dead Joseph, while we are aware of the aching need in his mother, father and sister (mirrored in that of Sir Arthur Conan Doyle for his own dead son): this is Joseph's 'single exposure' in the film.

At the start of this chapter I observed the importance of arguments surrounding sight and absence in relation to the media fascination with child safety. In *Fairy Tale: A True Story*, we are once again reminded that when children 'disappear' their invisibility looms large. One final intertextual connection is with J. M. Barrie's *Peter Pan*, first staged as theatre in 1904 before being written up as a novel for children, *Peter Pan and Wendy*, in 1928. *Fairy Tale: A True Story* begins with a scene from *Peter Pan*, both helping to root the setting of the narrative in the right period and establishing the sense of darkness underlying children's play. What both texts also share is a conclusion revolving around the trope of the doll's house. As Wendy returns home to her mother at the end of the play she bids farewell to the orphan Peter, but not before her own mother has offered to take him in. When he refuses, she asks 'Where will you live, Peter?' to which he replies: 'In the house we built for Wendy. The fairies are to put it high up among the tree-tops where they sleep at night . . .'[37] As Susan Stewart observes, 'Occupying a space within an enclosed space, the dollhouse's aptest analogy is the locket or the secret recesses of the heart: center within center, within within within.'[38]

Toys can encourage extremes of possessiveness and self-centredness in all children, and perhaps the most internalising emotion of all – for both children and adults – is avarice, in which a miserly condition of self-fulfilment ensues. M. R. James's story 'The Haunted Dolls' House' (1923) is such a narrative of adult greed and its deathly effect upon children. Fittingly, the story opens in a shop, with a transaction between vendor and customer. The exchange between the two of them is as much one of repartee as it is economics: the opening gambit of the customer, Mr Dillet is an attempt to tease out the level of knowledge of his salesman: 'I suppose you get stuff of that kind through your hands pretty often?'[39] Both parties are clearly 'in the know' regarding the aesthetic value of the item that, however, quickly pales into insignificance the moment it is purchased. Immediately we shift, to the relief not just of the shopkeeper, Mr Chittendom, but also of his wife 'Thank God for that . . . I'd sooner it was him than another.' (p. 267)

The dolls' house in question is both an object of definite outline and value ('sixty guineas' is the sum upon which our narrator thinks they eventually settled (p. 267)) and one of utter indeterminacy. By daylight its layout is clear and conventional: 'When the front of the house was open you saw four large rooms, bedroom, dining-room, drawing-room and kitchen, each with its appropriate furniture in a very complete state' (p. 268). In the early hours of the morning, however, Mr Dillet discovers a complex combination of clarity and obscurity:

> though there was no light at all in the room . . . The effect was that of a bright harvest moon shining full on the front of a big white stone mansion – a quarter of a mile away it might be, and yet every detail was photographically sharp . . . with another shock he realized that, above the house, he was looking, not at the wall of his room with its pictures, but into the profound blue of a night sky. (p. 269)

As the miniaturist aspect of the tale suggests, it is as if Mr Dillet is watching a fairy enactment of a family drama. Certainly, theatricality is a key element of the story, as it is as if the dolls' house were a stage or, indeed, 'the box' which sits in the living room of our own houses and which projects, like a magic lantern, stories 'cut down to size' in the form of a variety of family sagas – always, as here, at the same time of night. The projection aspect of the narrative is reinforced as Mr Dillet peers at the house, apparently animated by its own illumination, and observes, 'You mean to show me something' (p. 270). Following the first performance we are told 'there would be a sequel' (p. 271), and just as the stage is unveiled by peeling back curtains prior to the performance, so, as Mr Dillet looks at the windows of the dolls' house, he realises that 'They would in real life have been shuttered or curtained . . . but, as it was, there was nothing to intercept his view of what was being transacted inside the rooms' (p. 270).

The first of the two resulting revelations casts the 'fairy parents' in the lead roles and, as is conventional in drama, the performance opens with both sitting centre-stage. They are 'plotting', and gradually we discover that their plot concerns an elderly man (father to one of them), in bed upstairs. Elements of the 'dumb-show' or the silent cinema tradition appear to characterise this performance, as their gestures are artificially demonstrative, where one might more conventionally expect them to be furtive:

> every now and again [they stopped] to listen, as it seemed . . . When the man left the window he seemed to leave the room also; and the lady, taper in hand, remained standing and listening . . . [Hers] was a hateful face, too; broad, flat and sly . . . The front door slowly opened and [the man] stepped out and stood on the top of the *perron*, looking this way and that; then turned towards the upper window that was lighted, and shook his fist. (p. 270)

As one might expect in a narrative concerning toys, these two characters are not simply play-acting, but engaging in play. Though acting out the role of dutiful daughter and son-in-law, their plan is to murder the father(-in-law), a plot which they hope will result in financial gain. While he is invalided in his bed, the daughter enlists the nurse's help in administering a poison draught, following which, and after a brief period of calm, the old man suddenly jolts awake: 'He was a sad and terrible sight – flushed in the face, almost to blackness, the eyes glaring whitely, both hands clutching at his heart, foam at his lips' (p. 271). Throughout the text, emphasis is placed upon the expression each of the characters has on his/her face and the ill-fitting nature of that expression in relation to their actions. Here, the grotesque visage of the old man is apparently mirrored in the 'horrified' look on his daughter's face at the news, except that we know this, too, to be a dumb-show (p. 271).

It is the subsequent revelation that we find the more chilling, however. Following the old man's funeral, though the parents are shown dressed in mourning, they act with jocularity. Standing beside their children's beds, the father play-acts the haunting of the children by the recent corpse, though unbeknownst to him our representative, Mr Dillet, has already witnessed the dead body rise from its coffin:

> the father was seen to go on tiptoe out of the room, taking with him as he went a white garment that hung on a peg near the door . . . A minute or two later . . . A bent form of sinister shape stepped across to the truckle-beds, and suddenly stopped, threw up its arms and revealed, of course, the father, laughing. (p. 272)

Where the father finds this sick game comedic, the children are genuinely terrified. Left alone by their parents, the nurse drowses, affording their grandfather (or, at least, a risen monster in his form) entry: 'The seer does not like to dwell upon what he saw entering the room: he says it might be described as a frog – the size of a man – but it had scanty white hair about its head. It was busy about the truckle-beds, but not for long' (p. 272). What haunts here is the similarity evoked, for readers of the twenty-first century, not so much with the ghost as with the abusing parent or guardian. Like such figures of contemporary domestic monstrosity, this ghoul rises after dark, creeps into children's bedrooms and 'plays about' with them in the privacy (read 'secrecy') of their homes. James R. Kincaid is right: 'Demonizing [the paedophile] . . . we call loudly for his presence',[40] and perhaps this is the father's error in acting the part of the one whom he most (at least apparently) loathes. In all these texts the Gothic takes on a kind of pathological direction, tracing an obsession in society which cannot make up its mind whether it is appalled or enthralled by children and the dangers by which, in their name, *we* are haunted. Having progressed from Bly, to Cottingley, to the world of the doll's house, in chapter 2 we now turn to face the Gothic mansion in its full size, and explore those structures within which those fears materialise.

2

Building Suspense: Architectural Gothic

❦

Daphne du Maurier's *Rebecca* (1938) is arguably the most iconic of all twentieth-century Gothic narratives and Manderley its structural centrepiece. As solidly constructed as any Gothic castle, Manderley is nevertheless the product of a ghostly dream:

> Last night I dreamt I went to Manderley again . . . and for a while I could not enter, for the way was barred to me . . . Then, like all dreamers, I was possessed of a sudden with supernatural powers and passed like a spirit through the barrier before me.[1]

It is this ambivalence between architectural intimidation and the alluring fragility of the boundaries between fear and desire that has characterised the Gothic since its earliest inception. From Mrs Radcliffe's 'mouldering walls of dark grey stone' and 'edifice[s] . . . invested with the solemn duskiness of evening', through to Walpole's Strawberry Hill, Stoker's view of Dracula's Castle, 'from whose tall black windows came no ray of light, and whose broken battlements showed a jagged line against the moonlit sky' or Carter's version of Bluebeard's lair in *The Bloody Chamber*, 'with its turrets of misty blue, its courtyard, its spiked gate . . . at home neither on the land nor on the water, a mysterious, amphibious place', buildings enclose our internalised fears.[2] As Mark S. Madoff observes, 'The locked-room mystery is characteristic of the Gothic. It nearly is the

Fig. 4 Giovanni Battista Piranesi, *Carceri d'Invenzione*, Plate XIV, *Untitled* (The Gothic Arch) © The Trustees of the British Museum.

Gothic.'[3] Yet, how important that 'nearly' is, for as we become increasingly fascinated with the mind and the body as containers for the ego, we also find flesh and psyche operating as surrogate interior chambers.

The psychological dimension inherent in architectural design is nothing new. The work of the eighteenth-century Venetian artist and architect, Giovanni Battista Piranesi (1720–78) is often cited as an early inspiration to more recent Gothic writers and artists, handed down through the Romantic Movement.

According to Anthony Vidler, in *The Architectural Uncanny* (1992), Coleridge's own 'fantasies of the architectural sublime' and, through his, Thomas de Quincey's, were inspired by a 'faulty recollection of Piranesi's Carceri etchings ... in which the prison etchings, variously described as dreams, drug-induced deliria, and prisons of the mind, take on the aspects of labyrinths through which the artist wanders'.[4] Vidler dislikes such slippage between the materiality of Piranesi's architecture and its psychological inferences, and one might argue that Eve Kosofsky Sedgwick feels similarly, though approaching from a different perspective:

> The confusion of the stairways is, of course, only symptomatic of the
> fact that it is impossible to organize the spaces in any of these prints

into architectural space. Architecture delineates and places in relation
to each other an inside and an outside. In the *Carceri* it is impossible to
construct in imagination the shell that would delimit this inside from
a surrounding outside ... density of detail and the complete lack of
open 'sky' space make it impossible to imagine them as being in any
sense outside.[5]

Nevertheless, all literary forms rely upon our ability to draw symbolic
readings from material ingredients and, in a twentieth-century
context, Piranesi also lays an important foundation for the work of
another psychologically resonant artist whose work is architectural
in focus, the Dutch modernist, M. C. Escher (1898-1970) (see fig. 5).

Where Escher's drawings are a complex combination of clarity and
obscurity, daylight filling 'Relativity' (1953) while simultaneously
conveying a lack of grounded perspective (where does inside become
outside and ceiling become floor, for instance?), the murk of Piranesi's
'Gothic Arch' renders it (as its unofficial title suggests) characteristically
Gothic. To return to Kosofsky Sedgwick's observation, in Escher there
is a similar lack of clarity in the boundaries between 'interior and
exterior', but a dissimilar relationship to transparency.

Escher's use of transparency is characteristically modernist; as Mark
Edmundson observes, 'By creating dwellings and offices that had
no room for clutter and ornament ... you removed the dead hand
of the past' In the Gothic, of course, 'dead hands', not to mention
the past, are central, and it is for this reason that Escher may, at first
glance, seem modernist rather than Gothic, as 'The eye travel[s] out
into the sky from the glassed-in study or office and [sees] no end
to its dominion' (Escher even dispensing with the glass). By contrast,
the Gothic embraces what Edmundson calls 'tricky shifts and hidden
meanings, unplumbable depths'. There is an evident lack of clutter
in Escher's work (a tray with a bottle and jug, two potted plants, one
sack and a ewer appear to be the only 'props'), matched by the minimal
clothing worn by the fifteen figures. Nevertheless, despite the fact that
a breezy lack of windows seems to suggest easy movement from inside
to outside, there are a number of shut doors and partially obscured
rooms which are carefully screened off from the observer. Here the
Gothic intrudes, for 'Relativity' appears to *show* transparency while
simultaneously suggesting that clarity and light are no proof of a lack

Fig. 5 M. C. Escher, 'Relativity' © 2009 The M. C. Escher Company-Holland.
All rights reserved. *www.mcescher.com.*

of secrecy: there may well be skeletons lurking in those closets. Nor
do the ideological contradictions of such aspirational towers go un-
noticed: 'One saw one's own image, vague, spectral (haunting),
looking wanly back as one stared out through the great panes of glass.'[6]

As is generally agreed among critics, as the nineteenth century
progresses the Gothic moves away from the country towards the city,
culminating in what Allan Lloyd-Smith identifies as the 'abhuman
Gothic horror ... [of] urban squalor and misery ... among a polyglot
immigrant population'.[7] During the twentieth century the relationship between architecture and the uncanny equally moves away from
the traditional image of the haunted house, and perhaps even the
haunted labyrinths of those claustrophic, foggy London streets
depicted in Stevenson's *The Strange Case of Dr Jekyll and Mr Hyde* (1886)
and its many cinematic adaptations, to new metropolitan signifiers
of the architectural uncanny.

Haunted geometries I: Kipling, 'Swept and Garnished'[8]

This does not preclude *any* instance of domesticated haunting in the twentieth century. Take Rudyard Kipling's story, 'Swept and Garnished' (1915), written during the First World War, in which Kipling uses the ghost story form to show how German military aggression haunts its own people. Frau Ebermann is a well-to-do German woman suffering from a fever, during which she is 'visited', first by one child and then by five young children. In generic terms it is a story situated on the boundaries between Gothicism and hallucination, falling quite clearly into Todorov's definition of the literary fantastic and dependent upon reader hesitancy for effect.[9] The entire frame of the tale is traditionally Gothic, set as it is entirely within one room, in which there is reiterated reference to locked and unlocked doors and the questioning of the means via which entry and exit of the children is effected. Unusually, however, rather than the innocent interloper intruding into a world of dark secrets, these children, in intruding, bring that dark world with them; to rework Mark Madoff's reading of the relationship between inside and outside a little, 'The[se] protagonist[s penetrate] . . . the boundary between outside and inside *because* the outside is open, obvious, familiar and unsatisfying in its simplicity and rationality; *because* the inside is closed, obscure, exotic and alluring.'[10]

Class is a crucial theme of the story: the central protagonist lives in a 'comfortable' Berlin flat and employs a servant, but race is also ravelled up in the social 'mix'. This is a story aimed at placing German military might squarely in a negative spotlight and Frau Ebermann's secure sense of her own class position is to be interpreted as a form of national arrogance. Nevertheless, Kipling gives Frau Ebermann narrative point of view, aimed at provoking a tension encouraging both our identification with her and, simultaneously, choreographing a separation that enables us to cloak ourselves in that sense of innate superiority readers are encouraged to adopt in all texts. As part of this characterisation (one might say caricature), Frau Ebermann is attributed with a personality privileging rationality and order over emotion and intuition. Hence, the very first words of the story inform us (initially it seems by an omniscient third-person narrator, but quickly we realise this is actually free indirect thought): 'When the first waves of feverish cold stole over [her] she very wisely telephoned the doctor and went to bed.'[11] Repeatedly, we are told she is balanced, logical and measured in her actions and thoughts, so much so that the key symptom demonstrating her illness hinges upon a misplaced object spoiling the visual balance of the room:

> Of a sudden she noticed that an imitation-lace cover which should have lain mathematically square with the imitation-marble top of the radiator behind the green plush sofa had slipped away so that one corner hung over the bronze-painted steam-pipes . . . She tried to get up and set the whole thing straight, but the radiator at once receded toward the horizon, which, unlike true horizons, slanted diagonally, exactly parallel with the dropped lace edge of the cover. (p. 226)

As we will see later, geometry is often used as an accompaniment to the Gothic, as if a disturbance in one element of the senses is sufficient to inject a sense of the uncanny into others. In literary terms one is also reminded, here, of Virginia Woolf's short story 'The Mark on the Wall' (1921), in which the female protagonist, once again framed within her own domestic environment, suddenly espies 'a small round mark, black upon the white wall, about six or seven inches above the mantelpiece'. Woolf's story is not Gothic, but it does incorporate elements of a shadow-world, literalised in its apparently three-dimensional projection from the wall, before retreating into banality: 'Ah, the mark on the wall! It was a snail.'[12] Where Woolf delays and then resolves hesitancy, however, Kipling sustains it. The psychological element of the Gothic is developed further through the introduction of the servant with the lexically symmetrical name 'Anna', whose own preferred method of humouring her employer is to give visual form to this nominal symmetry, restoring the cloth to its former position by 'measur[ing] the equal margins' either side of it with her knuckle (p. 227).

Such attention to detail should also be addressed to the wording of the passage. Here, the repetition of the adjective 'imitation', combined with the later use of the phrase 'bronze-painted steam pipes', draws attention to the presence of modernity. Though arguably designating the impoverishment of nature in favour of artifice, it also incorporates the presiding discourse of logic to imply the presence of industrialised 'civilization' in the face of the barbarism of war. At the time Kipling's story was first published, Freud had not written his landmark essay 'The Uncanny' (1919), but certainly this domicile perfectly embraces the characteristics Freud will later identify with the *unheimlich*, namely the rendering of the familiar unfamiliar by the presence of a small but irrevocable shift in one's relationship with one's own home (even if the central heating removes us from the literal comforts of a hearth). Furthermore, as we saw in chapter 1, there is something especially uncanny about misplaced or disappeared/ reappeared children: 'Frau Ebermann had had children of her own, but they were all grown-up now, and she had never been a child-lover in any sense' (p. 227).

Frau Ebermann is a married woman with an absent husband and, in that sense, the presence of his absence, signalled by the married female prefix 'Frau', equates her with the huge numbers of European women whose husbands are missing and dead at this time. Thus Kipling's story prioritises the political over the personal and speaks of *mass* child-maiming and murder, rather than the individual victims we encountered in chapter 1. In being confronted by these ghosts, Frau Ebermann is free from personal accusation only to become subject to national guilt:

> That is a lie. There cannot be a hundred even, much less a thousand . . .You should have been more careful. You should not have run out to see the horses and guns passing. That is how it is done when our troops pass through. My son has written me so. (p. 233)

In terms of military history, Andrew Rutherford tells us that the precise event to which Kipling is believed to be referring in the story is the German invasion of neutral Belgium, during which 'atrocities, including the murder and mutilation of children' were conducted by troops adopting a 'deliberate policy of "frightfulness" (*Schrecklichkeit*)'. Here Rutherford cites John Terraine, who claims that, during the First World War, *Schrecklichkeit* was 'designed to frighten the civilian population into absolute submission with the least possible diversion of German military strength'.[13] By the end of the story Frau Ebermann perceives her room to have become bathed in blood, a spillage which follows her refusal to believe the children's testimony, in response to which 'the elder girl' comments 'Oh, but look, lady!', at which 'Frau Ebermann looked and saw' (p. 233). Though we are not permitted to see what she sees, that the maid returns to find Frau Ebermann on her knees, staunching a puddle with the misplaced cover from the radiator, implies that it is indeed blood.

Through the children's presence, questions of play and lack of play arise. That the children intrude is clear and that the woman 'naturally' associates children with disruption and lack of control is also clear. On one level she is right to do so: the children do not 'belong' in her house and they climb on her furniture, 'boots and all' (p. 230). When she reprimands the first girl for 'finger[ing] and upset[ting]' her things, (p. 227), however, the narrator's description of the child's conduct ('investigating everything that came in her way – the yellow cut-glass handles of the chest of drawers, the stamped bronze hook to hold back the heavy puce curtains, and the mauve enamel, New Art finger-plates on the door' (p. 227)) suggests she is curious, not destructive. Similarly, when the children climb onto the sofa, they do so to sit down, not to bounce and they stand on one leg rather than two through fatigue, not to hop. In fact, it is the protagonist herself who comes closest to game-playing. First she tests Anna's memory in relation to the placing of various objects in the room, akin to the 'memory tray' game played at children's parties. Secondly, she asks the children (we are told 'twenty times') 'why you do not go away – why do you not go away?' (p. 230). The obvious allusion to 'Twenty Questions' here, a game in which one tries to establish, through deduction, the nature of a mystery object, typically beginning with the question 'Is it animal, vegetable, or mineral?', also evokes the unasked question shadowing the one that *is* asked, namely: of what nature *is* this apparition? Moreover, the two (not-) games reinforce the fact that it is in relation to the presence and position of her own 'known' objects that Frau Ebermann tries to negotiate her way through the unknown.

Haunted geometries II: Eco, The Name of the Rose

The presence of two world wars in the first half of the twentieth century obviously shapes many of the historical foundations of the

Gothic, but that does not prevent writers continuing to revisit its medieval foundations. Nor does the ever-increasing percentage of people owning their own homes during the century require *all* Gothic buildings to 'shrink to fit'. Indeed, in terms of the role played by architecture in the twentieth-century Gothic novel, one would be hard pressed to find a better illustration than the fourteenth-century monastic setting of Umberto Eco's *The Name of the Rose*, first published in Italian as *Il nome della rosa* (1980) and translated into English by William Weaver in 1983.

The structure of this novel is complex, and begins before the narrative 'proper' opens, with a Preface by Eco himself in the guise of the frame narrator, dated 5 January, 1980, making claims for the authenticity of the manuscript upon which his novel is based. The means by which he claims to have acquired it is, as is typical in the Gothic, labyrinthine and involves several hands and questionable sources. This narrative 'tease' initiates a presiding structure of writerly play in which the reader delights, but in the truth of which we never actually 'believe'.[14] This section is relatively protracted, but its function is to prepare us in the solving of conundrums, for this is how the novel 'proper' will continue. Thus is Eco/the implied author established as 'discoverer' and 'authenticator' at the same time as he is discredited as a 'mere' teller of fictions.

The Name of the Rose is a challenging book which propels its reader into a detective-like role. Concerned as the novel is with the serial murder of a number of the monks, we can position *The Name of the Rose* alongside other key texts, such as Stevenson's *Jekyll and Hyde* or Sir Arthur Conan Doyle's *The Hound of the Baskervilles*, as Gothic narratives provoking the question of what differentiates them from detective fiction. Immediately preceding the implied author's Preface, the reader is provided with a map of Melk Abbey, where the narrative events take place, clearly identifying the precise layout of each building and its walled location. Such early clarity, however, is another 'trick', for from this point the pace of the narrative proceeds by means of an uneven generic rhythm, alternating between compelling moments of murder/mystery storytelling and the intrusion of cliffhanger 'teases', such as that which concludes the 'Sext' chapter in the 'Third Day' section; 'I did not find [Ubertino]; indeed, I did not find him until evening. And so my curiosity stayed with me, for other events were occurring, of which I must now tell' (p. 195). Slowing down the overall pace are lengthy and, in truth, turgid passages of medieval Catholic dogma and counter-dogma. As such, the reader is forced to experience at first hand the frustrated rhythm of the detective: we, too, are looking for a truth, the revelation of which is, as this is, a retrospective narration, withheld from us as obstructively as the cul-de-sacs of the labyrinth in the Aedificium impede the progress of our two main protagonists, the 'learned Franciscan, Brother William of Baskerville' and his junior partner and our primary narrator, the 'young Benedictine novice', Adso (p. 13). Adso it is who is the author of the manuscript which Eco claims to have found, a manuscript he writes in his old age. Such a concertinaing of time, place and memory are therefore in conflict with the visual clarity afforded by the map.

Nevertheless, layout and structure function as importantly as mechanisms towards progress as they do as means for delay. Hence, one of the first things Adso shows us is the architectural significance of the Aedificium, the most important building in the abbey and the area in which most of the narrative interest lies. Again, geometry is central to both its splendour and its mystery:

> This was an octagonal construction that from a distance seemed a tetragon ... Three rows of windows proclaimed the triune rhythm of [the abbey's] elevation, so that what was physically squared on the earth was spiritually triangular in the sky. As we came closer, we realized that the quadrangular form included, at each of its corners, a heptagonal tower, five sides of which were visible on the outside – four of the eight sides, then, of the greater octagon producing four minor heptagons, which from the outside appeared as pentagons ... each revealing a subtle spiritual significance. Eight, the number of perfection for every tetragon; four, the number of the Gospels; five, the number of the zones of the world; seven, the number of the gifts of the Holy Ghost. (pp. 21–2)

Furthermore, here we have rendered explicit the fact that architecture is itself a text, upon and through which messages of scripture appear. Later, when we see the doorway to the church, we find it ornamented with messages of divine warning, requiring Adso to identify, immediately, with the same role of 'reader as detective' required of us: 'I realized the vision was speaking precisely of what was happening in the abbey ... and how many times in the following days did I return to contemplate the doorway, convinced I was experiencing the very events that it narrated' (p. 45). In *The Name of the Rose* Madoff's locked room is, indeed, the mystery, but what we eventually discover is that the hidden room at the heart of the monastery turns out to hold the key to a room which we *never* enter, for to do so means death. Trapped behind 'the wall that flanked the stairs' (p. 458) is the abbot, whose pursuit of the murderer, who turns out to be Jorge of Burgos, leaves him fatally encased inside a hollow space, enabling Jorge to block all means of exit and abandon him to suffocation.

The Gothic aspects of Eco's text, however, rely upon more than simple architecture to convey the uncanny. As Adso and William explore the library area of the Aedificium, they find the architectural maze to have been artificially 'enhanced' by means of a number of human irritants:

> Holding the lamp in front of me, I ventured into the next rooms. A giant of threatening dimensions, a swaying and fluttering form came towards me, like a ghost.
>
> 'A devil!' I cried and almost dropped the lamp ... [William] seized the lamp from my hands and, thrusting me aside, stepped forward with a decisiveness that to me seemed sublime. He also saw something, because he brusquely stepped back. Then ... [h]e burst out laughing.
>
> 'Really ingenious. A mirror!'
>
> '... you are frightened by your own image ... enlarged and distorted.'
> (p. 172)

Such partial obscurity of 'clear-sight' is a repeated trope of this novel, for one of the distractions by which both we and characters are impeded in the plot is the disappearance of William's glasses midway through, which the glazier has such difficulty replacing that, for a time, 'the most satisfactory lens was an emerald color, and as he said, he did not want parchments to seem meadows to him' (p. 196). William's long-sightedness may partly explain his interest in prismatic lenses, but his ability to use this knowledge in order to decipher this particular trick of the light and dispel the rumours of monsters and phantoms is more likely to be due to his interest in the thirteenth-century monk and scholar Roger Bacon (1214–92), believed to have been the first person to use lenses to correct vision. Lenses, therefore, offer a further angle on the skewed relationship between sight and actuality while, at the same time, enabling sufficient of the uncanny to be retained for Adso to consider, much later in the book: 'the magic of mirrors is such that even when you know they are mirrors they still upset you' (p. 239).

One of the problems faced by the reader, and the reader's representative, William, is that the intellectual calibre of all the possible suspects in this text is extremely high and Eco is not above reprimanding us by proxy as William gives Adso a 'ticking off', exhorting him, 'the scholar's first duty is to learn languages!' (p. 362). Certainly, this reader cannot help but stand in awe 'alongside' Adso, as even William struggles to outmanoeuvre, not simply the murderer, but those who would protect him, in the guise of protecting the library. Puzzling his way to the location of the 'finis Africae', we discover William requires, in order to do so, knowledge of Latin, Greek and Arabic, biblical and secular mythology, astrology, science and logic. At the end of all this, he is still left with a riddle, which William summarises in the following terms: 'First of all we have to know what Venantius meant by "idolum". An image, a ghost, a figure? And then what can this "four" be that has a "first" and a "seventh"? And what is to be done with them? Move them, push them, pull them?' (p. 209). It takes him a further 250 pages or, to put it another way, between Vespers on the third day and After Compline on the sixth of a seven-day narrative span, to realise that

> 'primum et septimum de quatuor' does not mean the first and seventh of four, but of *the* four, the word 'four'! For a moment [Adso] still did not understand, but then [he] was enlightened: 'Super thronos viginti quatuor! The writing! The verse! The words are carved over the mirror!' (p. 458)

In other words, this sub-theme of glass surfaces and lenses plays its own role, not just in the concealments of secrets, but also their revelation. Returning to the mirrored room later, William finds a concealed entrance revealed by the pressing of the letters 'q' and 'r'. Adso is triumphant: 'Two hours after compline, at the end of the sixth day, in the heart of the night that was giving birth to the seventh day, we entered the finis Africae' (p. 460).

Adso's sense of triumph is deserved, for the revelation is shown to have been due, in part, to him. The seeds of this involvement are sown far earlier on, in the Compline section of the second day. Searching the page left behind beside Venantius's desk in the Aedificium, Adso accidentally catches the underside of the page with his lamp. William's initial irritation quickly gives way to pleasure as he perceives a hidden script appearing on the reading surface of the page. Adso recalls, 'Slowly, as if an invisible hand were writing "Mane, Tekel, Peres", I saw some marks emerge' (p. 163). The phrase 'Mane, Tekel, Peres' is the phrase that reveals itself as 'the writing on the wall' in the biblical Book of Daniel, chapter 5. There, as here, revelation of the words is not enough, for Daniel is called on to translate the meaning of the phrase for King Nebuchadnezzar, which he does as follows:

ME-NE: God hath numbered thy kingdom, and finished it.
TE-KEL: Thou art weighed in the balances, and art found wanting.
PE-RES: Thy kingdom is divided, and given to the Medes and Persians.[15]

In the Bible, Daniel's skill is drawn upon because the wise men of the court cannot interpret the sign. Here, Adso is called in to copy out the hidden text, because this is when William's glasses have been stolen by 'an unknown'. Like Daniel, Adso tells us: 'And so I did, without knowing what I was copying.' As I have argued elsewhere, the biblical Daniel is our original 'super-reader', one who not only has greater insight into the symbolic nature of an encrypted text, but is sufficiently astute to 'translate' it to his advantage.[16] Brother William is similarly able and has a promising apprentice in Adso. What this comparison also prompts is the realisation that Adso's ultimate revelation is similarly conveyed through dreams, a feature utterly in keeping with the novel's period setting, for to the medieval scholar 'dream-visions' were a crucial type of prophecy through which God revealed, to the sleeper, truths otherwise obscured and leading to a higher Truth.

Much later on in the text, during the Terce section of the sixth day, Adso falls asleep while praying. He dreams a grotesque dream of carnivalesque abandon involving a feast attended by a litany of sacred 'Fathers', from Adam through to Jesus (and including Daniel himself), not to mention a variety of saints and brethren whose company is added to by 'Roger of Bacon on a flying machine' (p. 431). There is also a dreamt version of the girl with whom Adso enjoys sexual intercourse earlier in the text and who is later burnt at the stake for sorcery, leaving Adso bereft at the injustice of her fate but powerless to intervene. However, the dream enables the prevention of other deaths, for as Adso guiltily dreams of the woman's abuse, torture and death, culminating in this host of biblical 'Greats' being caught up in 'universal slaughter' (p. 433), the profanity jolts him awake, but not before he dreams,

> William emerging from the labyrinth and carrying in his hand [Roger of Bacon's] magnet, which pulled him rapidly northward. 'Do not leave me, master!' I shouted. 'I, too, want to see what is in the finis Africae!' 'You have already seen it!' William answered, far away by now. And I woke up . . . (p. 435)

Once again, here the convoluted relationship between dreaming and understanding operates as the metaphorical equivalent of the tortured cartography of the library. Only once Adso has learnt to chart the complexities of interpretation can he chart its architectural application. Hence, on waking and revealing his dream to William, the latter realises that Adso, too, has learned how to 'super-read' and has merely to add the companion text outside the dream to provide the missing link between dream-text and detective denouement. As William informs him, 'It is the *Coena Cypriani*' (p. 437), a book that poisons its readers because the offending pages have been stuck together with toxic paste, stolen by Jorge from Severinus's laboratory.

On one level, the centrality given to manuscripts and books in this text enables it to offer up a celebration of the printed page. Take, for instance, the Book of Hours, which William examines early on in the library, and which is so incredibly small that it would fit into the palm of the hand. The writing was tiny; the marginal illuminations, barely visible at first sight, demanded that the eye examine them closely to reveal all their beauty . . . The entire margins of the book were invaded by miniscule forms that generated on another, as if by natural expansion, from the terminal scrolls of the splendidly drawn letters . . . (p. 77)

At the same time, this expression of the miniature is also, paradoxically, the container for hyperbole, in the marginal illuminations that crowd the empty spaces between the text and which fracture the clear sense of a boundary distinction between text and no-text. In that sense we see that books (and their contents) can never be fully 'contained' and this is the danger that is explored in *The Name of the Rose*, one that can only be dispelled fully through their burning. So the library itself takes on a type of Gothic monstrosity because of the precarious relationship between the contents and their housing:

> Until then I thought each book spoke of the things, human or divine, that lie outside books. Now I realized that not infrequently books speak of books: it is as if they spoke among themselves. In the light of this reflection, the library seemed all the more disturbing to me. It was then the place of a long, centuries-old murmuring, an imperceptible dialogue between one parchment and another, a living thing, a receptacle of powers not to be ruled by the human mind . . . (p. 286)

The Gothic is, of course, a book-ish form, hence the presence of so many hidden manuscripts, from the account, written 'in old faded ink and in the most beautiful hand', that initiates James's *The Turn of the Screw* to the bathetic 'washing-bill' that Catherine Moreland discovers at Northanger Abbey.[17] In Eco's novel, however, because reading and writing take on a sinister – almost a murderous – feature in themselves, we are doubly sucked into (almost ingested by) the text, swallowed up as absolutely as the abbot walled up behind the stairs. Though books are certainly the monks' downfall, for us they are even the 'walls and floors' through which we enter this abbey and, as we consume these pages in our appetite for more, we risk catching sight of ourselves, much like Adso does in the grotesque mirror, in the guise of Jorge, as he gorges himself (the pun with his name bouncing off the page before us) at the end of the text. Like him, we have willed these deaths, but unlike him we offer no mitigating 'higher' goal: we have simply delighted in our own gratification, for that is what the Gothic offers.

Suburban and rural monstrosity: Clive Barker and Iain Banks

Few novels play more insistently upon the allure of self-gratification than Clive Barker's novel *The Hellbound Heart* (1986). Barker's novel is set in suburbia, in the 'upgrade' home of a young couple, Rory and Julia, married for four years. The house, 55 Lodovico Street, is a bequest, handed down jointly to Rory and his brother Frank on the death of their grandmother, but, as the two brothers are estranged, Rory has little compunction about moving in without Frank's permission ('He's got no interest in property'[18]). Its history, then, is already framed by death, the front bedroom being described by Julia as 'a dead woman's womb' (p. 38), a comparison that gives the lie to her husband's hopes that their move will result in a new family. In this respect the couple are already distinct from the rest of the neighbourhood, for though the houses are collectively described as 'well-dressed' and the children 'well-pressed' (p. 22), there is a sense of the ghostly to this house's unfurnished shell: '"It's not quite what I expected", Julia commented' (p. 20).

When reading any twentieth-century Gothic narrative and encountering a central protagonist called Frank, evocations of Mary Shelley's *Frankenstein* (1818) are inevitable. Though Frank is no scientist, he is of a mathematical bent and certainly looks to invent new ways in which sexual gratification can take him beyond the limits of mere pleasure: 'sighs, and languid bodies spread on the floor underfoot like living carpet . . . virgin whores whose every crevice was his for the asking and whose skills would press him — *upward, upward* — to undreamed of ecstasies . . . He would be exalted by his lust, instead of despised for it' (p. 9). The extent to which Frank's desires take him beyond the limits of the human will be discussed more fully in chapter 3, but for now it is important to look at how it is housed within the frame of conventional suburbia. Frank, it turns out, both is and is not in the house, as we already know by the time we have encountered Julia and Rory. The opening is taken up entirely with Frank, whom we have watched engaging in the puzzle of Lamarchand's Box.

> The device had been constructed by a master craftsman, and the riddle was this ... there simply seemed to be no way into it, no clue on any of its six black lacquered faces as to the whereabouts of the pressure points that would disengage one piece of this three-dimensional jigsaw from another.
>
> Frank had seen similar puzzles ... products of the Chinese taste for making metaphysics of hard wood – but to the acuity and technical genius of the Chinese the Frenchman [Lamarchand] had brought a perverse logic that was entirely his own ... Only after several hours of trial and error did a chance juxtaposition of thumbs, middle and last fingers bear fruit: an almost imperceptible click, and then – victory! – a segment of the box slid out from beside its neighbours. (pp. 1–2)

Once again, then, we witness geometry, that sub-set of mathematics designed to best show off the symmetry of all that is good, put to profane use. What Frank unwraps is a looking-glass world which, much like Adso's terrifying mirror in the monastery library at Melk, throws his own image back at him in 'distorted, fragmented' form (p. 2). However, where Adso's adversary, at least in that passage, turns out to be harmless, no such reassurance awaits Frank. Where he had hoped to find, within the box, a conventional fantasy gateway into an anti-conventional pleasure-dome reminiscent of Samuel Taylor Coleridge's 'Kubla Khan' (1798),[19] what he finds instead is a breach in the invisible membrane screening off our world from one of hideous exploitation by a demonic and sadistic alien species belonging to the Order of the Gash, who – once the partition slides back – seek out their licentious prey and drag them to hell.

Despite the fact that Frank acquires Lamarchand's Box from a man ironically named Kircher ('*Kirche*' being the German word for 'church'), and then chooses to bring it into this disused house, the minute it enters it seems to invest the walls around it with its own monstrous aura. This is undoubtedly helped on by his erection of an altar of votive offerings: 'Bones, bonbons, needles. A jug of his urine – the product of seven days' collection – stood on the left of the

altar, should they require some spontaneous gesture of self-defile-
ment. On the right, a plate of doves' heads' (p. 4). As the acts of
violence and murder progress, however, we find Frank's remains
walled up behind the plaster, and the wall itself transformed into a
version of Lamarchand's Box: 'The wall seemed to be coming apart,
segments of it shifting and dislocating like a magician's prop, oiled
panels giving on to hidden boxes whose side in turn collapsed . . .
[Julia] watched fixedly . . . while pieces of the world came apart in
front of her eyes' (p. 48).

Early on in the narrative it is only the front bedroom, the one in
which Frank experiments with the box, which absorbs an atmosphere of haunted dread. As the narrative progresses, however, and
Frank enlists Julia in his mission for blood, we find Rory reduced
to a pulpy mass of flesh in the bedroom, Julia dressed as a headless
bride clad in her wedding dress and Frank's body 'unsewn' at the top
of the stairs (p. 160). Only Kirsty, Rory's 'good girl' friend, the woman
jealously cut adrift by his marriage to Julia, manages to escape and,
as she does so, the corporeal desecration enacted within the body of
the house projects itself outwards onto the architecture:

> The hallway danced. One moment an abattoir (the walls running
> scarlet); the next, a boudoir (powder blue, canary yellow); the moment
> following that, a ghost-train tunnel – all speed and sudden fire.
> . . . The fireworks in the hall threw some light ahead of [Kirsty] into
> the dining room, enough to see that it was already bewitched. There
> was something moving over the floor . . . and chains cavorting in the
> air. (p. 148)

Thus is suburbia revealed as only deceptively cosy in structure, in
actuality enabling the housing of nightmare within its bounds, a point
to which we will return in relation to *What Lies Beneath*.

We have already gestured towards *Frankenstein* in the resonances
that attach themselves to Barker's Frank, but for readers of the
contemporary Gothic another Frank comes to mind, namely Iain
Banks's Frank Cauldhame, central protagonist of his debut novel,
The Wasp Factory (1984), published two years before *The Hellbound
Heart*. Here, too, we have a loner drawn towards murderous games,
whose acts are framed by similarly ritual practices:

I showered carefully . . . Sometimes, when I have to make precious substances such as toenail cheese or belly-button fluff, I have to go without a shower or bath for days and days; I hate doing this . . .

. . . Next the shave . . . I take the same number of strokes of the same length in the same sequence each morning. As always, I felt a rising tingle of excitement as I contemplated the meticulously shorn surfaces of my face.

I blew and picked my nose clean, washed my hands, cleaned the razor, nail clipper, shower and basin, rinsed out the flannel and combed my hair.[20]

The Wasp Factory is set on a small island adjoining Porteneil, in the Scottish Highlands, from the night-time shores of which the oil rigs can be seen twinkling like monstrous sea-creatures. As such peripheral but potent signs of industrialism suggest, at the heart of this landscape is a parody of the machine age, and this resides in the very wasp factory of the title. So, where Barker's Frank purchases his toy, Banks's Frank manufactures his from a clock face, 'which used to hang over the door of the Royal Bank of Scotland', augmented by an ingenious system of pulleys and trapdoors (p. 120). Into it he inserts the wasp and, via a sequence of 'twelve corridors through little wasp-sized doors', the insect chooses its own fate (p. 121). What is striking, comparing Lamarchand's Box with the wasp factory, is the importance of the artistry involved in both of their construction. Banks's protagonist goes to some pains to inform us of the regular maintenance he gives to his contraption to ensure no obstruction to the (clock-)hand of Fate and pleasures in its 'well oiled and balanced' workings (p. 121). Barker's Frank likewise glories in the 'fluted slot[s] and oiled peg[s]' of the Box (p. 2).

Where Barker offers us a twentieth-century suburban haunted house, the Cauldhames's ('cold homes') residence is a more tradition-ally isolated Gothic mansion, cut down to size by the democratisation of the family line. Like Barker's Rory, Banks's protagonist's father has an aversion to sleeping in 'the big bedroom on the second floor', something Frank puts down to 'too many unpleasant (or pleasant) memories' (p. 17). Where Barker's Frank ensures he has free rein in the front bedroom through a combination of uncanny and demonic practices, giving off an eerie aura, leading Julia to call it the damp room and leaving it 'untouched. *Unentered*, indeed, except for these few visits of hers' (p. 38), Frank Cauldhame keeps the presence of his wasp factory a secret in the loft, using his father's physical infirmity so to do:

> That stick is the symbol of the Factory's security . . .
>
> My father can't climb up the narrow ladder from the top floor; and even if he could, I know he wouldn't be able to negotiate the twist you have to make to get from the top of the ladder, round the brickwork of the chimney flue, and into the loft proper.
>
> So the place is mine. (pp. 10–11)

Unlike in *The Hellbound Heart*, though many of the events of *The Wasp Factory* are determined by Frank's relationship to his family home (not to mention the secrets that his father constructs in relation to his/her own sexual identity), the house itself is considered less important than the land around it. In part this is due to the family's typically aristocratic roots, so in keeping with earlier Gothic forms:

> The family has been in this part of Scotland for about two hundred years or more, from what I can gather, and we used to own a lot of the land around here. Now all we have is the island . . . The only other remnant of our glorious past is the name of Porteneil's hot-spot, a grubby old pub called the Cauldhame Arms . . . (p. 15)

Cartography is crucial in Banks's book. Frank controls and maintains a clear sense of identity through an intimate relationship with his environment; measurements are one means for achieving this, coupled with the ritual naming and charting of sites. Again, this begins as a family obsession:

> Ever since I can remember there have been little stickers of white paper all over the house with neat black-biro writing on them. Attached to the legs of chairs, the edges of rugs, the bottoms of jugs, the aerials of radios, the doors of drawers, the headboards of beds, the screens of televisions, the handles of pots and pans, they give the appropriate measurement for the part of the object they're stuck to. . . When I was a child I once went round the house tearing all the stickers off; I was belted and sent to my room for two days. (p. 11)

Later, Frank adopts a similar system himself, but allows it to mutate slightly by introducing into the equation a superstitious (indeed, Gothic) belief that these objects might actually exercise agency of their own. Hence, his construction of not only the wasp factory, but a series of dams, whereby he attempts to impose his own control upon the elements: 'The pleasure comes from the elegance of the compromise you strike between where the water wants to go (guided by gravity and the medium it's moving over) and what you want to do with it' (p. 25). In this respect we once again discover the importance of boundary negotiations and the manner in which our own sense of perspective is affected by our relationships with the lines we cross (literal and metaphorical). For Frank, control itself is a boundary negotiation, but one in which he tries consistently to stack the odds in his own favour. In this sense Frank is a traditional Gothic villain.

What both *The Hellbound Heart* and *The Wasp Factory* demonstrate is the manner in which environment, at the end of the twentieth century, is as deeply ingrained with issues of haunting as it was during the Victorian period, and how both rural and metropolitan landscapes remain ripe for the uncanny. Such we find, even beyond fiction, in Peter Brooker's late twentieth-century glimpse of the 'blackened brick wall of [a London] office building', as he 'wait[s] for a late train on London Bridge station'. Though this is rooted in a postmodern, post-industrialised, professional context, it immediately takes him on an imaginative journey in which 'A confused image of Melville's *Bartleby the Scrivener* came to mind. His clerk's desk looked out upon the black wall of a neighbouring building on Wall Street ...Weren't native New Yorkers strangers to the city's past?' In other words, as we situate ourselves within contemporary urban culture we are simultaneously placed and displaced; Brooker begins with a precise geographical locale before moving onto an imaginative one. Simultaneously, he moves from a situation of belonging to one of initial geographical distance and then philosophical estrangement. He need not, in this process, give literal voice to the Gothic, for its haunting effect is laid bare in his surrounds: 'on the other side of stark co-existence there is estrangement: the look of the unknown, and the risk and threat this brings'.[21] Such estrangement meets its zenith in the London of the Blitz, as we see in Elizabeth Bowen's story, 'The Demon Lover' (1945).

London Gothic: Elizabeth Bowen and Sarah Waters

Bowen's 'The Demon Lover' is an intriguing story of the un-explained in relation to death and desire, not dissimilar in that regard to those with which we ended chapter 1 and, of course, in the case of *Photographing Fairies*, we are dealing with the Gothic as it is inscribed upon a cultural landscape of collective mourning during the First World War. Bowen's narrative moves us forward to the Second World War and the architectural desecration of bombed-out London. Her character, Mrs Kathleen Drover, is a married mother who returns to the family home in London from the countryside, to which she and the children have been evacuated. The time-frame of Bowen's narrative is quickly narrowed down with the arrival of a letter, the nature of which shocks Kathleen into staring into the mirror, where she is 'confronted by a woman of forty-four'.[22] The frame narrows further as we then learn that the letter, though it could have remained lying there for weeks, carries 'today's' date (p. 662) and that the present time of day is six o'clock, as the church clock strikes. This is a story the very frame of which is bound utterly by time:

> Dear Kathleen: You will not have forgotten that today is our anniversary, and the day we said. The years have gone by at once slowly and fast. In view of the fact that nothing has changed, I shall rely upon you to keep your promise. I was sorry to see you leave London, but was satisfied that you would be back in time. You may expect me, therefore, at the hour arranged. Until then . . .
> K (p. 662)

The protagonist is connected to the letter's author by a space of twenty-five years, but the nature of that connection is initially unclear until he leaves, when his legacy to her becomes a veiled threat, affirmed as a speech act: 'I shall be with you . . . sooner or later. You won't forget that' (p. 663). Through simple mental arithmetic we realise Kathleen would have been nineteen years old at the time of her unspecified 'promise'. Immediately, the narrative propels us into another chrono-tope, one in which a young girl and soldier make their farewells before he leaves for the Front. It is August, the same month as that of the fictive present, and it is 1916, which sets the fictive present at

August 1941. This story, then, is framed by the horror of two world wars and, along with it, a sense that one war ghosts another. As Kathleen contemplates her intervening married life, her vocabulary establishes a sense of time concertinaing: 'in this house the years piled up, her children were born and they all lived till they were driven out by the bombs of the next war' (p. 664). Bowen has already used one derivation of this unusual verb phrase, 'piled up', in the story's opening, where she describes 'piling up ink-dark, broken chimneys and parapets', silhouetted against a darkening skyline (p. 661). What seems difficult to overlook, here, is the colloquial phrase 'pile', used for a large (typically Gothic) castle or mansion. What is conveyed is how architecture can embody a sense of personal emptiness and so, despite this house having no natural connection with the dead lover, it takes on the qualities of being haunted:

> Unable, for some minutes, to go on kneeling with her back exposed to the empty room, Mrs Drover rose from the chest to sit on an upright chair whose back was firmly against the wall. The desuetude of her former bedroom, her married London home's whole air of being a cracked cup from which memory, with its reassuring power, had either evaporated or leaked away, made a crisis – and at just this crisis the letter-writer had, knowledgeably, struck. The hollowness of the house this evening cancelled years on years of voices, habits and steps . . . To rally herself, she said she was in a mood – and for two or three seconds shutting her eyes, told herself that she had imagined the letter. But she opened them – there it lay on the bed. (p. 664)

Kathleen's relationship to her house in many ways resembles that of Charlotte Perkins Gilman's unnamed protagonist in her 1892 story, *The Yellow Wallpaper*, a narrative that tends now to be read as a study of *fin de siècle* attitudes towards women's 'hysteria', but which was originally read and published as a ghost story. As it opens we learn that Perkins Gilman's character is staying there as a tenant: 'It is very seldom that mere ordinary people like John and myself secure ancestral halls for the summer.'[23] As in that text, there is something almost transactional in Kathleen's approach to the house, as if it is to be protected as an asset, rather than a family home: 'the part-time caretaker she shared with some neighbours was away this week on his holiday, known to be not yet back. At the best of times he did not look in often, and she was never sure that she trusted him' (p. 661). As in *The Yellow Wallpaper*, Bowen's house is 'shut up', and the punning relationship between shuttered and silenced accrues around both dwellings. In each case, the marital relationship is implied to be one which has 'cooled'; hence, as Kathleen identifies a sense of 'desuetude' in her marital bedroom, Perkins Gilman's protagonist and her husband sleep in separate beds, purportedly to aid her mental health.

The sense of distance between Bowen's protagonist and the house continues as the story progresses, as if there is a direct connection between the cracks in the architectural structure caused by the bombing, and the appearance of the intruder. Again, a very similar dynamic is in evidence in *The Yellow Wallpaper*, where it is the space which opens up between the walls of her room and the paper on them which enables the mysterious woman to enter her chamber. It is as if, in 'The Demon Lover', it is through this type of space, rather than the more conventional one of a letterbox, that the letter appears, placed directly onto the hall table by an unknown party – evocative, perhaps, of Edmundson's 'dead hand'. Here, then, though civilian casualties shadow the presence of 'The unoccupied houses opposite [that] ... meet her look with their damaged stare' (p. 666), the scars this woman bears are imprinted upon her by a much more domesticated milieu and, again, carry echoes of *The Yellow Wallpaper*: 'Since the birth of the third of her little boys, attended by a quite serious illness, she had had an intermittent muscular flicker to the left of her mouth' (p. 663).

In 'The Demon Lover', as the sense of the *unheimlich* and its connection with the family home builds, Kathleen decides to leave, but her descent down the stairs is met with 'a draught that travelled up to her face. It emanated from the basement: down there a door or window was being opened by someone who chose this moment to leave the house' (p. 666). As she nears the taxi rank she finds one waiting; its engine starts as she approaches and its driver needs no instruction before embarking on the required U-turn. It is as if her marriage and subsequent naming (Drover) has driven her towards this moment, hence the nature of the horror as she comes 'eye to eye' with the driver's face:

Mrs Drover's mouth hung open for some seconds before she could issue her first scream. After that she continued to scream freely and to beat with her gloved hands on the glass all round as the taxi, accelerating without mercy, made off with her into the hinterland of deserted streets. (p. 666)

Though the concealed mask of the driver's face suggests its identity might well belong to the lost soldier, her equally faceless husband, William (conventionally shortened to 'Bill', of course) is potentially implicated as a partner in the transaction, 'steering' her towards the settlement of the debt. As Eve Kosofsky Sedgwick argues, summarising René Girard,

> Through the readings of major European fictions, Girard traced a calculus of power that was structured by the relation of rivalry between the two active members of an erotic triangle. What is most interesting . . . is [his] insistence that, in any erotic rivalry, the bond that links the two rivals is as intense and potent as the bond that links either of the rivals to the beloved . . .[24]

No such calculus attaches itself to women in Waters's *The Night Watch* (2006), a novel also set in inner London during the Blitz, in which haunting is once again given an architectural form: 'it was the last surviving building in what had once, before the war, been a long terrace; it still had the scars, on either side . . . the zig-zag of phantom staircases and the dints of absent hearths'.[25] Unlike Waters's earlier novel *Affinity*, *The Night Watch* is not easily labelled a Gothic narrative but, as we will see in chapter 4, it draws directly upon Terry Castle's argument of the apparitional lesbian and questions of sociocultural 'ghosting' in its treatment of the phantom existence of lesbian couples. Additionally, certain passages describing the inner-city landscape of London during this period are explicitly Gothic in mood:

> Pimlico had an odd sort of haunted feel – the feel of having until recently swarmed with lives, which had all been violently extinguished or chased off . . . Kay and Mickey had once or twice walked along the edge of the river after their shift was finished. The place was uncanny: quieter, in its way, than the countryside would have been; and the

view down the Thames, to Westminster, was all of humped, irregular masses – as if the war had stripped London back, made a series of villages of it, each of them defending itself against unknown forces, darkly and alone. (p. 180)

Kay Langrish, the character with whom the text opens, identifies herself, in the early stages of the novel, in a manner again reminiscent of Perkins Gilman's *The Yellow Wallpaper*:

sometimes she walked restlessly about, just as lunatics were said to. And other times she'd sit still, for hours at a time – stiller than a shadow, because she'd watch the shadows creeping across the rug. And then it seemed to her that she really might be a ghost . . . (p. 4)

Waters's novel adopts a retrospective chronotopic shift, whereby the first section of the narrative – from which this passage is taken – is dated 1947, the second 1944 and the third 1941. In the middle section we follow Kay's work as an ambulance worker, a period coinciding with her romantic involvement with Helen Giniver, with whom she lives in a flat 'north of Oxford Street, in a sort of mews or yard off Rathbone Place' (p. 199). Following a particularly bloody night's work, collating the dismembered limbs of a woman and her young children, Kay returns to the flat and, after a delayed reaction, 'started to shake . . . Soon she was shaking so hard she could barely keep the cigarette in her mouth or sip from her drink. It was like the passing through her of a ghost express-train' (p. 201).

Here we have a similar phenomenon to that suffered by First World War shell-shock victims, a condition which Elaine Showalter identifies as a form of male hysteria. In comparing Kay's symptoms (albeit momentarily) with those of hysteria, one is immediately aware of the ideological dangers inherent in doing so, it being a term that has dogged women since the nineteenth century. At the same time, it is also a term that has been associated with powerful female politics:

In England at the turn of the [twentieth] century, hysteria, feminism and political speech merged in the popular mind. Women who spoke out in public for women's rights were caricatured as 'the shrieking sisterhood' . . . [and i]n 1910 Arnold Ward warned that giving women the vote would 'incorporate that hysterical activity permanently into the life of the nation'.[26]

Hence, not only is hysteria 'not a single, consistent, affliction like malaria or tuberculosis' but 'a vast, shifting set of behaviors and symptoms – limps, paralyses, seizures, coughs, headaches', it can also be seen to be 'a product of women's social circumstances'.[27] On one hand, this observation might further weaken the character of Kay: after all, the social circumstances in which she is acting, here, are not conventionally female at all, but male: she is a pioneer whose conduct of her job as a wartime ambulance worker paves the way for other women to follow in her footsteps. Read unhelpfully, one might argue such symptoms show Kay unable to cope with a 'man's job'. Yet, because of the retrospective narrative trajectory of *The Night Watch*, we have learnt, by this point in the text, that the insecure relationship Kay has with buildings in the first pages of the novel is itself set in train by the loss of Helen, not by inhabiting 'a man's world': 'she had a secret, persistent dread of coming back and finding that the place had been hit, was in flames or ruins' (p. 200). We have to wait, in fact, until the last few pages of the book to realise that Helen did first come to her as the survivor of a bomb blast:

> The dust fell away. The skin beneath was pink, plump, astonishingly smooth. Kay brushed a little longer, then moved her hand to the curve of Helen's jaw and cupped it with her palm ... unable to believe that something so fresh and so unmarked could have emerged from so much chaos. (p. 470)

Designer bathtubs and drowning in air: What Lies Beneath

That something fresh and shocking emerges from the rubble of the past is a clear metaphor for the Gothic itself. According to Allan Lloyd-Smith, American Gothic narratives emerge out of a tradition lacking in 'a feudal past, or those relics so important to the English or European Gothicist, castles and monasteries and legends', and, as such, require an impetus latching onto 'what it was about castles ... feudal aristocracies and monastic oppressions that had made them so potent for their contemporary audience'. What he identifies as characteristically 'American' are 'The shadows of patriarchy, slavery, and racism, as of Puritan extremes of the imagination and the political horror of a failed utopianism'.[28] It is perhaps no surprise that it is sunny Hollywood where one finds the epitome of these shadows in the twentieth century, and they loom large over the almost dazzling whiteness of Zemeckis's box-office pleaser, *What Lies Beneath* (2000), starring Michelle Pfeiffer and Harrison Ford.

What Lies Beneath is a film in which architecture, not least the architecture of professional suburbia, is framed by an almost sublime fascination with empty space. In that respect it reflects the kind of deceptively dazzling transparency of Escher's 'Relativity' and is shown, once again, to use light to hide darkness. According to Halliwell's *Film, Video and DVD Guide, 2005*, *What Lies Beneath* is a film that 'can't quite decide whether to settle for being a thriller or a supernatural chiller',[29] but I cannot agree; it is quite obviously a ghost story. What does complicate its generic identity is, firstly, the fact that it is set primarily in daylight – or at least artificial light – and, secondly, and partly because of that, that it operates as an implied commentary on the suburban existence of an American patriarchal elite. This is a very traditionally constructed milieu in which the men leave during daylight hours, enabling full focus to fall upon the women – none of whom appears to be 'employed' in the traditional sense – and it is during these empty daylight hours, that the haunting takes place. To quote Vidler:

> At the scale of the house, too, its roof removed and replaced by a garden, its cellars filled in and its first floor open to the park, its horizontal windows and terraces encouraging the ceaseless flow of light and air, modernism proposed to consign the cluttered interiors and insalubrious living conditions of centuries to oblivion. By these means it was thought that disease, individual and social, might be eradicated once and for all, and the inhabitants of the twentieth century rendered fit for the marathon of modern life.[30]

As the credits roll at the beginning of the film we find ourselves submerged in water of unknown depth; we are in an elemental realm that fleetingly returns us to Freud's intrauterine state of 'burial alive' or what is referred to in Szilagyi's *Photographing Fairies* (discussed in chapter 1) as 'the stream of filth running beneath the surface of respectable life',[31] a shadow layer which gives more than a hint of the reasoning behind the vicar in that text having been named the Reverend Drain. What breaches the unknowability of our positioning as voyeurs at the opening of *What Lies Beneath* is a sudden rupture of the credits as the surface breaks and we are propelled suddenly into the first frame of the film 'proper', thrust from the murky depths of a river or lake into a surface that gleams pure white, the luxury bathroom of an upper-middle-class family; what is framed centrally and with clarity in that moment of revelation is a close-up full-face shot of Claire (played by Michelle Pfeiffer), our lead protagonist.

Water, in fact, is the key element in *What Lies Beneath*, but what leads to the presence of the sublime in the movie is not water in its natural state as much as in its meeting point with post-industrial suburban culture. The sublime attaches itself to the power of the repressed, manifest in this film as Madison, a dead student and Claire's husband's former lover, whom he murdered a year previously and whose body he has disposed of, somewhere underwater. This is in fact a neighbourhood in which women are condensed into elemental status: Claire comes to signify air – clear, *clair*, clarity itself – Madison the element in which she resides, water. Wife and mistress (air and water) have formerly combined to produce the atmosphere most productive of male success, becoming, in the process, invisible. This is all about to change: Madison is a ghost with a traditional sense of architectural significance and haunts by eating away at the structure of the house, beginning with the front door; Claire returns one day to find the door opening of its own accord. Subsequently, Madison enters through a variety of portals, including the computer screen, but her defining realm 'inside' is the bathtub, site of the meeting point not only of air and water, but also of civilisation and disgust, where 'what lies beneath' are the drains, conduit for the detritus of middle-class existence.

From a historicist view it is interesting to consider the role of the subterranean sewer system, the hidden necessity to the filling and emptying of the bathtub. In her book *Victorian Babylon* (2000), Lynda Nead explores the relationship between a preoccupation with the geographical mapping of the city and its drains and the regeneration that paralleled it on the surface of the street, through attempted improvements in the transport system and recreational spaces, both of which related to questions of mobility, literal and cultural (the upward mobility of the class system), and which especially impacted on the relationship between women and the public arena. What is interesting about this, according to Nead, is that the very problems the planners set out to solve were also highlighted by the implementation of reforms:

> Sewerage created a new urban aesthetics . . . It also created a new street architecture of decorative drinking fountains, which symbolised the modern city's dedication to hygiene and flow. But stagnation and blockage could not be eliminated from the city. In spite of the modernisers' dreams, the experience of the city streets remained one of physical proximity and streams of people immobilised within confined spaces.[32]

It is this type of paradox between upward mobility ('modernisers' dreams', to use Nead's phrase) and female 'immobility' that strikes home most clearly in *What Lies Beneath*. No wonder these women keep appearing in the bath: designer bathrooms, those signifiers of postmodern capitalist success, gleam in the face of that which one is encouraged to believe we may no longer need to contemplate, namely the gutter. Yet, this is a house with a blockage, and one which employs sanitation and its designer disguises to draw attention to the manner in which the futures of these affluent women are tamped, to the advantage of their male partners.

Narratologically, *What Lies Beneath* opens by drawing attention to but also refusing to 'spill' a pre-existing story. Claire is in 'recovery', but from what neither we – nor apparently she – are at first aware. Claire tells her therapist that she has had some kind of 'empty nest episode' and on a surface level she has: the film opens on the day when her only daughter leaves for college. However, emptiness applies not just to 'nests': considering this is a suburb, what is most apparent is the all-pervasive emptiness that translates into vastness. Panoramic shots play across the water, where either nobody obstructs the view, or by which Claire herself becomes dwarfed; huge houses contain no sound, no children play and only one other woman seems to live here, Mrs Mary Feur. This is a neighbourhood constructed in order to draw attention to an unsettling absence that is as much environmental as it is uncanny. Early on in the film it appears as if Claire is 'drowning in air'.

In this conflict between air and water we come to the means by which senses become skewed in relation to perception, a narrative ploy that finds metaphorical realisation in the use of bathroom condensation. Like a number of twentieth-century Gothic narratives, elements of self-parody are planted in the text. One such moment involves a failed seance, set up by Claire and an unnamed friend. The use of such conventional Gothic tropes is shown to be misplaced in this suburban milieu, a point that carries well when Claire's friend takes one cynical look at the Ouija board, ponders its cultural obsolescence and asks her where she found it, to which Claire replies 'K-Mart' (an American supermarket chain). Nevertheless, the frisson established by the use of the conventional Gothic is taken up by its postmodern successor, 'the ghost in the machine'. Claire having waved off her friend and put away the Ouija board, as she re-enters the house alone the computer screen comes to life. This scene works through the construction and reinforcement of boundaries, while simultaneously permeating them. As the screen illuminates, the viewer gains full view of it in a mirror, a presence missed by Claire, who is further down the hallway on the other side of a partition wall. Because Madison 'is' water she belongs to the realm of the submerged, which is also, in this context, the realm of the abyss or the 'beyond' (the other side of the screen), and one question that intrigues the viewer is whether or not the keys of the keyboard are being physically depressed as the letters 'MEFMEFMEFMEFMEF' scroll like a compulsive obsession across the screen. This refusal to allow us sensory access to that information sustains a lack of clarity about on which side of the glass Madison is to be found.

Another instance of narratologically skewed perception is in the role adopted by Mary Feur. She is the decoy phantom, the spirit whom Claire and her friend court unsuccessfully at the seance – not least because she is still alive! However, there are many ways in which her presence 'ghosts' Madison's. Like the dead woman she is also, for much of the film, seen only in glimpses, heard rather than seen, or espied through holes in the wooden fence. As her name suggests, where Claire is air and Madison water, Mary Feur represents fire. She and her husband argue aggressively and make love passionately. At one point she asks Claire if she has 'ever felt so completely consumed by feeling for someone that you felt you couldn't breathe'. Their fiery relationship unsettles Claire, who wrongly believes Mary to be the victim of domestic violence – and later of murder – a decoy narrative that is later shown to be an outward projection of fears that will return to haunt Claire in her own marriage.

Why, then, is Mary Feur in the film? It's a question that bothers the spectator, until we realise that only through Mary can Claire and Madison meet. To pursue the elemental analogy to its logical extreme, only through heat can air and water mix, and without that fire the steam that Claire needs to turn beauty into passion (here, the crime of passion that results in her husband's death) will remain lost. Indeed, the means via which Claire is literally brought into contact with Madison against her will is in the recurrent filling of the bathtub with hot water, resulting in the steam escaping beneath the bathroom door, obscuring the reflecting surface of the mirror, signalling to Claire that an encounter with the abyss beckons. As an aside, it is crucial that in order to empty the brimming bathtub Claire has to lean across it, not just forcing her into a face-to-face encounter with the dead, but to arouse our fears of the possible presence of another (human) assailant, who might come from behind and drown her.

Intriguingly for Hollywood, this is actually a film in which the women join together to destroy the male predator, Norman (Harrison Ford). Once he learns Claire knows he has murdered Madison, the film climaxes in a stereotypically drawn-out Hollywood domestic violence sequence, Norman anaesthetising his wife before attempting to drown her in the bath. Portraying Claire as paralysed but conscious, the film presents us with a postmodern version of 'burial alive'. Part of Norman's pleasure is that she will witness herself dying in the bath, just as he – and, of course we – witness her death from our safe vantage points. However, the bathroom fittings turn against him, as his sinister suggestion that Claire's death will afford him a closer relationship with their daughter fuels a final, desperate lunge by Claire which causes him to slip on the wet floor and crack his head open on the washbasin, enabling Claire to flee. The remaining film sequences track their mutually weakened bodies engaging in a slog to the death which culminates in a twist on the conventional stalker narrative mixed with a twist on the Hollywood car-chase. To cut short an overly contrived final sequence, both end up underwater, bringing the elemental realm of the film full circle, and, with Madison's help, Claire drowns her husband and resurfaces. As Lisa Hopkins puts it playfully, at the end of *Screening the Gothic*:

> When the Gothic began as a genre, it was located primarily in Italy and dealt with the habits of those who were different from its original readers in nationality and, above all, in religion. Now it finds its most urgent energies in the home, in the presence of those most like, and most nearly related to, those who read and watch it . . . It may be safe to get back into the water, but what about the bath?[33]

In *What Lies Beneath*, we have seen the suburb set up as an arena for the sublime, one in which beautiful dreams are architecturally drawn, wealth is simultaneously assumed and erased (no money changes hands at all), and women are present, but only visible in their absence. The film ends with Claire having tamed the river and presuming a safe return home. However, as Bowen's The Demon Lover' shows us, such returns are never straightforward, and this ending evades the question of Freud's 'compulsion to repeat' or, to put it more architecturally, 'Nothing disappears completely. . . In space, what came earlier continues to underpin what follows'.[34] Hence, *What Lies Beneath* leaves us with no mechanism for being able to resolve the family trauma it drowns: what will Claire tell her daughter? In leaving this ending unresolved, Zemeckis's film enables such questions to pertain to more than one family. The Gothic may take as its focus one family, but its consequences always apply to society at large. In effect, this proves to be a film about contemporary respectability and its deceptions, whose skeletons lurk within but reach beyond the dazzling façade of one district. In chapter 3 we come on to examine that aspect of the Gothic which prioritises such irresolvable returns perhaps more than any other: the monster narratives of Gothic inhumanity.

3

Gothic Inhumanity

One could take any century in isolation and identify within it acts of gross inhumanity inflicted on the part of the State: the Crusades (1200s to 1400s), the hanging, drawing and quartering of male prisoners convicted of High Treason in England (1241–1798), the use of the guillotine in France for prisoners of both sexes (late 1700s and 1800s), the Napoleonic Wars (1799–1815), the Potato Famine in Ireland (1845–1849), the Peterloo massacre in Manchester (1819), the annexing of vast areas of Africa and Asia by various European powers. In the twentieth century, however, one cannot help but observe that lists of atrocity at a variety of hands accumulate: two world wars, the Holocaust, the bombing of Hiroshima and Nagasaki, the war in Vietnam, the assassination of crucial leaders such as Martin Luther King and President Kennedy, the imprisonment of Nelson Mandela. As we move into the twenty-first century we have already seen the 9/11 attacks on the World Trade Center, leading to the imprisonment without trial of detainees in Guantanamo Bay and related political controversies, such as those surrounding 'extraordinary rendition' and acts of prisoner abuse. While one might argue that none of these is, in itself a 'Gothic' event, each is an inhuman event and, collectively, one can see how such an accumulation works to inspire and reinforce an age in which a Gothic aesthetic flourishes.

According to Jean-François Lyotard, the inhuman is best understood in terms of its extinction alongside 'the human':

While we talk, the sun is getting older. It will explode in 4.5 billion years. It's just a little beyond the halfway point of its expected lifetime . . . That, in my view, is the sole serious question to face humanity today . . . Wars, conflicts, political tension, shifts in opinion, philosophical debates, even passions – everything's dead already if this infinite reserve from which you now draw energy to defer answers, if in short thought as quest, dies out with the sun.[1]

At the same time, landscape takes on a crucial significance for Lyotard: 'Deserts, mountains and plains, ruins, oceans and skies enjoy a privileged status in landscape-painting, rather as though they were by definition without any destiny. And they are therefore disconcerting [*dépaysant*].'[2] In a volume titled *Inhuman Reflections* (2000), Howard Caygill discusses the prevalence of the location of the desert in the traveller's tale, a landscape he takes back to the biblical wilderness and 'the site of journey, trial, encounter with the divine and natural inhuman and finally redemption'.[3] It is, he argues, at 'extreme[s] of heat and cold' that one most clearly feels the limitations of what it is to be human.

In his recent essay, 'Terrorism and the uncanny, or, the caves of Tora Bora' (2008), David Punter also focuses upon desert terrain, examining the relationship between terrorism and the uncanny, identifying governmental phrases such as 'homeland security' as an extension of debates surrounding the interrelationship between the *heimlich* and the *unheimlich* and the terrorist, especially, perhaps, the suicide bomber, as one 'about to be fearfully liberated into a different, unimaginable realm . . . an inconceivable freedom around which the ghosts of martyrdom and posterity hover'. In Punter's discussion of caves, prompted in part by his reading of a poem by Kamal Mirawdeli, 'Tora Bora 2002', Punter argues that 'the symbolism of caves is in part as entrances to, or exits from, the underworld, places from which strange exhalations breathe, and to enter which might involve encounters with monsters'.[4] Here, one cannot help but be reminded of E. M. Forster's *A Passage to India* (1924), a novel exploring the limits of inhumanity in the shape of early twentieth-century British colonialism, which meets its climax in the Marabar Caves:

Caves appeared in every direction – it seemed their original spawning-place – and the orifices were always the same size . . .

'Shout!' he commanded.

When they had done this for a while, the guide explained that to shout is useless, because a Marabar cave can hear no sound but its own . . . The place was so confusing; it was partly a terrace, partly a zigzag, and full of grooves that led this way and that like snake-tracks. He tried to go into every one, but he never knew where he had started.[5]

The 'reality' of what happens in this cave is shut up, but just prior to this scene, Aziz, an Indian doctor and the point-of-view character, has entered one of the caves with an English woman named Miss Quested. Alone in the caves, we are first introduced to her thoughts about Dr Aziz's physical attractiveness ('What a handsome little Oriental he was . . . She did not admire him with any personal warmth, for there was nothing of the vagrant in her blood, but she guessed he might attract women of his own race and rank') before she addresses him with a series of impertinent questions relating to his own family, which he tolerates, but by which he is insulted ('to ask an educated Indian Moslem how many wives he has – appalling, hideous!'). We are told, at this point, that he drops the hand by which he is guiding her, although Miss Quested appears unmoved: 'She followed at her leisure, quite unconscious that she had said the wrong thing, and not seeing him she also went into a cave'.[6] Suddenly she disappears, sparking Aziz's frantic search, until he discovers she has left already in another woman's car, an unexplained flight she will blame on Aziz having sexually assaulted her. In essence, the whole encapsulates Jean-François Lyotard's vision of the inhuman as: 'The opposite of a place . . . The grey that drifts over the sea after a storm. It is not that you get lost . . . but that [the] meanings are lost.'[7]

Considering the contemporary political significance of Tora Bora, Punter summarises the transformation in this landscape with the help of America in the 1980s, who militarised it, 'for use by the mujahideen during the Soviet occupation' before it became home to Osama bin Laden. In the near future a new phase in its history beckons: 'Osama bin Laden's secret caves hideout is being converted – into a £5.3 million tourist resort. Hotels and restaurants are being constructed on mountains overlooking the al-Qaeda chief's Tora

Bora refuge in Afghanistan, reports *The Sun*.' Earlier on in 'Terrorism
and the uncanny' Punter turns, with the help of the psychologist James
Hillman, to one possible differentiation between the terms 'underground' and 'underworld':'The underground, while frightening, is
nevertheless populated – with spirits, with gods, with souls ... perhaps
not with "life as we know it", but nonetheless with life of a sort ...
The underworld, on the other hand, is empty, cold, desolate: there
is nothing there.' Punter has just chilled us with the connection we
might draw between entering the caves and that old Gothic favourite,
burial alive, which he explains more resonantly still, as 'being for
ever unheard as we bang on the lid of our coffin'.[8] What he does not
go on to discuss, however (and which I thought he would), is the subterranean connection which jumps out at us in relation to 'our' own
homeland and its perceived (in)security, namely the London Underground, site of the 5 July bombings. The Tora Bora caves are both
(incredibly) old and, as Punter's mention of the new resort demonstrates (improbably) new. Like the Gothic, they may manifest themselves
differently in response to the precise historical moment by which they
are defined, but the fear itself will remain unchanged. The suicide
bomber, of course, enacts a living death, the act a momentary illustration of the point at which the human becomes inhuman as the
body explodes. In those dark tunnels of the London Underground,
how many of 'the lucky ones', surrounded by unimaginable carnage,
human remains that would certainly come into the category of 'life
[not] as we know it', feared they would be 'for ever unheard as [they]
bang[ed]' on the walls, doors, floors of their carriage coffins?

Bestiality and the Gothic: Sir Arthur Conan Doyle and Leonora Carrington

As we have already begun to see, London features as an innately
Gothic city throughout twentieth-century literature, from Joseph
Conrad's *The Secret Agent* (1907), which Punter also discusses in his
essay, to Sarah Waters's *The Night Watch* (2006). Among those writers
with whom we connect the London Gothic, after Stevenson (in *The
Strange Case of Dr Jekyll and Mr Hyde*) we surely have Sir Arthur Conan
Doyle, primarily through his detective series featuring Sherlock

Holmes and, of course, Baker Street. In *The Hound of the Baskervilles* (1902), comparatively little of real Gothic horror attaches itself to London, except for Holmes's greeting of his friend and colleague Lestrade, to whom he promises 'we will take the London fog out of your throat by giving you a breath of the pure night air of Dartmoor', coupled, earlier on, by the uneasy sense that both Baker Street and its visitors are being watched:

> At that instant I was aware of a bushy black beard and a pair of piercing eyes turned upon us through the side window of the cab. Instantly the trap-door at the top flew up, something was screamed to the driver, and the cab flew madly off down Regent Street.[9]

The key Gothic element of this narrative bears more resemblance to the deserts discussed above than to London, attaching itself to the barrenness of the Devonshire moorland, with its 'undulating downs, long green rollers, [and] crests of jagged granite foaming up into fantastic surges' (p. 66). It is here that we encounter the Great Grimpen mire, a topography linked directly with untimely death, as Dr Watson finds out on his first visit to Mr Stapleton, a naturalist who lives in Merripit House on the moor:

> Something brown was rolling and tossing among the green sedges. Then a long, agonized, writhing neck shot upwards and a dreadful cry echoed over the moor. It turned me cold with horror, but my companion's nerves seemed to be stronger than mine.
> 'It's gone!' said he. 'The Mire has him. Two [ponies] in two days ...' (p. 67)

It is in the midst of this unstable landscape that we also find Baskerville Hall, a fixedly stereotypical Gothic mansion:

> the house lay before us. In the fading light I could see that the centre was a heavy block of building from which a porch projected ... From this central block rose the twin towers, ancient, crenellated, and pierced with many loopholes. To right and left of the turrets were more modern wings of black granite. A dull light shone through heavy mullioned windows, and from the high chimneys which rose

from the steep, high-angled roof there sprang a single black column of smoke. (p. 57)

This house is a real throwback to the more conventional Gothic villas of the eighteenth and nineteenth centuries, and the presence of the moorland and its potentially bottomless marshes also recalls Edgar Allan Poe's 'The Fall of the House of Usher' (1845), with its 'black and lurid tarn', into which the house will sink at the end. Neither are the names of the central villains particularly distinct, Roderick in Poe's case, Rodger in Conan Doyle's. Both houses make a gloomy impression upon their visitors: Poe's narrator tells us that 'with the first glimpse of the building, a sense of insufferable gloom pervaded my spirit', unrelieved on entering to find 'sombre tapestries . . . , [an] ebon blackness [to] the floors', and, in the interior, a 'large and lofty' room, with windows which were 'long, narrow and pointed, and at so vast a distance from the black oaken floor as to be altogether inaccessible from within'.[10] Watson finds, in Baskerville Hall, an apartment which is 'large, lofty, and heavily raftered with huge balks of age-blackened oak . . . [and a] high, thin window of old stained glass', the whole being 'all dim and sombre in the subdued light of the central lamp' (p. 58). Though Watson finds his own room in a more modern wing of the house, the central rooms remain 'place[s] of shadow and gloom' (p. 59) and even the new owner is moved to admit that 'it isn't a very cheerful place' (p. 60).

In such a conventional Gothic setting it is no surprise that family portraits take centre stage, a literary trope handed down from the aristocratic tradition of early Gothic times, with their collective emphasis on the inheritance of 'bad blood'. These include pictures, 'from the Elizabethan knight to the buck of the Regency' (p. 60), at the heart of which is a 'Cavalier . . . .[in] black velvet and lace' (p. 138), the first Sir Hugo, painted in 1647, around whom arises the family curse. This takes the form of a legend concerning 'a foul thing, a great, black beast, shaped like a hound, yet larger than any hound that ever mortal eye has rested upon' (p. 13), claimed to have caused Sir Hugo's death as he, in turn, hunted a young woman to death on horseback. Supreme among those horrors resides the sight of the animal, witnessed by the three men who followed, one of whom dies of shock, the other two surviving as 'broken men for the rest of their days' (p. 14).

What sets the present-day narrative in train is the death of the former inhabitant of the house, Sir Charles Baskerville, a popular figure of the local gentry, praised for his 'amiability of character and extreme generosity' (p. 15), his body having been discovered in the grounds of the hall, reputedly surrounded by footprints bearing resemblance to a 'gigantic hound' (p. 20). Uncannily, Sir Hugo is said to resemble exactly Rodger, the younger brother of Sir Henry Baskerville, the new inheritor of the Hall. Consider Elisabeth Bronfen's observation on the doubling commonly found at the heart of detective narratives:

> As harbingers of death the double incarnates the end of bodily existence, figures ephemerality and contradicts notions of wholeness and uniqueness due to the division of the self it traces, even as the double also incarnates the notion of endless preservation of the body, the beginning of immaterial existence. The revenant, occupying the interstice between two forms of existence – a celebration and a triumph over death – calls forth two forms of anxiety, i.e. the anxiety that death is finitude and the anxiety that death may not be the end.[11]

The Hound of the Baskervilles is certainly a narrative about doubling, from the family legend that appears to be re-enacted by the suspicious death of Sir Charles, to the uncanny resemblance between the seventeenth-century rogue, Sir Hugo Baskerville, and the 'late' Rodger Baskerville – himself doubled, as we later discover, in the form of his son and heir, a man whose existence is unknown prior to Holmes's revelation of it at the end of the text, but who turns out to be the 'original' of whom the disguise of Jack Stapleton is a double. In this respect, death is, indeed, demonstrated to be simultaneously 'finitude' and 'not . . . the end', a point that explains Holmes's realisation, as he inspects Sir Hugo's portrait later on in the text, that 'The face of Stapleton had sprung out of the canvas' (p. 139).

So, 'detective fiction tells two stories, the story of the crime and the story of the investigation',[12] and, from this perspective, given the information about family resemblance Holmes amasses even before visiting the house, one might well ask why it takes him as long as to chapter 13 to inspect the portraits. However, Holmes's view of art is treated as utilitarian. After being told that he 'had, in a very remarkable degree, the power of detaching his mind at will' (p. 41), Watson refers to a visit to a Bond Street art gallery, as if to a leisure break from the investigation. Once there, we are told, 'For two hours the strange business in which we had been involved appeared to be forgotten, and [Holmes] was entirely absorbed in the pictures of the modern Belgian masters' (p. 41). Rather than pointing to the contemplation of a connoisseur, however, Watson immediately continues by telling us that, 'He would talk of nothing but art, *of which he had the crudest ideas*, from our leaving the gallery until we found ourselves at the Northumberland Hotel' (p. 41 – my emphasis). Nevertheless, Holmes's own viewing of the portrait *is* prefaced by the assertion: 'Excuse the admiration of a connoisseur . . . Watson won't allow that I know anything of art, but that is mere jealousy, because our views upon the subject differ' (p. 138). Shortly, he expands upon this 'difference': 'My eyes have been trained to examine faces and not their trimmings' (p. 139). In other words, he is a connoisseur of criminology, not art.

On occasion, however, Holmes finds himself the subject rather than the agent of the artistic gaze, as in the following scene detailing the first impressions of Dr Mortimer, the visitor who brings to Holmes the manuscript in which is written the family legend:

> You interest me very much, Mr. Holmes. I had hardly expected so dolichocephalic a skull or such well-marked supra-orbital development. Would you have any objection to my running my finger along your parietal fissure? A cast of your skull, sir, *until the original is available*, would be an ornament to any anthropological museum. It is not my intention to be fulsome, but I confess that I covet your skull. (p. 8 – my emphasis)

This increasingly Gothic portraiture of Holmes's skull operates as both a celebration of his life and an eager anticipation of his death. In this regard the murder cases upon which he pounces so enthusiastically appear both to renew his own vitality and invite contemplation of his fate.

Other doublings are at work in the text, however, and they revolve around a strange triadic structure pulling together the hound, Holmes and Selden (the murderer at large on the moor), who roams around like the hound itself and, on one occasion, is compared directly to it: 'Somewhere there, on that desolate plain, was lurking this fiendish man . . . like a wild beast' (p. 56).The very first thing we learn about Holmes, is that, like both the hound and the criminal, he has a nocturnal habit ('save upon those not infrequent occasions when he stayed up all night' (p. 3)). Later, there is a fleeting similarity between the expressions used to describe Holmes and that describing the hound. Recounting the old family legend, Dr Mortimer reads that, following the discovery of Sir Hugo and the maid's body, the hound can be seen 'plucking at' and then '[tearing] the throat out' (p. 13) of Sir Hugo. Later, as Watson enters the sitting-room at Baker Street, he finds Holmes's tobacco smoke 'took me by the throat' (p. 26). Oblivious to Watson's discomfort, Holmes refuses to allow him to open the window:'I find that a concentrated atmosphere helps a concentration of thought.' Continuing with the words,'I have not pushed it to the length of getting into a box to think' (p. 28), obviously brings to mind his or Watson's coffin.

If the shadowy aspects of Holmes's character introduce moral complications, more are introduced by the interface between class, rank and death – for some deaths are clearly 'more important' than others. Sir Charles's death turns this narrative into a 'case', whereas the maid in the original 'Sir Hugo' legend is merely a bit-part player in an embedded Gothic tale. Furthermore, although the convict's death is seen as important, it takes on full narrative resonance only because he is found clad in the garb of the aristocrat and so is mistaken for Sir Henry. Issues of doubling and portraiture attach themselves even here. As Holmes approaches the victim, the initial focus upon its head shifts to contemplation of the skull, resonant of Mortimer's fascination with Holmes's, but this one is 'crushed' amid a 'ghastly pool' of blood (p. 129). The narrative method of portraiture regarding Selden is interesting. As the tale unfolds he comes ever more clearly into focus, much as if he were an image developing on photographic paper. At first he is portrayed in caricature as 'the Notting Hill murderer' (p. 56), then, as Holmes and Watson start to track the hound, his appearance is conveyed through synecdoche ('Over the rocks . . . there was thrust out an evil yellow face, a terrible animal face, all seamed and scored with vile passions' (p. 97)), before, though only in death, his features come fully into focus. Here delay combines with ever finer detail. First, Selden is face down, reinforcing the mistaken belief this is Sir Henry; then we see a beard, a detail that delights

Holmes ('Now he was dancing and laughing and wringing my hand'), for now he knows it is not Sir Henry; only then do we see, in full frame, 'the beetling forehead, the sunken animal eyes' that reveal this as Selden (p. 131).

Throughout this book, as in *The Name of the Rose* (discussed in chapter 2), the metaphor of reading and writing is prevalent. In true Gothic tradition the case is set in train by the presence of a manuscript, supplemented by reference to newspaper clippings from *The Times*, and sustained, between chapters 8 and 10, by letters written by Watson to Holmes. These are followed up by Watson's own diary entries, which, on 16 October, refer to the discovery in Sir Charles's grate of the charred fragments of a letter sent by a mysterious woman, L.L. (Mrs Laura Lyons). In part, of course, such devices are narrative necessities (and in this case sometimes clumsily conveyed), but they do work to enhance the Gothic rather than the detective aspects of the text. In the use of the legend as storytelling device at the start, Conan Doyle structures the narrative as a ghost story: the content happens at a remove in time and space from the action and is relayed by a character not directly involved, who passes on the story on behalf of another (in this case Sir Charles Baskerville) to a group of similarly privileged men in an interior of Gothic architecture and situation.

At the heart of these narrative convolutions, nevertheless, one finds two key foci of inhuman monstrosity. The first is the hound, described as a

> dreadful shape . . . Fire burst from its open mouth, its eyes glowed with a smouldering glare, its muzzle and hackles and dewlap were outlined in flickering flame. Never in the delirious dream of a disordered brain could anything more savage, more appalling, more hellish, be conceived than that dark form and savage face which broke upon us out of the wall of fog. (pp. 150–1)

The second is another 'dreadful shape', this time discovered in a locked bedroom in Merripit House, to which Holmes, Watson, Lestrade and Sir Henry all race in the hunt to accost Stapleton. Here they discover Stapleton's wife, bound to a beam and gagged, a body 'so swathed and muffled in sheets which had been used to secure it that one could not for the moment tell whether it was that of a man or a woman' (p. 153). Freed, she leads them across the Mire after him, but all we discover is that Stapleton has disappeared:

> If the earth told a true story, then Stapleton never reached that island of refuge towards which he struggled in the fog upon that last night. Somewhere in the heart of the great Grimpen Mire, down in the foul slime of the huge morass which had sucked him in, this cold and cruel-hearted man is for ever buried. (p. 156)

So we return to this theme of burial alive, a trope with which the story leaves us; in so doing, it follows the tradition of monster narratives everywhere, where the actual boundary between the monster's death and life is left uncertain as they retreat into mist, mire or, as in the case of Frankenstein's monster, moral darkness:'He sprang from the cabin window ... upon the ice raft which lay close to the vessel. He was soon borne away by the waves and lost in darkness and distance.'[13] The interface between the natural and the unnatural (death versus murder), and the natural and the supernatural ('the strongest and most savage' dog in the possession of a London dealer (p. 160), transformed, by the application of a phosphorescent paste, into a monster with 'flaming jaws and blazing eyes' (p. 161)), is rendered especially forceful in the use of the interface between human malevolence and animal desperation.

Leonora Carrington (b.1917) is a British writer whose work plays along precisely the same fine line between monstrous humanity and bestiality. Her work is similarly characterised by hybridity; though clearly macabre in tone and Gothic in register, her writing is often categorised as surrealist, partly through her association with the famous twentieth-century surrealist painter, Max Ernst (1891–1976). In her story 'The Débutante' (1939), translated and anthologised by Angela Carter in her classic edited volume of stories, *Wayward Girls and Wicked Women* (1986), we encounter a narrative about a young girl from an aristocratic family whose sense of alienation from 'polite' society is so acute that her instincts are to socialise with animals, including a hyena she meets at the zoo, whom she invites to replace her as a guest at the May Ball. The subtext to this story implies a difficult relationship between the girl and her mother, such that the girl believes her mother will not notice the substitution, provided the hyena arrives disguised and when the ball is crowded. Additionally, when her mother calls by her room earlier, though she notices the bad odour, she simply instructs her daughter to 'take a bath perfumed with my new salts before this evening'.[14] As preparations for the evening unfold, the key conundrum becomes how to disguise the hyena's hairy face, a difficulty overcome by the hyena's decision to kill and eat a maid, salvaging her face for a mask.

Clearly what we have here is a dismantling of the boundary markers between humanity and inhuman behaviour, where the trappings of decency are worn like a masquerade costume. The implied class commentary, previously discussed in relation to *The Hound of the Baskervilles*, demonstrates what is here depicted as a literal expendability of individual members of the lower classes, such that the servants' own full status as human beings is implicitly called into question. The actual killing of the maid is erased from view as the protagonist 'turn[s her] face to the wall so as not to see' (p. 23,) but this also has the effect of removing the narrative significance of 'the kill' on social as much as moral terms. The deed done, our 'heroine' waits upstairs and it is here the story shifts from being a narrative of bestial violence to one of the Gothic: 'After about an hour came the first sign of bad luck. A bat came in through the window uttering little cries. I am terribly frightened of bats. My teeth chattering, I hid behind a chair' (p. 24).

Carrington's writing is full of bats, often combined with rats or toads, and their close connection with vampire narratives often fits the general bloodthirstiness of her writing. Both a portent of violence downstairs and a heralding of the return of her mother, here we sense the bat is primarily a metaphor for the bloodsucking aristocracy, coupled with the horror of her 'respectable' family. To a degree, and as the bat suggests, there is a harking back to traditional Gothic tropes and symbols in Carrington's work that is missing in many Gothic writers of the twentieth century. This feature is especially clear in her story 'As They Rode Along the Edge' (1937–40), detailing an encounter between the Church and witchcraft.

The witch in this story carries the suggestive name Virginia Fur: simultaneously a virgin and characterised by profanity, she embraces a moral darkness such that 'one couldn't really be altogether sure that she was a human being'.[15] Surrounded by one hundred cats, Virginia Fur devours whatever meat she can hunt on the mountainside, including 'lost sheepdog, and occasionally mutton or child, though this last was rare since no one ever came there' (p. 4). One day on the road she encounters a priest called Saint Alexander, who invites her to his church in an attempt to convert her to Christianity. Tellingly, what he uses to persuade her are the pleasures of the churchyard:

> 'My friend! Every night there are apparitions, and you really have to see the graveyard, really, it's a dream! . . . I promise you, on the head of little baby Jesus, that you'll have a beautiful spot in my graveyard, right next to the statue of the Holy Virgin.' (p. 4)

What she discovers on her arrival, however, is that the playthings of this 'saint' are potentially more sordid than her own:

> About a hundred yards from the Church of Saint Alexander there was what he called 'my garden of the little Flowers of Mortification'. This consisted of a number of lugubrious instruments half buried in the earth: chairs made of wire ('I sit in them when they're white hot . . .'); enormous, smiling mouths with pointed, poisonous teeth; underwear of reinforced concrete full of scorpions and adders; cushions made of millions of black mice biting one another – when the blessed buttocks were elsewhere. (p. 5)

This description places the transgressions of the Reverend and Mrs Drain (see chapter 1) utterly in the shade. Where Linda Drain drapes herself sensually before the altar eating chocolates, Saint Alexander performs a miracle involving the conjuring up of the Lamb of God in 'a cloud like sour milk'. No sooner is the cloud evoked than the priest's voice breaks, at which instant the cloud bursts and the cats fall upon the Lamb and devour it. Clearly, what we have here is a profane re-enactment of the Holy Communion, followed first by the sacking of the church by this unholy Virgin(ia), who 'fill[s] her bag with holy plates', then by her swift departure, accompanied by bats and moths (p. 6).

In the second half of the story, Virginia Fur has a carnal encounter with a wild boar. Having viewed the seduction from the beast's point of view, following his proposition, Virginia

spat into the stewpot and put her lips into the boiling liquid . . . With
a savage cry . . . she jumped around Igname [the boar], tearing her
hair out by the roots; Igname stood up, and together they danced a
dance of ecstasy. The cats caterwauled and stuck their claws into one
another's necks, then threw themselves in a mass onto Igname and
Virginia, who disappeared under a mountain of cats. Where they made
love. (pp. 8–9)

A traditional dance of savagery, akin to a dance of death, this frenzy
is matched by what we have seen of the masochistic desires of the
priest. Hence, demonic and inverted mirroring is set up as a key
metaphor in the tale. What are stressed are both the narcissism and
the ceremonial pomp of Igname, as he prepares himself for Virginia's
seduction:

No animal or bird ever looked so splendid as did Igname in his attire
of love. Attached to his curly head was a young nightjar. This bird with
its hairy beak and surprised eyes beat its wings and looked constantly
for prey . . . A wig of squirrels' tails and fruit hung around Igname's
ears, pierced for the occasion by two little pikes he had found dead
on the lakeshore. His hoofs were dyed red by the blood of a rabbit
he had crushed while galloping, and his active body was enveloped by
a purple cape which had mysteriously emerged out of the forest. [He
hid his russet buttocks, as he did not want to show all his beauty at one
go.]
   He walked slowly and with great dignity . . . As he was passing under
an oak tree, Igname saw a rosary hanging down among the leaves. He
knew there must be a body attached to this rosary, and he heard a shrill
and mocking laugh from above.
   Any other time, thought Igname, and he'd be laughing on the other
side of his face . . . (pp. 7–8; square brackets in original)

Note, here, how the nightjar on Igname's head recalls the 'blind
nightingale' Virginia swallows during her aforementioned escape
from the church. In the cape that superficially 'conceals' Igname's
buttocks, we also, and paradoxically, have a narratorial *display* of the
buttocks (through the very reference to their fineness). In this respect
the passage also mirrors the reference made to the priest's buttocks

and their 'hidden presentation' to the biting black mice in the hole in the graveyard. Once again, though they are hidden from our readerly 'gaze', they are presented vividly to our mind's eye, and hence are displayed in their nakedness, where the text only pretends to conceal them. In that respect, we also acknowledge the presence of the priest in the very description of Igname, a suggestion conveyed towards the end of the quoted passage, in which the priest is simultaneously hidden and present in the rosary that dangles from the tree. As the priest mocks Igname, this is tantamount to self-ridicule, and hence as narcissistic a gesture as Igname's adoration of himself in the lake, 'Every evening when the moon was shining' (p. 7).

Carrington's story turns into one of sexual rivalry and deathly vengeance once hunters appear in the forest and slaughter Igname. A badger informs Virginia that Saint Alexander led them to the boar, and the birth/death cycle is completed as Virginia returns home to give birth to a litter of boars, she and the cats feasting on all but that which most resembles Igname. Her attentions now turn to Saint Alexander and, accompanied by all the beasts of the forest, she tracks him to the pulpit. By one of those fictional coincidences typical of fairy tales, the corpse of Igname has, that day, been brought to the altar, but it is Saint Alexander who is sacrificed, falling prey to slaughter by the beasts.

One of the key traditional elements of Gothic fiction, shared by Carrington with Eco's *The Name of the Rose*, is the depiction of the traditional Catholic Church as an establishment based upon depravity and avarice. Sexual perversion is masked by the trappings of holiness, and those who are most trusting are typically those most at risk. There is also a traditional sense of competing worlds in the text: church and churchyard versus forest and the ruined village. Entry of one territory equates with entry into moral darkness, and so we are back to the conventional idea of Gothic interlopers moving between worlds and finding themselves affected by resulting horror. What is less orthodox is the fact that, here, the balance between worlds is far more even than is conventionally the case, in that *both* priest and witch represent knowing depravity. It is this resistance to the conventional coordinates of morality that also endows Carrington's Gothicism with a surrealist flavour. Like Escher's etchings (see chapter 2) or the ride conclusion to Hex (see Introduction), all certainty about vertical and horizontal boundaries is removed as we struggle to orient our reading within an amoral miasma.

Occasionally, as in 'The Skeleton's Holiday' (1938), comedy over-takes Carrington's sense of the macabre. Here, the eponymous pro-tagonist rejoices in the sacrifice of his fleshly burden: 'Sometimes he danced a few steps to the tune of Saint-Saëns's "Danse Macabre". But he did it with such grace, with such guilelessness, in the manner of midnight dances in romantic, old-fashioned graveyards, that nobody seeing him would have thought of anything unpleasant' (p. 17). More often, however, her stories operate along a very dark plane indeed, such as in 'The Sisters' (1939) which, like Elizabeth Bowen's 'The Demon Lover' (discussed in chapter 2), opens with the arrival of a suitor's letter. Where Bowen's protagonist is tyrannised by a letter from the dead, however, here Carrington's protagonist, Drusille, is courted in fairy-tale style by a living king. What haunts Drusille is not her lover but her sister, Juniper. An example of the 'living dead', Drusille imprisons Juniper in the attic in a monstrous development of the Bertha Mason motif first introduced in Charlotte Brontë's *Jane Eyre* (1847). In Carrington's hands we find a figure transformed not merely into a 'madwoman', but into a grotesque hybrid of woman and vulture:

> Perched on a rod near the ceiling, an extraordinary creature looked at the light with blinded eyes. Her body was white and naked, feathers grew from her shoulders and round her breasts. Her white arms were neither wings nor arms. A mass of white hair fell around her face, whose flesh was like marble.
>
> 'What have you brought me to eat?' she asked, jumping on her perch . . .
>
> . . . Drusille held out a glass of water, but Juniper shook her head.
>
> 'Not that, not today, I need red . . .' (p. 44)

The house inhabited by the sisters is of the conventional size and condition for a Gothic tale, the spiral staircases being 'peopled' by rats and bats and the story opening with an equally conventional Gothic storm (p. 44). Almost immediately, we recognise this to be a Gothic narrative characteristic of the sort of animal anthropomorphism we might expect to find in either a conventional or a Gothic fairy tale, for we encounter Drusille, accompanied by 'two toads [which] hissed this thought monotonously, "Drusille, my Belzamine, Drusille, my Belzamine"' (p. 43).

Vampires and bloodfests: Leonora Carrington and Clive Barker

As we have already seen, Carrington uses talking animals to draw attention to the limitations of humanity (especially in relation to perceived superiority based upon questions of morality or civilisation). As in the work of Carter, however, she also uses bestial characters to draw attention to ferocious appetite, be it for food or sex.[16] This element is best conveyed in 'The Sisters', for in the cellars 'the old wooden casks gave up their contents of blood, honey, and wine. Most of the servants were lying about the floor, dead drunk' (p. 43). Amid the delicious abundance of wine and honey, the presence of casks of blood returns us to *The Name of the Rose*:

> Outside the pigpens, swineherds were stirring a great jarful of the blood of the freshly slaughtered pigs, to keep it from coagulating. If it was stirred properly and promptly, it would remain liquid for the next few days, thanks to the cold climate, and then they would make blood puddings from it.[17]

Where, in Eco's text, food is reiterated as one of the few legitimate outlets for the monks' appetite, relished in all its richness and abundance, the following day that same jar of blood becomes a site of human slaughter, Brother Venantius being found dead, head-first, within it, his legs protruding in what Adso describes as an 'obscene position'.[18] In 'The Sisters', the phrase 'dead drunk' conveys, simultaneously, both the perils and the gluttonous pleasures that might accrue around servants in Gothic tales.

In this respect, Carrington's story is highly evocative of one of Angela Carter's own Gothic fairy tales, 'The Lady of the House of Love'. Carter's story is a vampire narrative drawing on elements of 'The Fall of the House of Usher', aspects of Miss Havisham in Charles Dickens's *Great Expectations* and moments derivative of Hammer Horror films ('Bats swoop and squeak outside the tightly shuttered windows').[19]

The eponymous Lady is a virgin of nocturnal habits, who spends her days in a coffin clad in a 'négligé of blood-stained lace' and her nights dressed in 'her mother's wedding-dress' (p. 96). Her key accessory is a pair of sunglasses that shield her eyes from any vestige of light, and her life is undisturbed until she is visited by a 'handsome bicyclist' (p. 105), holidaying and looking for a room for the night.

This is a narrative in which the question of sexual initiation is complex. The Lady may appear as virginal as Miss Havisham, but her appetites are rapacious and she devours all men who stop at the village fountain for a drink, lured into her abode by a mute old crone. Caught somewhere between the innocence of a child who catches rabbits for pets and the ravenous beast which cannot resist the allure of all flesh, 'hunger always overcomes her. She sinks her teeth into the neck where an artery throbs with fear; she will drop the deflated skin from which she has extracted all the nourishment with a small cry of both pain and disgust' (p. 96). On this occasion, as she draws the young man towards her and a similar fate, the cycle of death and desire is destined to be shattered, for this time the nervous vulnerability of the sexualised woman overcomes the urgencies of the beast:

> She is shaking as if her limbs were not efficiently joined together, as if she might shake into pieces. She raises her hands to unfasten the neck of her dress and her eyes well with tears, they trickle down beneath the rim of her dark glasses . . . When she takes off the dark glasses, they slip from her fingers and smash to pieces on the tiled floor. (pp. 105–6)

As she stoops to collect the fragments of shattered glass she cuts her thumb, which bleeds. Reacting to the child in her, the bicyclist places his lips to the wound and sucks and, as he does so, sets her free: 'In death, she looked far older, less beautiful and so, for the first time, fully human' (p. 107). The cost to himself and others, however, is the contraction of her *dis*-ease and, returning home, he takes with him a souvenir of the Lady in the form of a red rose. Carter's mischievous sense of humour erupts as he places it in his own 'tooth glass' (p. 107), while the thrill of the macabre returns as he leaves for battle the next day and the bloodfest that awaits.

In all such stories the symbolic sensuality of redness dominates, often in contradistinction to the culturally informed 'purity' of white. Juniper is a berry of purplish-red hue, and so perfect for conveying the vibrancy of shed blood, but, in 'The Sisters', what we also have (again, in similar vein to 'The Lady of the House of Love') is a vampire narrative dressed as a Gothic fairy tale. As the royal suitor arrives, Drusille leaves the attic in haste, forgetting to shut the door. As Juniper makes her escape, her presence within the house starts to drain the blood from Drusille's complexion, which becomes 'like the face of a ghost' (p. 46). At this point, the king starts to behave in kind, offering her a strangely worded cure: 'Kiss me . . . I shall eat your migraine' (p. 46). The culmination of the story sees Juniper at full strength, as she confronts and devours the servant Engandine, bringing us full circle to the horrors explored in 'The Débutante'.

Similar predatory seductions are central to Clive Barker's *The Hellbound Heart* (1986), partly discussed already in chapter 2. Frank is, like Rodger Baskerville, 'the black sheep' of the family, leading 'a life lived in delirium, or an appetite for experience that conceded no moral imperative'.[20] Julia, attracted to this 'smiling, seductive chameleon', makes love to him in her wedding dress one week before she marries his brother Rory (p. 37). It is this appetite for more that leads Frank to open Lamarchand's Box. What he finds, however, even his excessive desire for gratification cannot handle: a predatory race called the Cenobites, set on teaching him the mortal limits of what he thought was 'inhuman' desire: 'he saw nothing of joy, or even humanity, in their maimed faces: only desperation, and an appetite that made his bowels ache to be voided' (p. 7). This first encounter leaves Frank in a torment of sensual excess:

> He sucked his mother's milk, and choked; felt his sibling's arms around him (a fight, was it, or a brotherly embrace? Either way, it suffocated) . . . A short lifetime of sensations, all writ in a perfect hand upon his cortex, and breaking him with their insistence that they be remembered. (p. 15)

All that is left, by the next time we see him, is something that, though defined as human, certainly only exists at its very limits:

> the body had been ripped apart and sewn together again with most of its pieces either missing or twisted and blackened as if in a furnace.

There was an eye, gleaming at her, and the ladder of a spine, the
vertebrae stripped of muscle, a few unrecognizable fragments of anatomy
...That such a thing might live beggared reason – what little flesh it
owned was hopelessly corrupted. Yet live it did. Its eye, despite the rot
it was rooted in, scanned her every inch, up and down. (p. 49)

Barker's narrative explores the way in which humanity becomes
dehumanised, but also how adult masculinity moves in and out of
adolescence and even childhood. One of the early realisations that
confronts Frank, after his experiments with Lamarchand's Box, is
that all previous erotic yearnings are 'adolescent' in comparison with
the horrors that await; indeed, the more one compares this text with
The Wasp Factory (as we did in chapter 2), the more one realises that
Barker's vision of Frank demonstrates what might have happened
to Banks's Frank, ten years on, had he not discovered himself to be
female at the end of *The Wasp Factory*. It is this 'adolescent', yearning
sexual immaturity upon which Julia feeds in her determination to
find bodies with which to revitalise Frank. Having ensnared her prey,
she ponders 'why this was so very easy. Was it that the man was
plainly a victim ... born, did he but know it, to make this journey?
Yes, perhaps that was it' (p. 68). As she begins to undress him she
notes 'He was trembling, poor lamb. Poor, bleatless lamb', and, as
she toys with his expectations, he asks her, 'Is it a game?' (pp. 70–1).
At the same time, he is also a man who is *beyond* sexual maturity: 'If
the ring on his finger hadn't already given his status away, she would
have known him to be a married man by the underpants he wore:
baggy and over-washed, an unflattering garment bought by a wife
who had long since ceased to think of her husband in sexual terms'
(p. 72).

Frank Cauldhame's dark, adolescent trials are only one of the intertextual echoes resonating through Barker's text. At the point at which
Frank and Julia's first victim shrivels, 'sucked clean of marrow and
every vital fluid' to the point at which 'When [Julia] had parcelled
it up in [a] bag, it was the weight of a small child', (p. 76), we are
reminded of volume 4 of J. K. Rowling's Harry Potter series, *Harry
Potter and the Goblet of Fire* (2000), more specifically chapter 32,
'Flesh, Blood and Bone', in which we witness Voldemort's return to
fully-fleshed existence, following the earlier confrontation with the

infant Harry that pre-dates the seven volumes. At the start of this chapter we find Voldemort in a similarly sorry state to Barker's Frank:

> The thing Wormtail had been carrying had the shape of a crouched human child, except that Harry had never seen anything less like a child. It was hairless and scaly-looking, a dark, raw, reddish black. Its arms and legs were thin and feeble, and its face – no child alive ever had a face like that – was flat and snake-like, with gleaming red eyes.[21]

Again, it requires the death and mutilation of others to re-enliven the remains, firstly by extracting the dust of Voldemort's own father's buried body, then the 'willing' sacrifice of Wormtail's self-amputated hand, followed by the unwilling taking of a phial of Harry Potter's blood. All is flung into a cauldron, along with Voldemort's diminished remains, and Harry's own murderous side is revealed as he wills to some unspecified deity, 'Let it drown ... please ... let it drown.'[22] This whole scene takes place in a graveyard, adding maximum Gothic atmospherics, not to mention questioning its suitability for all child readers – this is arguably the darkest scene of the entire Harry Potter series and it has, as this comparison with Barker's novel shows, more in common with adult horror than with children's fantasy.

Returning to *The Hellbound Heart*, despite Julia's rejection of Rory on the grounds of his lack of 'manliness', one might argue that Julia's developing relationship with Frank is best seen as a form of profane child-rearing. Just as he, like Voldemort, resembles a child in his partially developed state, so he comes to replace the child (as surely as Voldemort wishes his own existence to replace Harry's) in Julia's marriage to Rory. So Julia dumps the remains of her first victim in the junk-room which, we are told, is 'Too small to be used as a bedroom (except perhaps for a child)' (p. 77). Later, as she enjoys her first moment of sexual congress with Frank in his re-enlivened state, she simultaneously casts herself in the role of an incestuous mother and as Frankenstein, engaging in sexual relations with his (her) monster:

> She had *made* this man, or remade him, used her wit and her cunning ... Then he was kneeling in front of her. His unfinished hands were at her hips, then his mouth.

> Forsaking the dregs of her distaste, she put her hand upon his head,
> and felt the hair – silken, like a baby's – and the shell of his skull beneath
> . . . with time she would have love from this hateful thing, or know the
> reason why. (pp. 97–8)

As *The Hellbound Heart* continues, a deviant model of the nuclear
family unit evolves, with Rory and Julia as 'parents', Frank as 'naughty
child', and Kirsty the jilted 'girl-next-door'. Only to Kirsty are all
Rory's guises irresistible, from 'the ragged line of his front teeth'
(p. 25) to childish jokes ('[the one] about a gorilla and a Jesuit . . . had
her choking on her drink before he'd even got to the votive candles'
(p. 45)). So entranced is she by Rory that she is even seduced by those
guises of Rory that do not come *from* Rory: 'It was Rory's voice, or
rather, a close approximation of it. More guttural, more self-regarding,
but the resemblance was uncanny enough to keep her rooted to the
spot while the beast shambled within snatching distance of her'
(p. 118). Here, Frank is acting out the final stages of the bloody
denouement that will leave three of the four members of this 'family'
dead. Clothing himself in dead Rory's skin, peeled from his body
by Julia and himself, Frank is 'wed to his brother's body, the marriage
sealed with the letting of blood' (p. 147).

Kirsty, entering the house, finds herself chased by this monster,
and herself propelled into a set of increasingly infantilising roles as
he mocks her with the taunting address, 'Poor baby', then 'Hush,
baby', and finally the moment at which his own doom is sealed:
'Frank's here, baby' (p. 157). Earlier on in the text he has taunted her,
similarly, with the phrase 'Come to Daddy' (p. 120), a phrase reiterated
in extremis as she returns, the degree of insistence conveyed by Barker's
use of italic font: '"*Come to Daddy*,"' he said (p. 146). As Fred Botting
observes, 'Gothic fiction is bound up with the function of the
paternal figure . . . More precisely, Gothic fiction can be defined as
a transgression of the paternal metaphor . . . As a transgression of the
paternal principle, then, Gothic fiction constitutes a game of loss and
recovery'.[23] We have seen this game-playing already: at such moments
we are returned to those shared cultural horrors inspired in us by the
desecration of childhood innocence, discussed in chapter 1. In this
instance, however, we long for the destruction of 'the child' and it
is with no small amount of ironic pleasure that we find Frank falling

into Kirsty's trap, as she tricks him into naming himself, enabling the Cenobite that has accompanied her to pick him out as 'rightful' prey: 'It said his name, lightly, as if calling a child out to play' (p. 157). Kirsty it is who 'leaves home', if not unscathed, at least alive.

Though the primary challenge to human 'respectability' in *The Hellbound Heart* resides in the depiction of the Cenobites, framing the threshold into their world is the suggested presence of animal horror. As Frank begins experimenting with Lamarchand's Box, success is heralded by a vision of 'A world of birds . . . Vast black birds caught in perpetual tempest . . . brittle, broken things that rose and fell and filled the dark air with their fright' (p. 6). Again, at the end of the text, as Kirsty looks back over her shoulder on fleeing the house, she sees 'everywhere – thickening the air like smoke – the ghosts of wounded birds, sewn wing tip to wing tip, and lost to flight' (p. 160). Written and read in the wake of Du Maurier's story 'The Birds' (1952) and Hitchcock's cinematic adaptation of it (1963), it seems that birds – especially crows, ravens or, here perhaps, blackbirds – often present an epiphany of inhuman or bestial horror, a world in which humanity loses its grip upon sensibility.

Monster birds: Du Maurier and Hitchcock

Du Maurier's 'The Birds' is set (despite the Californian setting for Hitchcock's film) in a seaside village on the south west (presumably Cornish) coast of England, and against a cultural backdrop of the cosy insularity of rural family life in the years following the onslaught of the Second World War. Though readers first familiar with Hitchcock's version may be surprised at the apparent cultural distinction between the two settings, and despite Hitchcock's own assertion to Evan Hunter, his screenwriter, that 'We're throwing away everything but the title and the notion of birds attacking human beings',[24] the two locations were seen to resemble each other in some ways. As Robert Boyle, production designer on *The Birds* observes,

I think Northern California always reminded Hitch of England. There was something about the weather which was very unpredictable. It was fog and rain and then sunshine and then fog and rain again. It was a moody, strange area both forbidding and foreboding. I believe that's what intrigued him: it had a kind of mystical quality.[25]

Though uncanny, one would be hard-pressed to describe the socio-cultural setting of Du Maurier's original as 'mystical'. Her central protagonist is a middle-aged farm labourer called Nat Hocken, a war casualty managing on a small pension and part-time labouring on a neighbour's farm. He is married with two children, and it is suggested that they are existing on more meagre means than he would have been able to provide, had it not been for his war-time injury ('Nat was said to be superior. Read books and the like'[26]). They live in a house without electricity and buy candles once a week with the groceries. Though Nat borrows the neighbour's car to transport supplies from the farm to the cottage, he does not own one. In fact, the relationship between machinery and monstrosity is far more of a theme in Du Maurier's original than in Hitchcock's reworking of the narrative, but it is a conflict that is surrounded, in itself, by a broader elemental disturbance much more traditionally Gothic in its focus:

> When [Nat] reached the beach below the headland he could scarcely stand, the force of the east wind was so strong. It hurt to draw breath, and his bare hands were blue. Never had he known such cold, not in all the bad winters he could remember. (p. 10)

It is as the weather's hostility starts to eat away at Nat's extremities that he notes the birds adopting a challenge to human supremacy, here configured in their ability to 'ride' the waves: 'What he had thought at first to be the white caps of the waves were gulls. Hundreds, thousands, tens of thousands ... like a mighty fleet at anchor, waiting on the tide' (p. 11). At this point the elements are in league with the birds, conveyed by the sinister susurration of the tide, itself anticipating the first bird attack: 'Oy*s*ter-catcher*s*, red*s*hank, *s*anderling, and curlew wat*ch*ed by the water'*s* e*dg*e; as the *s*low *s*ea *s*ucked at the *s*hore and then withdrew, leaving the *s*trip of *s*eaweed bare and the *s*hingle *ch*urned, the *s*ea-birds ra*c*ed and ran upon the bea*ch*es' (p. 2 – my emphasis). As the pace of this passage builds to a release of energy at the end, the racing and running of the birds on the sands on the one hand evokes, and on the other erases, the more usual activities of happy children on the beach. It is children, primarily, whom the birds target, in both Du Maurier's and Hitchcock's texts.

What makes 'The Birds' most horrifying is the alternating distance and proximity established and reinforced between the birds and the humans. On one level it is when contact is attained that the full distaste of humanity for the birds is felt, such as when the birds swoop to attack, gouge skin and blood and peck at characters' eyes. However, as Nat handles the corpses of those birds whose suicide attacks upon his house and family have resulted in them piling up on the sills, he considers that 'It was queer; he hated touching them. The bodies were still warm and bloody . . . He felt his stomach turn' (p. 27). Bloodshed is repeatedly transacted between birds and humans in this story. On the night of the first disturbance, Nat opens and shuts the window to frighten away the bird, but in the process 'feel[s] his knuckles wet [and] put[s] his mouth to the scratch. The bird had drawn blood' (p. 3). This blood is his, but later on, when Nat returns inside after a subsequent attack, he has to rebandage these hands, which are now 'sticky with the birds' blood, not with his own cuts' (p. 27). The first instance should have prepared us for such returns. Here, Nat's sucking, coupled with the placing of the bird at the threshold of the house, invites a reading of this passage as potentially vampiric, and thus invites the return and ultimate breach of more boundaries by the birds.

Part of this alternating pattern of proximity and distance resides in the symmetry established, from the start, in the reciprocal gaze between humans and birds. Eyes and vision are a key trope of the story, from the shared glances by which Nat and his wife communicate without scaring the children, through to the birds' assaults on human eyes. Just as Nat is shown to habitually watch the rituals of the seabirds on the cliffs, so the birds are depicted, between phases of attack, watching and waiting as the humans go on with their daily tasks. It is in relation to one of these early moment of 'watching' that we see farming the land being placed at the interface between humanity and the animals or, to put it another way, technology and nature. Hence, as Nat observes his neighbour, Farmer Trigg, astride his tractor, 'the whole machine and the man upon it [was] lost momentarily in the great cloud of wheeling, crying birds' (p. 2). Later we will learn that Trigg's proximity to the natural world clouds his ability to recognise its dangers. When Nat asks him about the precautions he has taken to secure his house, Trigg scoffs: 'Lot of nonsense. They like to scare you on the wireless' (p. 19). In this respect his response makes him no more enlightened than the metropolitan radio newscaster, who 'Nat had the impression . . . treated the whole business as he would an elaborate joke' (p. 13).

According to Carol Clover, a metropolitan viewpoint is assumed by the majority of horror narratives: 'People from the city are people like us. People from the country (as I shall hereafter refer to those people horror construes as the threatening rural Other) are people not like us.' Hence, the mere immersion of a Gothic reader into rural terrain already prepares him/her for an encounter with the monster: 'Going from city to country . . . is in any case very much like going from village to deep, dark forest in traditional fairy tales . . . rural Connecticut [or Cornwall, perhaps] . . . is a place where the rules of civilisation do not obtain.'[27] The distinction to be drawn between town and country is one that certainly obtains in both Du Maurier's story and Hitchcock's film. Nat makes much of the fact that geographical factors leave this farming community at the periphery of government interest, but, at the same time, both he and his wife know that: 'It's not only here, it's everywhere. In London, all over the country. Something has happened to the birds' (p. 11). As Nat watches the flocks swarm overhead, he realises that different species of birds have been allotted to different areas: the gulls will attack their home territory of the coast, while the 'rooks, crows, jackdaws, magpies, jays . . . [are] given the towns' (p. 16). Similarly, though much is made in Hitchcock's movie of the comparative isolation of Bodega Bay, Mitch's mid-week city neighbour telling Melanie Daniels that it is 'About sixty miles north of [San Francisco] . . . About an hour and a half on the freeway. Or two hours if you take the coast highway', and Hitchcock's direction in the script noting that 'The montage of SHOTS that follow [her journey] should alternate between the winding, twisting road and the ocean below', the start and end of the film are set in uptown San Francisco. It opens on bustling Grant Street in 'mid-afternoon, and there is a tempo and pace to the people walking, the doormen HOOTING for taxicabs, the police-men directing traffic', as Melanie Daniels (played by Tippi Hedren), walks along towards Davidson's pet shop.[28]

What is missing from Hitchcock's movie, despite Boyle's earlier observations about the local climatic conditions, is the obvious way in which the birds utilise elemental disruption as the catalyst for their assaults. In Hitchcock's version the disruption remains on the level of wild nature's attack on civilization. The scene operating as a possible companion to that in which Nat Hocken is struck by the sight of the gulls riding the crests is when Mitch Brenner looks down the road after Melanie's retreating car and notices 'the long line of telephone poles and wires and . . . something strange on the wires.' This 'something strange' turns out, once again, to be 'Hundreds of birds'.[29] Here, technology takes the brunt of the interface between humanity and monstrosity. It is the fear of being 'cut off' that is also alluded to here, an element of both Du Maurier's story and Hitchcock's film that is conveyed by the comparatively remote (at least in twentieth-century terms) communities which form the central locations for each.

Another distinction is worthy of comment, however. Where, in Hitchcock's film, machinery follows a horizontal plane, focusing on the motor car or outboard engine of a boat, not to mention the telephone wires, in Du Maurier's story it takes a vertical trajectory, centred upon aircraft. This enables a closer consideration of flight as one means by which humanity has employed technology to usurp the power of the birds – hence their retaliation. It also, of course, encapsulates a sense of apparent elevation ('pride coming before a fall'), explained in the 'crash and burn' inflicted upon the plane by the birds:

> Just then they heard a crash about two miles distant, followed by a second, then a third. The droning became more distant, passed away out to sea. 'What was that?' asked his wife. 'Were they dropping bombs on the birds?' . . . He did not want to tell her that the sound they had heard was the crashing of aircraft . . . What could aircraft do against birds that flung themselves to death against propeller and fuselage . . . ? (p. 25)

The centrality of air-strikes also enables a closer relationship to be established between the monstrosity of the birds and the monstrosity of the (then) recent war, characters alluding to or silently remembering the air-raids, providing a backdrop of entirely human catastrophe as a framework for this new terror from the skies: 'Why don't the authorities do something? Why don't they get the army, get machine-guns, anything?' (p. 21). More than once the birds are implied to have studied the devastating power of mechanised air-attacks as a prototype for their own f(l)ight tactics:

> Statement from the Home Office at eleven a.m. today. Reports from all over the country are coming in hourly about the vast quantity of birds flocking above towns, villages, and outlying districts ... House-holders are warned to see to their windows, doors, and chimneys, and to take reasonable precautions for the safety of their children. A further statement will be issued later. (p. 12)

While Hitchcock's movie jettisons this theme of human versus bird flight, he retains the 'bird's-eye view' of the camera to establish a sense of the birds studying and thereby outwitting humans, the most powerful instance of which is the scene in which the birds attack the gasoline station. This scene is, arguably, Hitchcock's equivalent of the aircraft crash in Du Maurier's original, the difference being that where the aircraft crash 'out of sight' (insofar as a reader can 'see' what is on the page), the attack on the gasoline station emphasises full frontal violence. The assault commences with a gull swooping on a driver filling up at the pump. The man's face is away from us as the gull strikes, but the attack is severe (possibly fatal) and leaves him prone. As the pump, pre-dating the days of automatic shut-off, continues to siphon gasoline across the forecourt, it is only a matter of time, in this film in which smoking is the norm, before a customer, distracted by Melanie's and others' attempts to attract his attention, drops a lighted match in the fuel, and is instantly engulfed in flames. The scene is tantamount to a critique of human excess. The first driver to be attacked has been drinking strong liquor in the diner; that he is 'the worse for wear' through drink is clear in his demeanour, a state which is intriguingly mirrored by the flood of gasoline pumping across the forecourt (which also, and simultaneously, operates as a reprimand of America's 'gas-guzzling' economy).

In Du Maurier's spartan alternative there is no such excess, although fuel remains a player in the battle. The lack of electrical lighting contributes centrally to the Gothicism: shadows loom large, outlines are unclear after dusk and, following the threat posed by the birds, the darkness is doubled by the additional presence of wooden boards at doors and windows. This reduction of clear sight feeds into the terror of 'damaging or losing one's eyes', which Freud insists to be one of the most powerful fears among children, and about which, he claims, 'Many adults retain their apprehensiveness . . . and no physical injury is so much dreaded by them as an injury to the eye.'[30] This is only one of several echoes of Freud's 'The Uncanny' in Du Maurier's text.

Following the initial attack by the birds, Nat goes outside to dispose of their bodies. Finding the ground so frozen that digging proves impossible, he decides to bury them on the beach. Making a pit with his feet, he starts to empty the sack of its contents, only to find that

> the force of the wind carried them, lifted them, as though in flight again, and they were blown away from him along the beach, tossed like feathers, spread and scattered, the bodies of the fifty frozen birds. There was something ugly in the sight. He did not like it. (pp. 10–11)

In this apparently fleeting instance of the reanimation of the dead, we have evoked the potent superstition that the dead might return to haunt, to maim and to attack – the very horror upon which all Gothic tales are based. In this story it is also the mechanism whereby the reader is encouraged to wince as Nat later handles the bodies of other dead birds, afraid that they, too, may suddenly rise and attack.

This is an aspect Hitchcock exploits to the full, using the stillness of live birds as an intimidating gauntlet, the length of which characters must creep along, agonisingly slowly, towards their car and presumed safety. In Hitchcock's *The Birds* a combination of real and fake birds were used on set. In some instances it was considered there was no substitute for 'genuine' attacks, including training individual birds to attack real people.[31] On other occasions fake birds on wires were used, such as in the scene when Melanie is attacked in the boat crossing the bay. What comes over in later interviews with the cast is the genuine uncanniness evoked by the birds' presence on set. As Rod Taylor observes, recounting his relations with the bird handlers: 'You look after a bunch of seagulls and ravens and crows and pigeons and God knows what else and you get very nervous.'[32]

This uncanny characteristic of the birds is the foundational element connecting the original and the cinematic text. Du Maurier's version provides an especially close rendition of one of Freud's key Gothic scenes, referred to in his reading of E. T. A. Hoffmann's *Der Sandmann* ('The Sandman') (1816), whose first-person narrator is also called Nat(haniel):

> It is a wicked man who comes after children when they won't go to bed and throws handfuls of sand in their eyes, so that they jump out of their heads all bloody, and then he throws them into his sack and carries them to the crescent moon as food for his little children, who have their nest up there and have crooked beaks like owls and peck up the eyes of the naughty children.[33]

At this point we recognise a number of unexpected connections between the passage in which Nat disposes of the birds' bodies on the beach and this one from Hoffmann's tale. Note the shared usage of the sack, the sand, the threat of pecked-out eyes, and also (and unexpectedly in the case of 'The Sandman') the imagery of the violence imposed by the hook of a bird's beak. Freud's reading of such tropes is typically blunt in its focus: 'an anxiety about one's eyes, the fear of going blind, is often enough a substitute for the dread of being castrated'.[34] Despite its apparently conservative nature, the Freudian reading of anxieties over blindness carries some weight in relation to Du Maurier's 'The Birds'. Nat is partly 'unmanned' by his war injury, which prevents him from fulfilling his full potential as breadwinner, a point gestured towards in relation to the lack of provisions in the house, something he seems to equate with a more modern version of wifely womanhood: '"We'd be better off in the old days," he said, "when the women baked twice a week, and had pilchards salted, and there was food for a family to last a siege, if need be"' (p. 15).

In this regard, however, we see further unexpected connections between Du Maurier's text and *The Hellbound Heart*, at least in relation to infantilism and the family unit. Nat's wife is clearly lacking: though mother to two children, her behaviour is repeatedly self-enfeebling, as she looks continually to Nat for basic guidance and reiterates injunctions for him not to go out and 'leave [her] alone with the children' (p. 26). In fact, it is partly her failure to fulfil the role of 'mother' that places Nat's ability to 'father' under scrutiny, alongside a not dissimilar comparison between Nat's masculinity and Farmer Trigg's. On the face of it, Trigg's masculinity is less in question than Nat's, hence his gun-toting response to the birds ('Jim and I are going to take a crack at them' (p. 18)), followed by his derision at Nat's more considered approach ('Garn. You're windy' (p. 19)). However, where Nat is shown to have fathered children in the biological sense – and as Johnny is pre-school in age, it is implied that this ability has been unaffected by his war-wound – the Triggs are childless. Furthermore, it is this more considered (one might say nurturing) brand of masculinity that the story ultimately affirms. As the attacks continue, Nat increasingly focuses upon the dangers the birds pose to children, not simply his own but other people's. Hence, as he enters the Triggs' desecrated farmhouse to find all three inhabitants dead (Mr and Mrs Trigg and the farmhand, Jim), he consoles himself with the words 'Thank God . . . there were no children' (p. 35), while at the same time fearing for those in the less substantial properties of the council estate: 'He thought of the children who had run across the fields the night before. "I should have known . . . I ought to have taken them home with me"' (p. 36). Though 'mothering' typically carries a nurturing quality absent in 'fathering', here the tables are turned. Du Maurier's narrative implies that the necessary reform of the human condition must include fathers learning better how to 'mother' their own young.

'Daddy's home!': Jekyll[35]

This manipulation of the family unit for Gothic effect is an element employed in a number of canonical Gothic texts, among them *The Strange Case of Dr Jekyll and Mr Hyde*. At first this seems an unlikely claim, not least because Stevenson's original is the story of a bachelor whose intimacies are entirely with other men. However, as psychoanalytic readings have gathered pace around the text, one of the most common interpretations offered is to read Hyde, the evil 'Other' into whom the 'good doctor' metamorphoses with the help of a chemical draught, as a form of repressed adolescent or 'child' self:

It is [their] anatomical dependency, among other things, that restrains Hyde within the limits of the newly born child; his rebellious and enraged behaviour consistently following those patterns that [D.W.] Winnicott associates with 'I AM moments' during the first year of life. So Hyde is repeatedly being reborn, ever renewing his infantile status at the same time that he seems to follow an adolescent rebellion.[36]

This is an aspect of the original fully exploited in a recent six-episode BBC television series simply titled *Jekyll* (2007), starring James Nesbitt in the leading role of Dr Jackman, a family man and research scientist at the Klein and Utterson Research Institute who finds himself descended from the original Henry Jekyll. This is a very 'knowing' drama which plays with accepted scholarship on Stevenson's original, as well as being an intelligent and creative piece of contemporary television. In episode 5, for instance, we suddenly shift period to the nineteenth century and Jekyll's house. Jekyll returns late and is greeted by the butler, whose own knowing gaze suggests Jekyll is returning from an encounter with/as Hyde. Learning that Hyde has confronted Alice, the maid, Jekyll goes to the kitchen. She tells him, 'He scares me. Mr Hyde scares me, but not as much as the man who asks the questions.' This 'scarier' man turns out to be Robert Louis Stevenson himself, who leaves a calling card and returns to document Jekyll's experience. Such a conceit is crucial to the drama's larger contention that Dr Jackman has inherited a family condition, not a tale.

We have already noted the retention of the 'child' aspect of the narrative. After the first really savage attack of the drama, Dr Jackman awakens the following morning at the laboratory to discover Hyde possesses a copy of Disney's *The Lion King and Other Disney Favourites* on CD, a discovery that prompts the following observation: '*He* has Disney favourites? ... My dark side likes Mary Poppins; no wonder I was bullied at school!' Hyde *does* like children's songs: one of the ways in which the switch between Jackman and Hyde is signalled is that Hyde whistles the tune to the children's nursery song 'Girls and boys come out to play'. Later in the drama we discover this signature tune is, much like Hyde's alias, Billy, the result of an earlier memory of trauma. On his honeymoon, Jackman goes to buy icecream from a mobile van for himself and his new wife, Clare, and it is the van which plays the nursery tune. While Clare waits she is accosted by

Jake and his gang. On Jackman's return Jake humiliates Jackman by daubing his face with ice cream before turning to Clare and tracing it around her mouth and chin with his finger, suggestively licking it, before pressing the cone to each of her coated breasts and sucking the cream from the left. Leaving, Jake taunts Jackman that he has left the other one for him, as 'you are her husband'. That enforced suckling/violation prompts Jackman's first full transformation into Hyde. He seeks out Jake, tortures him and then exacts his own oral revenge, tearing him to pieces with his teeth.

The ice-cream van and its music is a crucial signifier of childhood and it is equally significant that Hyde's victims are little more than adolescents themselves. For Hyde, it is the precariousness of the boundaries between adulthood and childhood that seems to trigger his transformations most effectively – especially when coupled with the assault upon the (maternal) breast. In the very last scene of the drama Jackman comes face to face with his birth mother, an apparently kindly elderly woman descended from Hyde, but whose alter ego turns out to be Ms Utterson, the brains behind 'Klein and Utterson'. As Jackman asks her how his father died, the question prompts her to 'change' and, replying that she probably killed him herself, she metamorphoses into Utterson, develops fangs, and the final close-up leaves us with a chilling invitation to her son: 'Come on, Sweetie, kiss Mommy, kiss Mommy, kiss Mommy.'

Orality, coupled with a sexually-driven, violent appetite characterises all the bloodletting episodes in this drama. Retrospectively, the whole makes greatest sense as a monstrous Gothic manifestation of the phallic mother (jocularly expressed, perhaps, as 'Who put the (Melanie) Klein into Klein and Utterson?'). So, in the attack which occurs prior to Jackman's discovery of the Disney CD, we watch Hyde taunt another delinquent victim who has been harassing his own girlfriend. This is Billy, whose name Hyde will take for use around Jackman's family. As Hyde rounds on Billy, he teases them with the words, 'Now, do you know what I call this, children? I call this the perfect start to an evening.' Billy, who has previously assumed Jackman to be the middle-aged, middle-class loser he was in the ice-cream scene, quickly learns the error of his assumption, and as he does so immediately switches from young man to frightened child, as Hyde enters the arena of 'games'. Giving him three chances to kill him first, Hyde informs Billy that the third will be followed by the breaking of his neck. As Billy's third and final attempt fails, Hyde embarks on game-show rhetoric: 'Oh well, Billy, thanks for competing. You've been great, but it's time to say "Good night" to the folks at home.' Playing with the language of television, Hyde also brings to the surface the rhetoric of 'happy families'. Here, as the scene becomes ever darker, the language of the child murderer resurfaces. Gripping him in a headlock prior to snapping his neck, Hyde tells Billy, 'The truth is . . . I don't get a lot of pleasure out of killing children.' Following a momentary pause, the snap is audible to the viewer, before Hyde continues: 'But I get enough.' As we watch 'Billy-Boy's' body slump to the ground we assume him to be dead. Hyde, turning to tyrannise his girlfriend, taunts her and sends her fleeing, but then jumps upon the stomach of prone Billy. The camera zooms in on Billy's face to show blood appearing at his mouth and Billy gasping in agony: Billy is paralysed – *un*dead.

Such 'play' recalls us to Barker's use of child-like invitations as a masquerade for bloody violence, a juxtaposition employed wonderfully in Steven Moffat's script in *Jekyll*. Hence, in a scene in episode 3 in which Hyde has Clare and (as Jackman believes) his boss and 'friend', the rather stiffly formal Peter, trapped in the basement of Peter's house, his rhetorical talents are given full rein once again, as he addresses Jackman, his alter ego: 'Hi, Daddy, this is *so* much better. Why! A woman, a tied-up old guy (OK, not sure where you're going with that one . . .) Mrs Jackman?! Oh, Daddy! You're spoiling me!' At the same time, the oratory games delighted in here (as much by the audience as Hyde himself) are ravelled up with a very similar darkness to that we examined in chapter 1, namely the predatory role of the child murderer, a role Hyde also performs as he takes Jackman's children (whom he cannot bear, clearly because of their rivalry for his 'Daddy's' attention) to the zoo. We should note that these boys are called Eddie and Harry, obvious modern equivalents of Edward (Hyde) and Henry (Jekyll) and, sure enough, it is Eddie who is continually in trouble. More significantly, he is the one who 'sees'; he spots Hyde sitting beside his father in the front passenger seat of the car as it approaches – something to which both Harry and Jackman are oblivious. In the same episode, Eddie finds himself 'placed' in the lions' enclosure as a mechanism for staging Jackman's transformation into Hyde, a scene that concludes with a blood-soaked Hyde performing 'The Lion Sleeps Tonight' in the centre of the lion enclosure, having saved Eddie and killed the alpha male of the pride.

Such knowing parodies always flirt with the boundary marker dividing horror from camp, a marker of surprisingly flimsy substance. In chapter 4 we will look at the role of the queer in twentieth-century Gothic narratives, a chapter which continues with *Jekyll*, opening with its use of the closet metaphor. Throughout this chapter we have witnessed the ease with which nature turns 'strange', from the sea-birds' 'restless, uneasy', flight through to Barker's protagonist's sexual deviance. What we turn to look at now is how the Gothic politicises this interface and, in the process, 'queers' the uncanny.

4

Queering the Gothic

❧

According to Gordon Hirsch, Robert Louis Stevenson's *The Strange Case of Dr Jekyll and Mr Hyde* deals in 'the corrosive presence of gothic passion',[1] an observation fully developed in the BBC drama series *Jekyll*, with which we concluded the last chapter. Where Stevenson absolves himself of the need to explore the effects of pathological doubling on a nuclear family, Steven Moffat's television script reintroduces the heterosexual (indeed marital) structure, but retains along with it a fear of the closet (the protagonist, Jackman, suffers from acute claustrophobia). Furthermore, a key aspect of Hyde's transgressive personality in *Jekyll* resides in flaunting an indeterminate and voracious sexuality that is as often openly camp as it is aggressively macho: 'First fag of the day, always hits the spot.'[2] In one episode, Jackman borrows a mobile phone from a fellow passenger on a train to call his wife, Clare. Having returned it, the passenger, who is depicted as outwardly gay, engages him in conversation: 'She isn't worth it by the way . . . Dump her, you'll feel like a different man . . . Now me, I always feel like a different man.' Utterly missing the homoerotic subtext, Jackman's obsession with his own condition results in him unwittingly encouraging the man's advances: 'Yeah, that's my problem, too.'

As the drama progresses, such homoerotic flaunting gathers pace and is a regular part of Hyde's sparring with Clare. As she demands to know where Jackman has gone, he replies: 'Search me, Love; he was here a minute ago, I turn my back and, whoosh! Not even a tip on the dresser: Men!' The parading of homoerotic play, however, culminates in a scene in which the Klein and Utterson Research Institute attempts to 'cure' Jackman by forcing him to confront his claustrophobia, locking him in a high-tech cage/coffin/closet which his boss, Peter, calls a 'Total self-contained life-support system'. Re-opening it (much) later, they discover Hyde chained inside, Jackman having disappeared, a revelation provoking the following conversation between Hyde and Clare, initiated by Hyde:

> 'Do you know how they killed your husband?'
> 'They put him in a box.'
> 'Yeah, they put him in a box . . . He was claustrophobic: all they needed, his biggest nightmare come true. Buried alive in a big, steel box . . . Can you imagine? Afraid of the dark, with your eyes pinned open. Wouldn't you just *die?*'

Compare this scene with the ending of Stevenson's original, set in Jekyll's 'cabinet': 'Poole swung the axe over his shoulder . . . the red baize door leaped against the lock and hinges. A dismal screech, as of mere animal terror, rang from the cabinet. Up went the axe again, and again the panels crashed and the frame bounded'.[3] What confronts the two intruders here is, once again, Hyde's body. Where Jackman's closet is situated at the centre of a stark, high-tech laboratory, Stevenson leaves Hyde surrounded by deceptively *heimlich* effects: 'the kettle singing its thin strain, a drawer or two open, papers neatly set forth' and the realisation that, as I discuss elsewhere, 'Jekyll is swallowed whole by the hostilities of the "closet".'[4]

Stevenson's narrative is widely accepted, today, to be a narrative about male same-sex desire, in which a group of 'clean-cut' professional men, Jekyll, the lawyer Mr Utterson, his friend Mr Enfield and Dr Lanyon find their group infiltrated by a 'pale and dwarfish [man who] gave an impression of deformity without any namable [*sic*] malformation', and whose actions bring them all into a state of dangerous exposure, including to sexually transmitted diseases such as syphilis, a disease so devastating in its effects upon Victorian society as to inflict monstrous transformations on the sufferer. As Jekyll's body vanishes, it is as if he has fallen foul of his own desires, for Jekyll self-diagnoses the inherent tendency in his condition that cries out for chemical alteration: 'the worst of my faults was a *certain impatient gaiety of disposition*, such as has made the happiness of many, but such as I found it hard to reconcile with my imperious desire to carry my head high'.[5] In *Jekyll*, Jackman is offered a fake life-narrative based upon the 'queer' practice of genetic cloning, re-explained to him as the evolutionary symptom of a deviant family tree. Peter tricks Jackman by appealing to his altruism: 'Hyde is a marvel; the next stage in human evolution, not a word of exaggeration – with Hyde we could cure every illness known to man. He's a blueprint for a better kind of human being; to have Hyde back is worth almost anything.' Peter follows these words by flicking a switch that fills the chamber with toxic gas, simultaneously donning a gas-mask. The aim is to kill Jackman and save Hyde, though Hyde plays him at his own game and wins. Thus Peter, believing both to be dead and the experiment a failure, bends over the body and removes his own mask. As he does so Hyde re-engages the oral weaponry discussed in chapter 3 and exhales into Peter's face, poisoning him before imprinting his own mouth on his in a deep and sustained kiss of death, the very mirror of what will prove to be Jackman's demise at his mother's behest.

Pathology becomes the supreme branch of medicine most open to a kind of Gothic inevitability. Some critics have suggested the Gothic to be a mode of writing requiring, even begging, a continual state of 'over-reading',[6] or, to put it another way, the reader is required to become a kind of textual hypochondriac (there is more to this than meets the eye, there is something unknown lurking beneath this diagnosis, I know it, I'm sure of it, is it this . . . ? is it that . . . ?). In this frame of mind it is a small step before any pathologist who, according to the *OED*, concerns him/herself with 'any variant or deviant condition from normal', becomes deviant him or herself: a necromancer, a grave-robber, the very origin of contagion. Simply add the adjectival suffix '-ological' to 'pathology', and meaning undergoes a further Gothic twist: now, the dictionary tells us, it means 'compulsively motivated' and, in the illustration given therein, most commonly 'a pathological liar'. Such wordplay is haunted by an earlier Gothic trace: Freud's own tortuous twisting back and forth in his essay 'The Uncanny' as he drags us from *heimlich* to the *unheimlich* and 'home again'. Such intelligent trickery lies at the heart of *Jekyll*.

But if argument and counter-argument attach themselves to the uncanny, such might also be said of the term 'queer'. Eric Haralson begins his book, *Henry James and Queer Modernity* (2003), with the observation that: 'Originally, the conceptual terminology of "queerness" (or "queer") drew its analytical and political force from the very quality that made it so appealing . . . a fluency or an indeterminacy of signification that was felt to be at once powerful and elusive.'[7] Citing Alfred Habegger, Haralson acknowledges the difficulties of reading politics that are 'obvious' in a contemporary context into a text in which they are, at best, covert or unwitting:

> Habegger leans on the authority of the *OED* to argue that James could not have been thinking of 'homosexual' when he wrote 'queer': 'James used the language of his time, not ours,' and the earliest use of the word in its latter-day sense, according to the *OED*, occurred in 1922, or 'six years after James's death.'[8]

Haralson both acknowledges the weightiness of this dictionary-based perspective and its limitations, 'Habegger's formulation seems too complacent about "the language of [the] time", as if usage were governed by a unitary standard', before citing three examples prior to 1922, the earliest of which falls 'as early as 1895, when a Boston professional man, by the Jamesian name of Wentworth, warned his gay friends to be cautious inasmuch as '"queer things are looked at askance since Oscar's exposé"'.[9]

Certainly, the word 'queer' has a number of resonances in Gothic writing, from Stevenson's Mr Richard Enfield, the 'well-known man about town' of *The Strange Case of Dr Jekyll and Mr Hyde*, who observes that 'the more it looks like Queer Street, the less I ask' to 'queer goings on' in general.[10] There are a number of instances in which such juxtapositions of cultural nuance enable aspects of an original Gothic text to be 'unwrapped'; in others, a non-sexual queerness can equally pertain, such as in the case of Nat Hocken, the central protagonist in Du Maurier's 'The Birds' (discussed in chapter 3), who identifies the sudden shift in the local meteorological conditions that heralds the coming of the birds as 'queer' and, later, forcing himself to handle the dead and bloodied corpses of birds recoils, perceiving this contact to be similarly 'queer'.[11] The Gothic is concerned with all aspects of queerness, but that does not detract from the fact that its nocturnal and secretive plots have often provided the framework for what might, at the time of their publication, have been considered 'deviant' sexual dangers, one instance of which is to be found in Henry James's story 'The Jolly Corner' (1908), of which James himself wrote, 'I was moved to adopt as my motive an analysis of some one of the conceivably rarest and intensest [*sic*] grounds for an "unnatural" anxiety, a malaise so incongruous and discordant . . . as almost to be compromising.'[12]

Jolly queer: Henry James

The narrator of James's story 'The Jolly Corner' is Spencer Brydon, a man returning to the United States of America after a spell in Europe, a return he experiences as 'foreign' or 'strange', struck as he is by 'the differences, the newnesses, the queernesses, above all the bignesses . . . that at present assaulted his vision wherever he looked'. Later, he identifies in himself 'the queerest and deepest of his own lately most disguised and most muffled vibrations' and becomes repelled by the interior of his own house, which has become to him 'for queerness of colour, some watery underworld'.[13] Despite the fact that Spencer is the point-of-view narrator throughout, he adopts a third-person narrative voice, suggestive of a splitting between the self who utters and the self of whom the story is uttered. This dual stance is maintained, not just in the type of narrator adopted, but in the 'ghosting' activity Spencer himself undertakes, tracking his own footsteps through the house at night. The owner/resident of more than one property, Spencer is a man of continual mobility, never 'at home' and choosing to come and go at all hours:

> He let himself in and let himself out with the assurance of calm pro-prietorship; and accident so far favoured him that, if a fat Avenue 'officer' had happened on occasion to see him entering at eleven-thirty, he had never yet, to the best of his belief, been noticed as emerging at two . . . it was as easy to do this after dining out as to take his way to a club or to his hotel. When he left his club, if he hadn't been dining out, it was ostensibly to go to his hotel; and when he left his hotel, if he had spent a part of the evening there, it was ostensibly to go to his club. (p. 272)

That there are two possible interpretations of his relationship with the house, one 'public' and one 'private', is revealed in a conversation he has with his friend Alice. She suggests that part of its uncanniness is enwrapped in the lack of furnishings and interior decor, of which we are told, 'he risked ... his gathered answer ... "For me it is lived in. For me it is furnished" ... since his parents and his favourite sister, to say nothing of other kin ... had run their course and met their end there' (p. 268). This is, then, a house of death – or, at least, death to the family, a connection which invokes in him an atavistic sense of shame:

> He knew ... that should he see the door open, it would all too abjectly be the end of him. It would mean that the agent of his shame ... was *once more* at large and in general possession ... It would send him straight about to the window he had left open, and by that window, be long ladder and dangling rope as absent as they would, he saw himself un- controllably insanely fatally take his way to the street. (p. 283 – my emphasis)

Here, sexual deviance and its relationship to double lives and nocturnal wanderings progresses by means of a series of closeted spaces linked to the closing and opening of doors and windows. It is when Spencer believes himself to be at the height of his sensitivities – perhaps manifested most metaphorically in his determination to leave all interior doors open to prevent any obstacle to his freedom to roam – that he suddenly finds himself confronted by those same doors having been closed, apparently by another hand, a pivot in the balance of power in the text that leads inexorably, from here, to a sense of doom. We recall, as discussed in chapter 2, Bowen's 'The Demon Lover', in which her central protagonist, having decided to flee the house, detects a draught emanating up the stairs from the basement and the sense she has that her steps have been anticipated by another: 'down there a door or window was being opened by someone who chose this moment to leave the house'.[14] Such draughts might be anticipated in 'The Jolly Corner', in which what fills the house are Spenser's wandering memories/memories of wandering:

> He had come – putting the thing pompously – to look at his 'property', which he had thus for a third of a century not been within four thousand

miles of; or, expressing it less sordidly, he had yielded to the humour
of seeing again his house on the jolly corner, as he usually, and quite
fondly, described it – the one in which he had first seen the light . . .
(p. 261)

Here, then, we are introduced to the word 'jolly', a term which is
obviously synonymous with the word 'gay' (in its sense of 'happy' or
'carefree'), in a narrative in which the house itself appears anything
but 'jolly' (and as for the corner on which it is placed, we learn in-
sufficient to reach any conclusions). In this passage we are also introduced to the concept of 'see[ing] the light', a phrase that is usually
employed to denote a form of self-realisation, although in this context,
followed as it is by 'in which various members of his family had lived
and had died, in which the holidays of his over-schooled boyhood
had been passed' (p. 261). it could also simply suggest he was born
there. Such ambivalences are, of course, typical of James, but they
operate creatively as a space from within which a narrative subtext
can emerge. However we read it, this is a haunted house, as the 'no-
nonsense' Mrs Muldoon, his housekeeper, informs Spencer: 'If he
should wish her for any reason to come in after dark she would just
tell him, if he "plased", that he must ask it of somebody else' (p. 265).

As Mrs Muldoon continues, this time addressing Alice, we find
another connection with Charlotte Perkins Gilman's *The Yellow Wallpaper*, discussed in chapter 2 in relation to 'The Demon Lover'. Here,
Mrs Muldoon insists that 'no lady could be expected to like, could
she? "craping up to thim top storeys in the ayvil hours"' (p. 265).
'Creeping', of course, is precisely what we find Perkins Gilman's protagonist doing at the end of her text and, as already argued elsewhere,
it is perfectly feasible to read *The Yellow Wallpaper* as the story of a 'respectable' middle-class woman walled up within the haunted house of a
sexless marriage, struggling to free the woman (in the wallpaper) that
she might be capable of being, if only she could struggle out from
behind the façade and 'join those women who are "out" in the world
that she sees beyond the window'.[15]

That Spencer is both furtive and 'ashamed' might be surmised by
his secretive behaviour, coupled with his outward projection of that
behaviour onto a 'strange' persona. Hence, his words to Alice echo
closely Jekyll's own struggle to maintain his presence in the face of

Hyde. Where, Jekyll insists, 'He, I say – I cannot say, I',[16] Spencer asserts 'He isn't myself. He's the just so totally other person' (p. 270). At the same time, in James's text Spencer not only 'crap[es]', he 'prowl[s]' (pp. 265–6), thus ensuring we read Spencer as predator rather than prey. As he identifies the presence of a shadow self who paces as he paces, much like the echo of his footsteps, what he feels is not anxiety but appetite – one not dissimilar to Frank's voracious sexual hunger in *The Hellbound Heart* (discussed in chapters 2 and 3):

> he had tasted of no pleasure as fine as his actual tension, had been intro-
> duced to no sport that demanded at once the patience and the nerve
> of this stalking . . . he found himself holding his breath and living in
> the joy of the instant, the supreme suspense created by big game alone.
> (pp. 273–4)

This sexual dynamic complicates the relationship between the house, death and haunting for, as is clear, it is Spencer that haunts the house, not the house (or its ghosts) that haunt Spencer. In this sense, one might argue that what he stalks is his own death, projected outwards onto the face of another:

> Rigid and conscious, spectral yet human, a man of his own substance
> and stature waited there to measure himself . . . what made the face
> dim was the pair of raised hands that covered it and in which, so far
> from being offered in defiance, it was buried as for dark deprecation. So
> Brydon, before him, took him in . . . his planted stiffness, his vivid truth,
> his grizzled bent head and white masking hands, his queer actuality of
> evening dress . . . he could but gape at his other self in this other
> anguish. (pp. 285–6)

Allan Lloyd-Smith observes, 'If "homosexual panic" was a common-place response to the defining of homosexuality in the late nineteenth and early twentieth century, "The Jolly Corner" might be considered as more or less its obverse, a "heterosexual panic"'[17] Ravelled up in this mirror image of Brydon/not-Brydon is a complex blend of familiar recognition (framed by the use of the mirror image through which homosexual affinity is sometimes couched in literary narra-tives), the characteristic competitiveness one expects to find in male–male confrontations between strangers (especially in relation to proprietorship and possession), the admiration of one 'upright' gent for another (note the combination of erect adjectives such as 'rigid' and 'planted stiffness', coupled with suggestive phrasing such as 'Brydon, before him, took him in') and, finally, shame in the covered face. There is nowhere for men like Brydon to 'come out' in the early years of the twentieth century, as Haralson's previous observations about the ripple-effect of Wilde's trial demonstrates. Instead, they are left to live a double life, fated to 'stay in the closet' and even, as here, have any exit into daylight blocked by fears of what revelations might bring:

> The hands, as he looked, began to move, to open; then, as if deciding in a flash, dropped from the face and left it uncovered and presented. Horror, with the sight, had leaped into Brydon's throat, gasping there in a sound he couldn't utter; for the bared identity was too hideous as *his*, and his glare was the passion of his protest. The face, *that* face, Spencer Brydon's? ... It was unknown, inconceivable, awful, disconnected from any possibility –! He had been 'sold' ... the presence before him was a presence, the horror within him a horror, but the waste of his nights had been only grotesque ... (p. 286)

Recoiling from this image of what he is or might be Brydon retreats into the arms of Alice, an ending clearly evocative of heterosexual marital compromise with a 'knowing' partner: 'You "like" that horror–?' 'I could have liked him. And to me,' she said, 'he was no horror. I had accepted him.' '"Accepted"–?' Brydon oddly sounded. 'Before, for the interest of his difference ... and it may have pleased him that I pitied him' (p. 291). An innate deformity is the inevitable result, however, and one of the key features of the appearance of the figure in the doorway is that two of his fingers have been amputated, suggestive of the excision of an integral part of himself, for in fact 'the horror' resides in Brydon's decision to embrace a wounded hetero-sexual 'normality' rather than be true to his (shadow) self.

In Sarah Waters's latest novel, *The Little Stranger* (2009), we find a ghost story tackling precisely the same concerns as James does here. Though written one hundred years after James's 'The Jolly Corner', its setting is only forty years later, just the other side of the Second

World War. Here we find the upper-class Caroline Ayres, a woman described as a 'natural spinster', who refuses to settle for a heterosexual marriage of convenience to the local doctor and who, though she will die before she is able to follow her goal, determines instead to leave for 'London, at first. But after that, perhaps America, or Canada ... Don't you see? I need to ... get out. Get right away. England's not good any more for someone like me. It doesn't want me.'[18] Spencer Brydon, it seems, is not the only protagonist to hope North America might provide a 'jolly corner' unavailable in western Europe.

The apparitional lesbian: Sarah Waters

One of the most influential pieces of work on queer theory directly informing our reading of the Gothic is Terry Castle's book *The Apparitional Lesbian* (1993). In that book she examines what she describes as 'female homosexuality and modern culture', beginning with a tribute to the work of the Hollywood actress, Greta Garbo. Discussing a trip to see Garbo in *Queen Christina* (1933), shortly following the star's death, Castle observes: 'I found myself struck by the uncanniness of it all: a lesbian actress, portraying a notoriously lesbian queen, in one of the classic heterosexual love scenes in Hollywood film. Wasn't it odd? Yet no one seemed to notice, except perhaps Garbo herself.' Thus, Castle continues, 'The lesbian remains a kind of "ghost effect" in the cinema world of modern life: elusive, vaporous, difficult to spot – even when she is there, in plain view, mortal and magnificent, at the center of the screen.'[19] Though not exclusively Gothic in frame or focus, one of that book's many strengths is its successful application of Gothic metaphors to a range of cultural artefacts that are otherwise untouched by the uncanny. For if the uncanny is as all-pervasive as thinkers such as Freud would have us believe, we should not be surprised to find it lurking in the shadows of all forms of literature, not simply those identifying themselves as Gothic.

Waters is one of the best contemporary examples of a writer for whom the 'queer' is synonymous with an aesthetic practice some-times overtly Gothic, but always (overtly or covertly) uncanny. In her use of performative masquerade, girls dressing as 'chaps', maids dressing, undressing and doubling up as their ladies, women running away with men but only in order to find other women, we find a perfect illustration of the way in which the shadow self haunts the self that is performed. So Nan, entering 'The Frigate' pub on Brick Lane with Florence, in *Tipping the Velvet* (1998), queries: 'I thought you said it was to be all toms here? There are blokes over there', to which Flo replies, 'Blokes? Are you sure? . . . Those are not blokes! Nancy, how could you think it?' As Castle says, 'When it comes to lesbians . . . many people have trouble seeing what's in front of them.'[20]

Waters also works directly with the social aspects of visibility and invisibility inspiring Castle's book. Just as Castle makes manifest the woman whom we literally see but whose presence is culturally erased ('Politically speaking, the lesbian is usually treated as a nonperson'[21]), so, in Waters's *Affinity* (1999) it is crucial that Ruth Vigers, Margaret Dawes's maid, is rendered invisible to us so that we do not 'see' what is so literally obvious once we open our readerly eyes: Ruth has exploited her own social invisibility in order to plant, by sleight of hand, the apparently supernatural tricks through which Selina seduces Margaret. Via such stealth, Selina and Ruth steal not only Margaret's money and her trust, but her identity:

> *Vigers*, I said then. *My servant*, I said. *Vigers, my servant, Selina's maid . . .*
> 'Vigers came to us from nowhere,' I said. 'From nowhere, from nowhere.'
> . . . Now I think I began to glimpse the whole, thick, monstrous shape of it. I said, 'There were letters passed, between Selina and Vigers? . . .'
> She has taken everything . . . And she has the money, and the tickets, and the passports marked *Margaret Prior* and *Marian Erle* . . .
> *I must think, Selina has taken my life, that she might have a life with Vigers in it!*[22]

Affinity, with its imposing architectural backdrop of Millbank Prison, sits relatively comfortably within a traditional Gothic milieu. *Tipping the Velvet* does so rather less, though even here there are several scenes in which London takes on a sinister hue. Waters has a specifically cartographic storytelling approach in her London novels, tracing the city's pavements so closely one is often tempted to track her characters' movements on a map. As she says herself:

I know London very well and I like walking around London and finding new bits to it, and I like reading about London's history, so I suppose because I notice London and because I'm always geographically situating myself within the context of London, it's hard for me to write about London characters who aren't doing exactly that, too.[23]

It is this contact between characters, their footsteps and the streets that provides both the homely and *unheimlich* aspects of Waters's terrain. Of course, we realise that even what might be termed a 'daylight' familiarity with the streets of London does not remove them from becoming sinister after dark. Hence, Peter Brooker's apprehensive response to familiar London surroundings as he journeys home one evening: 'No place for a woman to walk alone . . . But then a young woman passed me carrying a pair of sturdy heeled boots',[24] an observation that resonates, in Waters's *The Night Watch* (2006), with a conversation shared between Viv and (Robert) Fraser, a conscientious objector with whom Duncan was formerly in prison during the war. Accompanying her on her way to meet Kay, Fraser insists, 'I couldn't think of myself as a gentleman, and leave you on your own in streets like these.'[25] And yet, it is precisely in the company of Fraser, during one of those long walks through London, that we find Duncan's anxieties becoming provoked by a sudden shift in atmosphere, giving Fraser a shadowy presence:

They were passing through Hammersmith now, crossing cheerless residential streets; soon, however, at Fraser's direction, they made a turn. The feel of the area began to change . . . the air smelt sour, dark and vinegary. The dirt surface of the road fell away, exposing cobbles, and the cobbles were slippery, as if with grease. Duncan didn't know this area at all . . . He looked at Fraser and saw a stranger. The preposterous idea came to him that Fraser might be mad; that he might have lured Duncan here and be meaning to kill him . . . He pictured his own body, strangled or stabbed . . . He thought of his father and Viv being visited by policemen; being told that he had been found in this queer place, and never knowing why. (pp. 78–9)

Although *The Night Watch* is a book in which Waters explores a variety of social instances of what one might call 'the illicit' (extramarital sex, imprisonment for conscientious objection, suicide, self-harming, back-street abortion), Duncan is not infrequently a central conduit for the 'queer': 'Now he really began to panic . . . he'd grown too conscious of himself: his hands seemed odd to him, like a stranger's. His whole body felt queer and wrong' (p. 90). Duncan is also a character haunted by death, partly through the early death of his mother and partly due to the bloody suicide of his teenage friend, Alec ('Duncan had another, violent glimpse of the scarlet kitchen in his father's house' (p. 405)). Indeed, for Duncan there is a sense of liberation in the ghostly. As he slips undetected from Mr Mundy's house after dark, like Hyde he takes the back entrance and glories in the transformations enabled by darkness: 'The world seemed full, to him, of extraordinary new things. Nobody challenged him. Nobody seemed even to look at him. He moved through the street as a ghost might' (p. 154). Heading as he is for Fraser's house, only when he arrives and sees Fraser through the window does he hesitate, 'Again, Duncan felt, but less pleasantly this time, like a ghost' (p. 156).

The Night Watch, as its title suggests, is a novel framed by darknesses of a variety of kinds, literal and metaphorical. In the blackout scenes the scale of London's square mileage appears to diminish in keeping with the shortening of characters' visual capabilities, with the attendant result that buildings loom large. So Helen and Julia, taking a walk in the blackout, enjoy the seclusion afforded them by darkness:

> They walked cautiously around the tower, still hand in hand, guiding themselves by a set of broken railings and feeling for uneven ground. A flight of three or four shallow stone steps ran up to each of the two doors; they made their way up to one of these doors, and sat down . . . Helen looked for Julia in her cap and dark coat and could hardly see her . . . 'We might,' she whispered . . . 'be the only people alive in the City. Do you think there are ghosts here, Julia?' (pp. 340–1)

Whether ghosts are at large or not, death is everywhere: perhaps the most explicitly Gothic description of an air-raid occurs when a group of women discuss their work with bombed-out houses and Binkie tells Mickey, 'Dear girl, talking of pulling out bodies – did you hear what happened to the crew over at Station 89? Jerry struck a cemetery and hit the graves. Half of the coffins were blown wide open' (p. 246).

Amid all this talk of civilian death and military darkness is Julia, the crime novelist, whose war work involves documenting the ruins of bombed-out houses. As she tells Helen, 'We're recording ghosts, you see, really' (p. 251), but she also analyses her own fiction as 'a queer thing to [write] . . . while so many people are being murdered all around us' (p. 328). It is the very banality of death as an everyday occurrence that enables Waters's characters to speak of death in other forms: from a conversation Helen overhears between two girls in the park, talking about a murder reported in the newspaper ('Mustn't it be awful to be strangled? . . . They say at least with an atomic bomb it's quick' (p. 51)), through to a throwaway remark Helen herself makes: 'I do think children would make the most perfect little murderers, don't you?' (p. 17). This does not prevent death from having a genuinely Gothic (almost occult) significance at times, such as when Kay, who is playing cards in the ambulance station with her colleague Hughes, observes, 'It's like gaming with Death'. His response begins as comic Gothic, but ultimately turns into something genuinely uncanny:

> point[ing] a finger, then turn[ing] and crook[ing] it. '*Tonight*,' he whispered in horror-film tones.
> She threw a penny at him. 'Stop it.' . . .
> 'Hey, what's the idea?' said someone . . .
> Kay said, 'Hughes was giving me the creeps.'
> 'Hughes gives everyone the creeps.' . . .
> Hughes did his Death-act, then, for Partridge . . . When two more drivers passed through the room, he did it for them . . . Hughes got up and went to the mirror and did it for himself. He came back looking quite unnerved.
> 'I've had a whiff of my own grave,' he said, picking up his cards.'
> (p. 177 – original emphasis)

Where *The Night Watch* is a novel dealing in death but adopting a predominately realist narrative mode, *Fingersmith* (2002) is pure Gothic and deals in what Sue, one of the two central protagonists, refers to as 'dark and fearful things'.[26] It begins in Dickensian London, literally so, in that it opens with a street performance of *Oliver Twist* at which Sue, one of the central protagonists, operates as a child accomplice to an older child pickpocket called Flora. Here the fear of Bill Sykes (*sic*) is instilled in Sue, a fear that will recur with the introduction of 'Gentleman', the villain in this text, whose arrival is heralded with the words '*Knock – knock – knock* . . . Like the knocking on a door in a play, when the dead man's ghost comes back' (p. 17). This is also, however, a London in official mourning for Prince Albert, as a result of which Paddington Station is 'hung with black' (p. 51). Such wall hangings evoke not only the death of the Queen's consort, but the many deaths of members of the criminal underclass, one of whom is reputedly Sue's mother.

If London is a bleak city, just as many Gothic tropes are to be found at Briar, the country house to which Sue goes to usurp Maud's fortune. Briar is a traditional Gothic house, 'rising vast and straight and stark out of the woolly fog, with all its windows shuttered, and its walls with a dead kind of ivy clinging to them, and a couple of its chimneys sending up threads of a feeble looking grey smoke' (p. 57). Though Sue exchanges the grinding poverty of Lant Street for the affluence of Briar, she immediately recognises the exchange as one of imprisonment ('I might as well have been put in gaol' (p. 61)), a realisation that almost immediately attaches itself to her feelings for Maud, for on laughing to herself about the 'beauty' of the conspiracy she believes she and Gentleman have hatched, 'the chuckle, I have to admit, was rather forced . . . for the house seemed darker and stiller than ever, now that she had gone [from the room]' (p. 71)). As Kate Ferguson Ellis observes, 'The strand of popular culture we call the Gothic novel can be distinguished by the presence of houses in which people are locked in and locked out',[27] and this is a distinguishing feature of Waters's work. One metaphorical extension of such enclosure imagery (especially linked to appetite) can be seen in *Fingersmith*, in Waters's continued use of shellfish imagery (begun in *Tipping the Velvet*, with its beginnings in a Whitstable oyster-parlour). So Sue describes Maud first as 'a pearl coming out of an oyster' (p. 79), then 'a lobster without its shell' (p. 83), before exclaiming, as their love is first consummated, '"You pearl!" . . . You pearl, you pearl, you pearl' (p. 142).

Unlike Astley's oyster-parlour, however, with its 'low-ceilinged, fragrant room . . . tables with their chequered cloths . . . the sweating slabs of butter . . . and [the waitress] with a rosy cheek, and a saucy manner and curls' (pp. 3–4), in *Fingersmith* the interior of Briar is far more reminiscent of the sterility of Poe's 'The House of Usher', and rather than the sensuality of Nan's visits to the music hall, where she revels in 'the glow of the footlights, the girls whose songs I loved to learn and sing' (p. 7), Maud arrives to discover that silence is the order of the day: ' "Walk softly!" says the [maid] in a whisper' (p. 186). What is also made clear to the reader, on *our* first encounter with it, is the bleakness within which the child is to be housed:

> Its walls were panelled all over in an old black wood, and its floor – which was bare, but for a couple of trifling Turkey carpets, that were here and there worn to the weave – was also black. There were some great heavy tables about, and one or two hard sofas. There was . . . a dead snake in a glass case with a white egg in its mouth. The windows showed the grey sky . . . (p. 65)

At the same time, and in strange contradistinction to the lack of sensual promise offered up by its walls, Briar houses a connoisseur's collection of literary pornography, and herein lies the reason for Maud's uncle having brought her to Briar on reaching pubescence, namely in order to read aloud to an assembled male gathering. Though the house is as sterile in shell as Maud's uncle is in the flesh, violence of a sexual nature is imprinted throughout, in both the bibliophilism and the 'family' crest:

> The plate bears his emblem, a clever thing of his own design – a lily, drawn strangely, to resemble a phallus and wound about with a stem of briar at the root . . .
> 'Sometimes,' I say, not looking up, 'I suppose such a plate must be pasted upon my own flesh – that I have been ticketed, and noted and shelved – so nearly do I resemble one of my uncle's books.' (p. 218)

Similar contradictions attach themselves to the treatment of Gentleman's arrival, under the alias of Mr Richard Rivers, for now, Maud tell us, the house has taken on the possibility of sensual promise:

> The house has opened its mouth, and is breathing.
> Then I know that, after all, this night is not like any other. As if

---

131

summoned to it by a calling voice, I rise . . . Then I hear the soft fall
of a shoe, and then another, still softer . . .

. . . [Mr Richard Rivers] is surveying the face of the house. He is
counting the windows.

He is calculating his way to my room! . . . Again my lamp flares, and
the window-glass bulges. This time, however, the house seems holding
its breath. (pp. 221–2)

It is not simply the encasement of sexual excess in the form of the
pornography that leads to this tension, but also the sexual activity
taking place between Maud and Sue 'under covers' and, prior to Sue's
arrival, between Maud and Agnes, her former maid. It is as if this stuffy
interior only precariously conceals the activities that go on behind
closed doors and, in this respect, we are once again reminded of James's
'The Jolly Corner'.

Haunting takes a variety of forms in *Fingersmith* and, early on in
the text, despite the horrors of Maud's incarceration, it is Sue who has
a superstitious dread of ghosts, jumping from her own skin at catching
a glimpse of Maud's nightdress hanging from the wardrobe door,
believing it to be 'Maud's dead mother, come back as a ghost to
haunt me' (p. 87). Maud, on the other hand, is inured to the dangers
of phantoms, having far more fleshly (or at least cadaverous) demons
to fend off, in the form of her uncle: 'They say children, as a rule, fear
the ghosts of the dead; what I fear most as a child are the spectres of
past lessons, imperfectly erased' (p. 195). So, when Maud later escapes
Briar, having avoided the temptation to murder her uncle in his sleep,
she indulges in an almost pleasurable contemplation of the fact that
the only reason she could ever anticipate returning would be to do so
in death, 'a neat, monotonous ghost, walking for ever on soft-soled feet,
through a broken house, to the pattern of ancient carpets' (pp. 287–8).
Here, of course, we hear clear echoes of Spencer Brydon's nocturnal
pacing around the house in 'The Jolly Corner', and, as the women
leave in *Fingersmith* (again by the back door), it is as if all the Gothic
nuances in the text have risen together in the landscape in which they
are placed: 'The bushes caught at the wool of our cloaks, and creatures
leapt in the grass, or slithered before us; and there were cobwebs,
fine and shining like wires of glass, that we must trample through and
break' (p. 152).

This passage recalls an earlier one in which Gentleman says one thing to Maud while conveying another:

> Do you know how careful my love will make me? See here, look at my hands. Say there's a cobweb spun between them. It's my ambition. And at its centre there's a spider, of the colour of a jewel. The spider is you. This is how I shall bear you – so gently, so carefully and without jar, you shall not know you are being taken. (p. 128)

The spider is, of course, a common female archetype in the Gothic, but it is both predator and, here, prey. The spider spins webs and therein lures her victim to its death, a plot in which Sue might actually be argued to be the fly (though she believes herself the spider), although in Part Two of the novel, narrated by Maud, it is her uncle who is described as 'perfectly and permanently aged; as flies remain aged, yet fixed and unchanging, in cloudy chips of amber' (p. 206). Indeed, towards the end of the novel, when Sue sees into the room in Lant Street and watches Mrs Sucksby embracing Maud, she describes Maud and Gentleman as 'two great spiders, they have spun their web' (p. 479), in which she believes the 'honest folk' in Mrs Sucksby's house have been unwittingly ravelled up. That, in the earlier scene, Gentleman suggests the webs to be strung between his hands is unusual, but nevertheless pertinent, for Gentleman is repeatedly shown using his hands to express one thing while concealing another. One might say this is the typical sleight of hand of the criminal, but his crimes are often of a sexual nature, as Sue knows from her witnessing of his behaviour earlier on in the text.

Towards the end of chapter 4, Sue accompanies Maud and Gentleman on a 'painting' trip. As she dozes and the two 'lovers' walk along together, Sue wakes to see Maud with

> her head upon his collar. Her skirt rose at the back, almost to her knees. And yet, her face she kept turned hard from his. Her arms hung at her side, like a doll's arms. He moved his mouth against her hair, and whispered.
>
> Then, while I stood watching, he lifted one of her weak hands and slowly drew the glove half from it; and then he kissed her naked palm. (p. 117)

Here, the (body) language of physical intimidation is dressed up as the (body) language of romance; Maud's posture apes that of the hanged mother, awkwardly combined with a strange form of 'head lock'. The 'kiss' to the hand might well be a bite, for the following day Sue observes her 'strok[ing] the spot upon her palm where he had yesterday touched his lips. Only now I saw, she was not stroking the flesh so much as rubbing at it . . . She felt his mouth like a burn, like an itch, like a splinter' (p. 125). Later, in Part Two of the novel, when we reread this passage as told from Maud's point of view, it is made clear that the impression made by his mouth is not literally that of a bite; instead, and more interestingly, he uses his mouth to 'brand' her lesbian: '"Excuse my whiskers. Imagine my mouth hers." . . . He pushes my glove a little way along my hand, he parts his lips . . . and I shudder . . . to know Sue stands and watches.' (pp. 276–7)

As first narrated by Sue in Part One, the image of Maud caught up in cobwebs recalls Miss Havisham in *Great Expectations*, whom Pip describes thus:

> Once, I had been taken to see some ghostly waxwork at the Fair, representing I know not what impossible personage lying in state. Once, I had been taken to one of our old marsh churches to see a skeleton in the ashes of a rich dress, that had been dug out of a vault under the church pavement. Now, waxwork and skeleton seemed to have dark eyes that moved and looked at me. I should have cried out if I could.[28]

It is a connection Waters goes on to make explicit in *The Little Stranger*, as a means of conveying Caroline's state of sexual limbo:

> Over the stable door was a great white clock.
> 'Twenty to nine,' I said, smiling, looking at the stuck ornamental hands. Caroline nodded. 'Roddie and I did that when the clock first broke . . . [It's] the time Miss Haversham's clocks are stopped at . . . We thought it awfully funny, then. It seems a bit less funny now, I must admit . . .'[29]

Fingersmith is free from such erotic stasis, however, and it is precisely following this encounter that Maud first comes face to face with genuine desire, as opposed (ironically) to that which is read about in books: 'I thought desire smaller, neater; I supposed it bound to its own organs as taste is bound to the mouth . . . This feelings haunts and inhabits me, like a sickness. It covers me, like skin' (p. 277). Gentleman's own response is pure bawdy derision, and his description of the 'care' he will take with Maud, to ensure 'you shall not know you are being taken', carries obvious references to the deflowering of a bride during intercourse. Ironically, of course, Sue and Maud have already 'deflowered' each other, something that is shown to be inscribed across their hands like a testimony. Smelling her fingers after sex, Sue considers, 'it smelt of [Maud]. The smell made me shiver, inside. The shiver was a ghost of the shiver that had seized me – seized us both – as I'd moved against her, in the night' (p. 142).

Earlier on in the text, Sue has offered to read Maud's cards and, like the nimble fingersmith she is, has 'sprung the pack' (p. 99). However, she is caught out herself when, instead of turning up the 'Two of Hearts, for lovers', the 'Queen of Diamonds' (p. 100) is revealed, something Maud's own account later reveals to us she witnessed, as she sees the expected card fall and chooses to grind it under her heel (p. 258). Later, with Sue in the asylum and Maud back at Lant Street, Mrs Sucksby enlists Dainty's help in dressing her new charge for her 'debut'. Finished in fine gowns and jewellery, Maud recognises the truth dealt by those cards: 'My heart beats hard again, "The Queen of Diamonds," I say' (p. 355). Victorian literary allusions present themselves again, here Thomas Hardy's *Tess of the D'Urbervilles* (1891) and the bloodstain 'about the size of a wafer' which reminds Mrs Brooks, the landlady in Sandbourne, of 'a gigantic ace of hearts' and which is, in actuality, evidence of a sexual crime, this time the revenge killing of Alec D'Urberville by Tess.[30] Analogous to this is the 'mark [of] crimson' Maud *thinks* must be upon her after Gentleman recognises her desire for Sue on the riverbank (p. 277) and the 'crimson bruise' (p. 144) *actually* left on Maud's 'breast . . . from where [Sue] had kissed her too hard' (p. 143). Dwarfing both in significance, however, is the mortal blow Sue inflicts upon Gentleman at the end of the novel: 'There came, from a gash in his waistcoat, a bubble – like a bubble of soap, but swirling red – and then a spurt of blood, that fell and struck the floor with a splash – an ordinary splash, like water or soup would make' (p. 504).

Caught in the midst of a horror narrative within a Gothic narrative (namely the marriage and exchange plot set within the frame text), the sweetness of Sue and Maud's union is frequently recast in nightmare terms, as here, when they are awaiting the bridegroom on his and Maud's wedding night:

> She kept her fingers upon my head and pushed my mouth too hard against hers; and she seized my hand and took it, first to her bosom, then to where the blankets dipped, between her legs. There she rubbed with my fingers until they burned.
> The quick, sweet feeling her kiss had called up in me turned to something like horror, or fear. I pulled from her, and drew my hand away. (pp. 160–61)

However, at the end Sue has learnt to embrace haunting, if not ghosts, as she returns to Briar and recognises that it is haunted by the ghost of her own mother, whom she had always believed to be Maud's; secondly by the meal-table which, just like Miss Haversham's, is still set for dinner, but now 'covered all over with dust and cobwebs, and the apples had rotted', and thirdly by a visual manifestation of Castle's apparitional lesbian, such that Sue herself now 'made no sound, and might have glided – as if I were a ghost. The thought was queer' (p. 540). When she finally locates Maud right at the heart of Briar, sitting at Mr Lilly's desk, it is as if Maud has, indeed, become the spider at the heart of the web and she is spinning yarns of her own: 'To find you here, all on your own, writing *books like that –* !' (p. 546).

Nevertheless, despite the commonly held view that Waters offers up a positive ending to *Fingersmith*, it strikes me as potentially sinister. Notice how Maud decides to weave Sue further into her plot(s) by initiating her into the reading/writing process:

> she *led* me to the fire and *made me sit*, and *sat beside me*. Her silk skirts rose in a rush, then sank. She put the lamp upon the floor, spread the paper flat; and began to show me the words she had written, one by one. (p. 548 – my emphasis)

As Maud coerces Sue into this seated posture the rushing/rustling of the silk mimics the strand projected from a spider's abdomen as it weaves in another thread. Imposing literacy upon Sue poses a further 'threat', for where one usually connects reading with liberation, in

Fingersmith it always results in imprisonment. Indeed, earlier on Maud openly envies Sue her *il*literacy 'Not read! Ah, Susan, were you to live in this house, as the niece of my uncle, you should know what that meant' (p. 69). While one might argue that the dispatching of Mr Lilly removes any such threat from the text, as we saw in chapter 1, those who grow up under a system of abuse generally turn abuser themselves. Thus, in employing Sue as amenuensis Maud has a carbon copy of her own former self upon whom to re-enact tyranny. It is indeed when dealing with the villainy of women that Waters is at her strongest, even (perhaps especially) in the face of utter desire, and this is surely a much more fitting portrayal of the sexual for a Gothic frame.

HIV/AIDS and the Gothicising of male homosexuality: Patrick McGrath

Over the last two decades, one might argue that writers such as Waters are giving a much needed positive antidote to a hostile backlash against homosexuality, prompted by the AIDS pandemic, and not infrequently explored through literary and cinematic depiction of vampirism. As Mark Edmundson observes, 'AIDS does lend itself readily to Gothic depictions. It's a condition that inhabits its victims, haunts them, often for more than a decade before making itself manifest. It is associated with some act in the distant past, often a socially stigmatized act.'[31] As a number of critics of the Gothic have asserted, among them Nina Auerbach, it is the presence of blood-focused desire that enables these anxieties about polluted or corrupted blood to take wing: 'Once the etiology of AIDS became clear, blood could no longer be the life; vampirism mutated from hideous appetite to nausea.'[32] In relation to these questions and some of the ways in which they are countered 'head on' by Queer Gothic, one might do worse than look to Patrick McGrath's short story 'The Angel' (1988).

Patrick McGrath is a writer for whom the 'queer', in all the senses explored above, features centrally. This story pre-dates his publication as a novelist, but its queer aspects continue to inform those works, too. In his first, *The Grotesque* (1989), we encounter Sir Hugo Coal, the traditional Lord of the Manor, who inhabits a typically Gothic mansion named Crook ('Black against that darkling air, no line straight, it seemed a great, skirted creature that rose by sheer force of will to thrust its wavering gables at the sky'). Paralysed by a brain haemorrhage, brought on by a violent struggle culminating in an enforced kiss with his butler, Fledge, Sir Hugo lives in a state of living death and narrates to us a first-person narrative implicating both his wife and future son-in-law, Sidney, in a range of licentious activities with Fledge. 'Speaking' silently to us from behind the brick wall of a persistent vegetative state, the novel is framed by death. During its course Sidney is murdered, a crime of passion for which Sir Hugo suspects Fledge, though it is publicly blamed on the gardener, who is hanged. As the novel ends, Sir Hugo sits in his wheelchair, his back to his wife and Fledge, who are dancing, 'as the wind freshens, and wails about the gables of Crook, blowing from the south'. Crook is, of course, a queer name, and Sir Hugo's view of 'the Queer' far from progressive. Speaking of Fledge, he describes him as a 'furtive, ruthless, doubly inverted creature . . . a homosexual of the worst type'.[33]

Spider (1990), McGrath's second novel, is once again about death and centres on a disturbed young man called Dennis, who suffers from 'Queer thoughts' and whose nickname, 'Spider', is the code-word in a pseudo-incestuous relationship with his mother, a woman who is murdered in her own kitchen, apparently by his father, though Spider's own involvement in that affair remains unclear.[34] In terms of the pathology discussed at the beginning of this chapter, however, it is McGrath's third novel, *Dr Haggard's Disease* (1993), concerning 'the diseases of the flesh', including those linked to sexual desire, which might interest us most. Again, the novel is told in the first person from the perspective of a physically enfeebled narrator, this time the eponymous Dr Haggard, who walks with a stick (personified as 'Spike') after having been thrown down the stairs by the Senior Pathologist, who is husband to Haggard's mistress, Fanny Vaughan. After he learns of Fanny's death from kidney disease, her son, James, befriends Haggard. The novel's chronology ends during the Second World War, in which James sees service as an airman and is wounded, following which Haggard attends him: 'and James, were I stitching the face of a beautiful woman I don't think I'd have taken more pains about it'.[35] The intimacy the two men share enables Haggard to see Fanny emerging from the form of her son. As the novel progresses the 'queer', previously

associated only with the body in its physically diseased form, begins
to take on an uncanny dimension. For it is during Haggard's physical
examination of his wound that he realises that James's penis is 'plump
and soft like a child's' (p. 157) and, a few pages later that James himself
'seemed to be growing paler, softer, quieter by the day' (p. 161).
Gradually Haggard realises that 'Explanation – *pathos* and *logos* – could
not begin to encompass what was happening to [him], the miraculous
change that was even now being effected by the movement of her
spirit into [his] body' (p. 169). It is perhaps the end of the text that
best suits our purposes, for at this point Haggard dreams of an angel
and realises he is dreaming of James: 'That I could even picture you,
poor sick boy, an angel . . . hairless, translucent, with tiny breasts and
a boy's genitalia' (p. 172). Driven by the need to see him, Haggard is
propelled into the form of a predatory monster, akin to those depicted
in chapter 1 of this book:

> Oh, the idea of it now, I shudder at it – I see myself skulking in the
> shadows of the big silent hangar . . . I see myself darting past the
> spitfires in the gloom of the hangar, a tiny limping figure in a black
> fur coat scuttling across a vast space of shadows and aeroplanes . . .
> What did I intend to do now? Come to you in the darkness? . . . I sat
> on the grass, in the shadows, with my back against the wall, feeling
> connected with you through the mere contact with the building in
> which you slept. (p. 174)

In part, the connection with the angel is based upon flight, in part on
James's physical symptoms (androgyny being the typical state of angels)
and in part it is the 'sniff' of death, for the last pages detail Haggard
cradling in his arms the dying boy. At this point, however, the same
rapacious homoerotic assault of which Sir Hugo accuses Fledge in *The
Grotesque* takes place, and the final passage of the book depicts Haggard's
penetration of James's lips in a scene that ravels up in its convolutions
labial penetration of the ghost of (a) Fanny and necrophilia:

> Then with a shock of violent exaltation I feel the sudden nearness of
> her spirit. Again she has entered your body, she had entered the
> ruined dying body . . . Your black lips parted, a gasp, a sigh, a word . . .
> I press my mouth gently to yours and probe for your tongue with my

own, probe with tiny darting flickers till I taste in your terrible burnt
head the fresh sweet wetness of the living tongue within – (p. 180)

In 'The Angel' we have a sustained exploration of the queer as it is
depicted in relation to homosexuality, vampirism and the 'undead'.
At the same time, this is a narrative exploring the suggestion that,
unlike in *Dr Haggard's Disease*, in which the term angel is used as a
metaphor or an endearment ('My Angel!' Haggard silently exclaims
on spotting James at the airmen's bar (p. 175)), in this story one of the
characters really *is* an angel (read monster). This is a metropolitan
story, set in New York with a visible and identifiable skyline and the
Chrysler Building used as a precise landmark. Death and the uncanny
permeate the story from the start, the 'liquid heat settl[ing] on the
body of the city like an incubus', and one's bodily activities 'devolve[d]
to a languid commerce of flesh and fluids, the ingestion and excretion
of the one by the other'.[36] Our retrospective narrator, Bernard
Finnegan, is a writer detailing his encounter with an elderly man,
whom he believes is Harry Talboys. The name Tal(l)boys is, of course,
symbolic of the masculinist framework for the text, along with (via
its homonymic connection with furniture) a certain stiffness and
awkwardness resonant of former grandeur – not to mention the
obvious play on 'closets' already encountered in relation to *Jekyll*.
Equally, in many ways the story reminds the reader of Oscar Wilde's
The Picture of Dorian Gray (1891), not least in the early narrative
encounter between some men who are 'knowing' and others who are
not. However, where Dorian is described as 'wonderfully handsome,
with his finely-curved lips, his frank blue eyes, his crisp gold hair',[37]
Harry's 'mouth had foundered somewhat, but the old man animated
it with lipstick!' (p. 2) and everything about Harry equates with soiling.
Our narrator describes him as

> a tall thin figure in a seersucker suit the grubbiness of which, the fraying
> cuffs, the cigarette burns and faded reddish wine stain on the crotch
> could not altogether disguise the quality of the fabric and the elegance
> of the cut. Very erect, very tall, very slow. (p. 1)

The reference to the vertical, inherent here in Talboys's erect gait, is
a recurring feature, from the 'Chrysler Building itself, rising like a

jeweled spearhead against the sky' (p. 10) to our narrator's sense, as he stares at the naked body of Talboys, that he (Bernard) had 'become detached from [his] own body and saw as if from high up and far away the two figures standing in the room' (p. 15). In part, this vertical perspective attaches itself to our conventional reading of angels as messengers from another (read higher) plane. Additionally, however, it derives from the phallocentrism inherent in the detailed study by one man of the 'queerness' of another, and there are frequent instances of puns around (de)tumescence, such as when Harry is described as 'lower[ing] himself stiffly toward an armchair' (p. 3) or when the narrator, wanting to draw out Talboys on the subject of his reminiscences about the 1920s jazz scene, contemplates being able to 'sink [his] probe with enough precision' to release the old man's memories (p. 6). Such references are, however, ironic in their piquancy for, rather like James's in *Dr Haggard's Disease*, the man's actual penis is anything but erect: 'He dropped his trousers and underpants. The corset extended to his lower belly, forming a line just above a hairless pubis and a tiny, uncircumcised penis all puckered up and wrinkled in upon itself' (p. 15).

This is a story about social disease and social paranoia, one which explores the ease with which male homosexuality can become both scapegoated and demonised in the wake of HIV/AIDS. By setting his story in Manhattan, where, currently, one in every twenty-five men is infected with HIV,[38] McGrath also draws attention to the fact that, though vertical metaphors can be read phallically, they can also be read hypodermically – after all, at the end of the story the Chrysler Building is described as 'a bleak gray needle against a thickening winter afternoon sky' (p. 16). In his book, *Death, Desire and Loss in Western Culture*, Jonathan Dollimore questions the tendency, among male homosexual writers and critics (as well as those hostile to them), to pursue an aesthetic connection between homosexuality and death:

> In certain hostile representations of AIDS, homosexuality and death have been made to imply each other: homosexuality is seen as death-driven, death-desiring and thereby death-dealing . . . Male homosexual desire has been regarded in diverse ways by gay people themselves – as death-driven, as revolutionary, as benign, as redemptive, as self-shattering, as impossible of fulfilment . . . on the one hand, this

connection of homosexual desire and death has been made by those who want homosexuals literally to die; on the other, it is also part of the homosexual history, as it is part of a more general cultural history.[39]

In this respect, in 'The Angel' McGrath interrogates the Gothicised relationship between male homosexuality and death as much as he appears to reinforce it. There is an innate irony of perspective which mirrors the 'knowing' or self-conscious elements of Gothic writing which we have identified in other contexts elsewhere in this book.

In order to carry off the dual perspective of voicing the stance of the one who represents (Harry/Anson) and the placing of a knowing distance upon that representation (through Bernard), a space needs to be opened up between the tale and the teller. Two typical Gothic tropes frame this narrative: the first is that it follows the structure of a ghost story, in that it is told in the first person, set in the past ('I was a writer in those days' (p. 1)), follows a hearsay dynamic, and concerns a queer tale about characters always at one or more stages of removal from us. The second Gothic trope works via the figure of the double. Here we revisit Elisabeth Bronfen's claim, already cited in chapter 3, that: 'The revenant, occupying the interstice between two forms of existence – a celebration and a triumph over death – calls forth two forms of anxiety, i.e. the anxiety that death is finitude and the anxiety that death may not be the end.'[40] In McGrath's story, our narrator (Bernard) tells the story of a man (Harry) who tells the story of a man (Anson), who then tells us the second man never existed: 'There was no Harry Talboys . . . I am Anson Havershaw' (p. 14). So what of the conundrum involving Harry and Anson? At the one time we are being asked to accept that these two men are distinct, a distinction dependent upon their very similarity: '[he was] a wealthy and sophisticated young dandy, "a much more polished character than I," said Harry, and he recognized the similarity between us at once; it amused him' (p. 7). At the same time, we are asked to believe that they are one and the same person, a fact that makes similarity and doubling obsolete. In one sense it may be an expression of the relationship between the self and the reflection in the mirror (something denied to vampires, of course), the mirroring metaphor being a not infrequent image in narratives representing same-sex desire; on the other hand, as the name 'Anson' (an(d) son) also implies, there may be a kind of Jekyll and

Hyde coupling here, whereby death emerges from the living (parental) host.

As Terry Castle observes, there is a distinction to be drawn between the cultural treatment of lesbians and gay men:

> When members of the House of Lords decided in 1921 . . . not to amend the antihomosexual Criminal Law Amendment Act of 1885 to include acts of 'gross indecency' between women, it was not because they deemed the threat of lesbianism an inconsequential one . . . but because they were afraid that by the very act of mentioning it, they might spread such unspeakable 'filthiness' even further. The result of such denial: the transformation of the lesbian into a sort of juridical phantasm.[41]

Nevertheless, and as we have seen, the comparative visibility of male homosexuality does not rid it of any association with the Gothic. As McGrath shows only too clearly in 'The Angel', in the wake of AIDS, instead of ghostly apparitions what we find are the haunted manifestations of cultural anxiety, in which the gay man figures as a form of living corpse:

> Harry's flesh had rotted off his lower ribs and belly, and the clotted skin still clinging . . . that bordered the hole was in a state of gelatinous putrescence. In the hole I caught the faint gleam of his spine, and amid an indistinct bundle of piping the forms of shadowy organs. I saw sutures on his intestines, and the marks of neat stitching, and a cluster of discoloured organic vessels bound with a thin strip of translucent plastic. (p. 15)

5

Survey of Criticism

Across the span of the twentieth century, our definitions of the Gothic, its films and its literatures have broadened tremendously, reaching ever outwards, perhaps almost beyond original recognition, though one of the reasons for the Gothic's continued popularity is its willingness to reinvent itself:

> because to Renaissance sceptics the Gothic ideal, wrought in castle and cathedral, seemed dark and thwarted beside the measure of a Parthenon, it came to pass in the early Renaissance, that the term 'gothic' took on a new and colored meaning, a meaning that masked a sneer.[1]

Alfred Longueil, whom we first met in the Introduction, uses his 1923 essay to trace out a journey we now readily accept as 'given', namely the manner in which eighteenth-century Gothic practitioners re-considered and revalued the cultural artefacts of the medieval period in order to rethink its relationship to their own present fears. What is striking about Longueil's reading of the Gothic is his association of it with 'clash and colour' rather than moonlight and pallid hues, though colour, in these terms, is not red, yellow and blue, but an 'interest in black letter', or the flourishes of Gothic script.[2] This para-doxical combination of exuberance and darkness is one of the sustaining features of the Gothic as it survives into and through the twentieth century. For instance, it is the feature enabling cultural consumerist interventions into the Gothic such as the Eerie Pub Company, which Catherine Spooner discusses in her book on the *Contemporary Gothic* (2006):

> The Eerie Pub Co. is a London-based chain of Gothic theme pubs and bars, all of which sport splendidly exaggerated Gothic styling, complete with gargoyles, bubbling test tubes and doors hidden behind fake bookshelves. One can order cocktails themed around the Seven Deadly Sins or chips on coffin-shaped plates, and pre-recorded hollow laughter rings through the toilets.[3]

At each stage of his essay Longueil painstakingly maps out the different routes taken by each variant meaning of the Gothic, careful to keep the architectural always away from the literary and to differentiate that aspect of the Gothic he associates (and to an extent denigrates) with the supernatural from a revisiting of the medieval. Critics such as Spooner do the opposite, not only examining traditional Gothic architecture as it informs contemporary art ('Jane and Louise Wilson's . . . video installation of an empty House of Commons, tracing the symbols and spaces of political power, tellingly marries Pugin's Gothic architectural idealism with the darker sensibility of the Gothic literary and cinematic tradition'), but similarly paying sustained attention to 'Goth' fashion, an aspect of popular culture which is largely ignored, still, by Gothic theorists. Like Longueil, Spooner takes this fashion trend back to the historical routes of literary Gothic, but the vast scope of interest in the Gothic that has developed in the intervening period between these critics' works enables Spooner to be more creative ('colourful', perhaps) in her arguments. For her, adolescence and 'dress up' are two key elements of all Gothic sensibilities:

> It seems a long way between Emily St. Aubert and a contemporary Gothic teenager like Buffy Summers, heroine of the film (1992) and TV series *Buffy the Vampire Slayer*, but historically distanced as they may be, Buffy and Emily clearly participate in the same tradition of representation.[4]

Comparisons between Longueil and critics of his own time also pertain. Bearing in mind that Longueil's essay is written four years after Freud's essay 'The Uncanny' (1919), it is striking to us, perhaps, that no mention of Freud (or psychoanalysis) occurs anywhere in it. In part this may well be that, though both are focused on a detailed consideration of one term, in each case that term is different (the 'Gothic' for Longueil and the 'Uncanny' for Freud). So dominant has psychoanalysis been to our understanding of the Gothic in the last twenty to thirty years, nevertheless (and certainly we are far more familiar with Freud than Longueil), that we tend simply to conflate the uncanny *with* the Gothic. Longueil's approach is not psychoanalytic, but one could argue that his essay is influenced by the unconscious, whether or not he is consciously influenced by (or even aware of) Freud.

Longueil's 'road map' of the Gothic identifies three differing routes taken by the term: firstly, 'a definite and recognized synonym for barbarous', then a cultural judgement centred upon all 'things mediaeval', then the 'supernatural'. What is intriguing, as he plots out his map, is his manifestation of the compulsion to repeat. So, differentiating between meanings one and two, he continues: 'This meaning is not an off-shoot of the first meaning, except in so far as the use of "Gothic" as a literary term in meaning one, helped to make easier its use as a literary term in meaning two. It is not an off-shoot of it.' The repetition of the phrase 'It is not an off-shoot of it' strikes us as clumsy, perhaps even suggestive of loose editing, a flaw that also occurs elsewhere in the essay, such as when Longueil observes, at the top of the fourth page of his article, 'The second meaning of "Gothic" is mediaeval', only to repeat two pages later, 'so the second meaning of "Gothic" as a critical term in the eighteenth century, is simply "mediaeval"'.[5] Though awkward to read, such compulsions are strangely fitting to a narrative mode we have seen to be excessive, insistent and reiteratively intertextual. It is a feature of which Freud is also guilty in 'The Uncanny', in the six-and-a-half-page investigation of the variety of usages of the word '*heimlich*' ('homely') and its antonym, '*unheimlich*' ('unhomely' or, as we more commonly use it, 'uncanny'). What it is to which both Longueil and Freud fall prey is something Freud himself defines as an impulse that 'forces upon us the idea of something fateful and inescapable when otherwise we should have spoken only of "chance"'.[6] This may explain why Longueil, who spends most of his article elaborating slowly upon shades of nuance, suddenly rushes to conclude his article with what strikes the reader as an unexpected minor outburst:'So – apart from its technical use in linguistics and architecture – run the ups and downs of"Gothic", from a race-term to a sneering-word, from a sneering-word to a cool adjective, from a cool adjective to a cliché in criticism.' Longueil, we suddenly realise, is irritated by the Gothic – or, at least, by what he considers its misuse – a fault he places squarely at the feet of readers. Speaking, earlier in the essay, of Horace Walpole's *The Castle of Otranto* (1764) and Clara Reeve's *Old English Baron* (1778), he asserts that,

> to the reading public the outstanding feature of these stories appears to have been, not their gothic setting, but their supernatural incident. Imitators and followers of Walpole and Reeve, therefore, being thrifty persons, and acutely conscious of the public's taste in best sellers . . . kept accenting this spectral side of the genre more and more, because there was a market for it.[7]

Here we have the reason for his irritation laid bare: Gothic sells, and that is both its greatest asset and its greatest weakness.

Questions of the body loom large in the Gothic; as the interface between fiction and criticism becomes closer, so does the overlap between them. One of the most innovative theoretical approaches to the Gothic emerges during the late 1980s with the work of Nicholas Abraham on cryptonomy. At this cultural moment, the concept of haunting takes the important shift away from belief in the occult towards a realisation of the self-destructive potential lurking within our own secrets and those inherited from others:

> It is a fact that the 'phantom', whatever its form, is nothing but an invention of the living . . . [it] is meant to objectify, even if under the guise of individual or collective hallucinations, the gap that the concealment of some part of a loved one's life produced in us . . . what haunts are not the dead, but the gaps left within us by the secrets of others.[8]

By situating the phantom as something innately linked to story-telling ('the gaps left within us by the secrets of others'), Abraham renders cryptonomy an especially fitting mode of Gothic investigation for readers and writers of narrative fiction. At the same time, it re-inforces its traditional situation within a family plot and across legacies, a pattern Abraham identifies as 'transgenerational haunting'. What remains complex about Abraham's theory is the fact that it carries a sense of contagion (a feature of a number of 'classic' Gothic tales such as 'The Fall of the House of Usher' or *Dracula*) but, unlike the physiologically visible conditions that writers such as Poe and Stoker use as the centrepiece for their narratives, cryptonomy is – as the references to gaps in the family narrative make clear – invisible or, in terms of the content of these untold stories, 'unspeakable'. These are the stories that are *not* told, that belong not to the narrators and characters we encounter but to those who come before and are already 'departed'. In that respect, cryptonomy sits perfectly within the realm of the postmodern or poststructuralist text, with its interrogation of the nuclear family unit, its narrative lacunae and its fractured narrative subject: '[This] phantom's periodic and compulsive return lies beyond the scope of symptom-formation in the sense of a return of the repressed; it works like a ventriloquist, like a stranger within the subject's own mental topography.'[9]

It is partly through psychoanalysis and partly through the post-modern that the Gothic, like its classic monsters, continues to metamorphose into ever more pertinent forms for today's culture. Technology has, surprisingly, provided a willing ally in this process, as phrases such as 'the ghost in the machine', or even the common usage of the term 'ghosting', in the sense of the blurring of the focus on a camera lens or television screen, underline. And perhaps there *is* something increasingly uncanny about inventions such as the telephone, in which disembodied voices visit us in our homes, or fax machines, which uncannily copy, as if in automatic writing, a message sent from hundreds of miles away by a disembodied hand. As Terry Castle puts it, in an interview with Michael Arnzen:

> Just about anything electronic has its uncanny aspect . . . Whenever something non-human can move on its own, respond to our move-ments, signal to us, answer questions, or image our bodies or voices

back to us in some luminous or resonant fashion, we confront, I think, a kind of cognitive *mise-en-abyme*.[10]

In his own monograph on the uncanny, Nicholas Royle identifies, at the end of the twentieth century, an all-pervasive sense of the uncanny within culture. By means of illustration, he cites an article in the *Guardian* newspaper which, on New Year's Day 2000, drew attention to the explosion in computing technology and scientific advances linked to genetic coding, before concluding: 'It feels uncannily as though human beings are finally getting to the roots of the tree of knowledge.'[11] In the run-up to the new millennium, many will recall such all-pervasive cultural anxiety fastening upon a precise mathematical difficulty: what would happen to all those clocks with digital date technology, once they moved from 99 to 00? It was feared that all microchip technology, from national and international databases to domestic video recorders and heating systems, might malfunction: unable to date not only 'zero hour', but 'zero year', time (and hence civilisation) might end. Of course, such fears proved groundless; digital timing technology was shown to deal with the new millennium as capably as did its analogue ancestor, hence was the master/slave dialectic upheld. What we are reminded of here, however, is how closely science fiction and the Gothic have come to exist in relation to each other: where once superstition lay at the root of the *unheimlich*, now, arguably, it is the machine age. Royle expresses it thus: 'The uncanny, then, is not merely an "aesthetic" or "psychological" matter . . . its critical elaboration is necessarily bound up with analysing, questioning and even transforming what is called "everyday life" . . . for example, in relation to notions of automation, technology and programming.'[12]

Royle details and traces a broad brief in his playful book, from the uncanny experience of the teaching scenario

There is something disgusting, incipiently uncanny perhaps, about the experience of repetition in talking to students, in memorizing or trying to memorize their names, in finding oneself seeming to say or being on the verge of saying exactly the same thing as one did an hour, or a day, or a year before

---

to the place of death within silence:

6

Silence, solitude and . . .

– Did you say something?
– I heard a voice.
– In your head?
– No, in yours.[13]

En route he engages in a detailed exploration of the concept of déjà vu, a concept which, he notes, is never mentioned in Freud's 'The Uncanny' but which frames it entirely. For Royle, 'There is no believing without the ghost of déjà vu' because 'This ghost haunts Freud's argument that beliefs that have been surmounted have not entirely been surmounted', a paradox that does seem to sum up any number of Freud's own illustrations, including the one Royle goes on to cite, 'the omnipotence of thoughts':

> We – or our primitive forefathers – once believed that these possibilities were realities, and were convinced that they actually happened. Nowadays we no longer believe in them, we have *surmounted* these modes of thought; but we do not feel quite sure of our new beliefs, and the old ones still exist within us ready to seize upon any confirmation.[14]

Having included the quotation, Royle uses Freud's own sense of engagement with his reader, through his adoption of the plural pronoun, as a mechanism for establishing a doubling paradigm for Freud in relation to his own text:

> Freud effectively presents himself here as a double, and imposes on his reader the same structure of being-two ('we' as Freud and the reader, but also the reader, you or me for example, as already a double): we non-religious, non-primitive, non-mystical people do not believe; and yet these 'surmounted' modes of thought 'still exist within us'. . . These phantom 'modes of thought' will have seen us coming.[15]

Throughout his book, Royle takes the uncanny in a variety of directions, to the extent that one can never anticipate what is coming next. Nevertheless, in so doing he also traces out some of the routes adopted by theorists and critics whose key concern is not the Gothic, but who employ metaphors of the Gothic (more particularly haunting) in their explorations into other subjects. The key exemplar of this for Royle is Derrida, who presides over Royle's reading(s) as central representative of deconstruction. For Royle, 'Another name for uncanny overflow might be deconstruction', an assertion he goes on to qualify in terms of how it renders the familiar text unfamiliar and frequently held assumptions about that text 'uncertain'. Similarly political and metaphorical in focus, Royle employs *Specters of Marx* (1993) as a virtual visual aid to his discussion of the crisis in British universities: 'At the centre of the book is the blackboard on which Derrida writes how badly the world is going' and again, 'The future, as Derrida says, belongs to ghosts. Ghosts don't belong to the past, they come from the future.'[16]

A technological focus on the Gothic equally characterises Fred Botting's latest book on the subject, *Limits of Horror: Technology, Bodies, Gothic* (2008). Botting shares Royle's playfulness of approach and delights in coinages such as 'Candygothic', which he defines as 'Pleasure and pain; horror and joy; candy bars and razorblades'. This he uses partly as a cultural framework through which to read monster narratives, such as Bernard Rose's film *Candyman* (1992), and partly as a mechanism for deconstructing the aridity of a culture in which sex is simply another form of commodification, 'a cycle of (boring) consumption'.[17] Coining another phrase, 'Disneygothic', Botting turns to 'the truth' as exemplar of the fabulous. This phrase refers directly to plans for an actual theme park in Sighisoara in modern-day Transylvania: 'A ghost castle, Dracula hotels and a "vampirology" centre had been designed'. Though these plans were axed, Botting continues:

> The Castle Hotel Dracula is open. Located in Bistrita-Nasaud, Romania, at an altitude of 3,600 feet in the Carpathian mountains, it is a mock-Gothic edifice with a turret nightclub built between 1983 and 1985 …At the time of building no references to Dracula were permitted: it was built for Nicolae Ceauşescu.[18]

On this basis, one assumes Botting would equally consider Alton Towers to be 'Disneygothic', though the comparison reminds us of the difficulty of rendering any architectural composite 'mock-Gothic', when all our key Gothic landmarks exist as artificial testimonies to an original authenticity that never was.

As we saw in the Introduction, this concept of the counterfeit is one Jerrold E. Hogle brought to our understanding of Gothic culture. In his landmark essay 'The Gothic ghost of the counterfeit and the progress of abjection', Hogle opens with a revisiting of the 'fakery' of Strawberry Hill before posing a conundrum which he identifies at the heart of our continuing fascination with the Gothic, even in the face of secular cynicism:

> If, then, the Gothic is so continuously based on ghostings of the already spectral, or at least resymbolisations of what is already symbolic and thus more fake than real, what does this basic and ongoing dimension of it have to do with the Gothic's cultural and psychological force in our culture over nearly three centuries?[19]

Certainly, our interest in, as much as our understanding of, the Gothic is rooted in our understanding of postmodernism as a network of theoretically complex discourses, a truth that makes contemporary Gothic seem highly remote from its first realisation by individuals such as Walpole. Part of the criticism levelled at postmodernism, aside from any perceived connection with the Gothic, is of its preoccupation with surfaces, commodities and performative identities at the expense of material concerns such as poverty, race and sexual discrimination. The appearance, indeed the cloak, the mask and the costume are the very epitome of Gothic identities, from the vampire through to the werewolf, and so one might well expect the parodic possibilities afforded the Gothic by commodification to play an important role in it. However, there remains a profoundly material element to the Gothic, manifest in the very use of blood, gore, weaponry and conflict. Hogle continues, it is the Gothic's 'grounding in the struggle between different discourses based on different class-based ideologies' that provides part of its ongoing appeal for students.[20]

Among those aspects of the Gothic that especially capture the imagination in the late twentieth century, one would have to single out the vampire, about which two key studies are particularly influential, Ken Gelder's *Reading the Vampire* (1994) and Nina Auberbach's *Our Vampires, Ourselves* (1995). Gelder's book particularly emphasises the role of eastern European politics in our understanding of vampire legend/folklore and film. After a brief discussion of the similarities between Tasmania and Transylvania he also opens his book with an analysis of media readings of the Communist regime under Ceauşescu, identifying within them a perspective on Romanian politics equating to Botting's return to Dracula's castle: 'The demonization of a communist tyranny by western journalists was nowhere more relentlessly pursued than here – bolstered by the easy availability of "on site" vampiric iconography.'[21]

Ethnic identity is the key theme of the opening of Gelder's study, one that takes him straight to questions of anti-Semitism and attendant fears of contagion present at the end of the nineteenth century, primarily in relation to the spread of syphilis and the nomadic characteristic attached both to vampires and Jewish migration, a theme from which he moves to questions of capital and financial greed. What Gelder recognises is that the figure of the vampire does not simply reside in literature of the late nineteenth century but, through Marx's allusion to vampires in *Das Kapital*, they are openly invited into the workaday world of industrial politics and the class struggle. Later, Gelder sustains a discussion of late twentieth-century vampire fiction and, most compellingly, vampire cinema, from *Nosferatu: A Symphony of Horror* (1922) through to Francis Ford Coppola's *Bram Stoker's Dracula* (1992). Here, he observes, 'it would seem that cinema is – and has been for some time – the rightful place of occupation for the vampire'.[22] In part this is because of its 'touring' nature (at least in its 'large screen' phase), though after that one might add that the purchase of a video or DVD personal copy becomes tantamount to inviting the monster over the threshold and into one's own home.

Just as Gelder insists on the prevalence of the vampire as cultural metaphor of the nineteenth century, so is he keen to emphasis its vitality at the end of the twentieth century. In his discussion of the British Hammer Horror films of the 1950s to 1970s, we briefly recall Longueil's use of Gothic colour to refer to an 'interest in black letter', or the flourishes of Gothic script. Hammer Horror films, by contrast, use colour at its most 'lurid . . . red and blue especially . . . developing their special effects accordingly'. This appetite for visual excess so clearly mirrors the vampire as a monster of excess that there can be little doubt about the suitability of the partnership between form and content. Overall, Gelder is cautiously 'upbeat' about the future of vampires: the vampire may be a figure of cultural excess rooted in wastage and becoming 'spent', but 'cinema "recruits" its audience, calling them back again and again'.[23]

Nina Auerbach (whose earlier book *Woman and the Demon: The Life of a Victorian Myth* (1982) informs part of Gelder's reading of anti-Semitism in relation to the vampire) publishes, one year after Gelder, her own book on vampires. Hers gives far more prominence to gender theory and, where Gelder's work is European in primary focus, hers is situated explicitly within a reading of American party political culture, from the presidency of Franklin D. Roosevelt through to that of George Bush Snr. As she explains, in relation to the rationale underlying her book,

> Vampires and American presidents began to converge in my imagin-
> ation, not because I think all presidents are equally vampiric (though all
> do absorb power from the electorate), but because both are personifi-
> cations of their age . . . the nervous national climate in which I
> imagined this book taught me that no fear is only personal: it must
> steep itself in its political and ideological ambience.[24]

Auerbach's cultural sweep is a wide one, taking in fashion, film and folklore as well as literature, but its focus remains political through-out, though the 'politics with a capital P' with which it opens also, on occasions, gives vent to personal politics, such as when she observes: 'For most of the young women who, like me, loved Hammer films in the 1960s and weren't sure why, these grins of aroused discovery were subliminal surprises in a waste of staked bimbos'.[25] Auerbach's study, then, is self-consciously left-wing and self-consciously feminist and, as its title assumes, it sustains the thesis, throughout, that monsters in film, fiction and poetry function as the outward projection of shared cultural anxiety. It is, however, in its treatment of the perceived connection between a resurgent fascination with the vampire and the AIDS epidemic of the 1980s and 1990s that it has had greatest impact on our cultural awareness.

In the final section of her book, titled 'Grave and Gay: Reagan's Years', Auerbach looks at the various means via which a genre previously associated with gleeful parody through the Hammer Horror movies becomes transformed into a genre of sickness: 'Once the etiology of AIDS became clear, blood could no longer be the life; vampirism mutated from hideous appetite to nausea.' However, for Auerbach it is through the backlash against homosexuality prompted by neuroses linked to the AIDS crisis that Queer Theory emerges as a positive means towards self-definition: 'In the Reagan-esque years, when reaction and AIDS seemed to petrify the future, critics longed for *im*permanence: Queer Theorists apotheosized a phantasmal, unsettled spirit. Even the countercultural vampire is a product, if a resistant one, of its age.'[26]

No survey of Gothic criticism would be complete without a consideration of film, a key exemplar of this being Barbara Creed's *The Monstrous Feminine* (1993), a landmark book in which Creed offers a sustained evaluation of Julia Kristeva's theory of abjection in relation to horror cinema. That Kristeva's title translates as *Powers of Horror* (1982) suggests it ought to have played a key role in our understanding of the Gothic, but in fact its influence upon it has been comparatively under-represented. Kristeva draws on the work of the cultural anthropologist Mary Douglas in exploring the relationship between self and not-self, a process of identity formation she roots in the child's relationship to the mother's body: 'As if the fundamental opposition were between I and Other or . . . Inside and Outside'.[27] In all monster narratives, such assignments of strangeness and belonging are fundamental, but Creed especially argues that it is the woman's body that is rendered most threatening of all in horror cinema:

> The female monster . . . wears many faces: the amoral primeval mother . . . vampire . . . witch . . . woman as monstrous womb . . . woman as bleeding wound . . . woman as possessed body . . . the castrating mother . . . woman as beautiful but deadly killer . . . aged psychopath . . . the monstrous girl-boy . . . woman as non-human animal . . . woman as life-in-death . . . woman as the deadly *femme castratrice* . . .[28]

One of the areas Creed especially addresses is the fragility of the relationship between woman as victim and as predator, which she summarises as 'castrator and . . . castrated'. Two sides of the same coin, Creed identifies the roles open to women in the horror genre either as one in which 'her body is repeatedly knifed until it resembles a bleeding womb', or as an embodiment of the '*vagina dentata* or toothed vagina'. The present/absent signifier of menstruation predominates in this form, for 'Victims rarely die cleanly or quickly . . . Close-up shots of gaping jaws, sharp teeth and bloodied lips play on the spectator's fears of bloody incorporation'. At times this can further complicate the self/other boundary, as shown in Creed's reading of the famous publicity poster for the film *Jaws* (dir. Spielberg, 1975), showing the open-mouthed shark rising to the surface where a young woman swims. Creed's accompanying caption titles the image 'Aquatic dentata' and continues: 'In *Jaws* woman and shark are closely linked through image and narrative', presumably through their physical proximity (and isolation), coupled with the fact that the savage teeth of the shark point directly at the woman's pubic mound.[29]

Another influential gender-oriented survey, brought out a year before Creed's, is Carol J. Clover's imaginatively titled *Men, Women and Chainsaws* (1992), a book focusing upon American horror narratives of the 1970s and early 1980s. She begins by considering the shifting nature of the audiences of horror films, noting the 'number of what I once thought of as unlikely people – middle-aged, middle-class people of both sexes – who have "come out" to me about their secret appetite for so-called exploitation horror'.[30] This would seem to map, quite closely, the general trend affecting the Gothic more generally. As Spooner explains, 'Goth' as a fashion statement is characterised, typically, as 'a predilection for black clothing in a combination of faux-period, Punk and fetish styles, elaborate jewellery, "vamp" make-up for both sexes, and dyed hair, also frequently black'.[31] Those who gravitate towards the Gothic as a literary, artistic or cinematic phenomenon, however, be they students, academics or general readers and tourists, cover a far more wide-ranging social palate than this implies and, in the academy, as this book began by noting, the Gothic has become more and more 'mainstream'. At the same time, the basic gender identification processes in play are dependent upon a typicality inherent in the demographic groupings comprising horror cinema audiences, and these Clover identifies, using 'what formal surveys and informal accounts there are', in the following terms:

> adolescent males hold pride of place. At theatre screenings, in any case,
> the constituencies typically break down, in order of size, as follows:
> young men, frequently in groups but also solo; male–female couples of
> various ages (though mostly young); solo 'rogue males' (older men of
> ominous appearance and/or reactions); and adolescent girls in groups.[32]

So Clover progresses to a consideration of how such social groupings map on to viewer identification. As Terry Castle does, in her Introduction to *The Apparitional Lesbian*, discussed in chapter 4, Clover opens her book with a discussion of the shaping effect one cinema visit had on her understanding of gender politics:

> This book began in 1985 when a friend dared me to go see *The Texas
> Chain Saw Massacre*. I was familiar with the horror classics and with
> stylish or 'quality' horror (Hitchcock, De Palma, and the like), but
> exploitation horror I had assiduously avoided. Seeing *Texas* ... jolted
> me into questioning for the first time the notion of the 'male gaze'
> and its assumption of masculine mastery.[33]

In summary, Clover challenges the received wisdom that male members of an audience identify solely with male members of the cast and thus, in the context of horror movies, use them as a method of giving imaginative vent to that part of their inner psyche that longs to maim, tyrannise and torture women. Instead, she argues, a far more complex and fluid gender identification takes place:

> To the extent that the possibility of cross-gender identification has been
> entertained, it has been that of the female with the male ... But if it is
> so that all of us, male and female alike, are by these processes 'made to'
> identify with men and 'against' women, how are we to explain the
> appeal to a largely male audience of a film genre that features a female
> victim-hero?[34]

Hence, despite the superficial presence of a male killer and a female victim (or even multiple all-female or female and male victims),

Clover argues the recurrent narrative formula is one in which the lone female survives. She it is who eradicates the killer, face to face, at which point all members of the audience will be cheering her on.

One of the most interesting observations Clover makes about the horror film more generally is its similarity to the folktale in significance: 'a set of fixed tale types that generate an endless stream of what are in effect variants: sequels, remakes, and rip-offs'. In that respect they perform a crucial storytelling function that overreaches their significance as individual films (or even, perhaps, a genre of films) and taps into a deeper function directly linked to cultural truths. In part this demonstrates the interpretative terrain they share with psychoanalysis: 'The house or tunnel may at first seem a safe haven, but the same walls that promise to keep the killer out quickly become, once the killer penetrates them, the walls that hold the victim in.' Later she turns to that section of Freud's 'The Uncanny' which compares burial alive to intrauterine existence. In Clover's hands, far from being the mother's womb, this 'Terrible Place' is the lair of the killer, a habitat that further confuses the gender identification of these movies:

> What makes these houses terrible is not just their Victorian decrepitude, but the terrible families – murderous, incestuous, cannibalistic – that occupy them ... Into such houses unwitting victims wander in film after film, and it is the conventional task of the genre to register in close detail the victims' dawning understanding, as they survey the visible evidence, of the human crimes and perversions that have transpired there.[35]

As both Clover and Creed observe, however, the comedic possibilities of such excesses are never far from the surface, and the audience are as likely to laugh out loud as to scream. Such ambivalences are the subject of William Paul's book *Laughing Screaming* (1994), in which Paul identifies both comedy and horror as communal forms of cinema well suited to outward expressions of fear and pleasure – sometimes in equal mix:

> In no other films are we so aware of other people in the theatre because in no other films are they so prompted by the film itself to make their

presence known. There is, then, a kind of loss of individuality . . . a loss that brings with it the gain of communal experience, a festive feeling akin to drunkenness.[36]

It is perhaps with such carnivalesque abandon (a sort of church of the profane) that we should conclude, rather than Longueil's 'sneer'. We have seen how the Gothic continues to haunt us throughout the twentieth century, even after we have ceased believing in 'ghosts, ghoulies and long-legged beasties'. In part it is that our fears require shapes through which they might become articulate (in the sense of 'possessing joints or jointed segments'[37]), in part because we marvel in the mysterious world of the special visual effect, superstition's technological substitute. Finally, however, our world is one so imbued with consumerism that the self-consciousness of the counterfeit has a value all of its own: once one exorcises the fear of the occult, the costumes and role-play of the Gothic remain 'to die for'.

6

Conclusion: Thriller *and* Stranger

In the last few months, two events of direct significance to the contemporary Gothic have occurred: the publication of Sarah Waters's
latest novel, *The Little Stranger* (2009), and the premature death of
the 'King of Pop', Michael Jackson. Jackson has surely epitomised the
twentieth-century Gothic (on and off stage) as well as anybody, an
identification that only partly relies on the worldwide success of his
Gothic album *Thriller* (1982), its title song and extended video (1983)
which, alone, sold over nine million copies. We have already considered
the role of haunted childhood in this book and, in the case of Jackson,
this has continued to define his adult life. Living a reclusive existence
in a ranch named 'Neverland' (after the land beyond death in Barrie's
Peter Pan), an estate described by Paul Theroux as 'a toytown wilderness of carnival rides and doll houses and zoo animals and pleasure
gardens', the presence of this personal theme park surely puts in the
shade Horace Walpole's fascination with his 'plaything', Strawberry
Hill.[1]

The stories that link Jackson to children and his own childhood
offer up the most Gothic aspects of Jackson's documented life. Sean
O'Hagan, in an *Observer* article, 'Tragedy of the Pop Genius who
Never Grew Up', refers to 'creepy sleepovers' at Neverland and then,
in reference to Jackson's own childhood relationship with Diana Ross,
writes of Jackson 'describ[ing] her creepily as his "mother-lover-
friend" with whom he shared his "deepest, darkest secrets"'.[2] The

Gothic elements of mass consumerism and popular culture (addressed in the Introduction) are also played out here: sadly, Jackson's story seems to have been driven by a death-narrative even before he died, again tied to issues of cosmetic surgery and 'enhancements'. Andrew Gumbel observes, 'It is still too soon to say for sure how his eventual death unfolded, but it is already clear that behind the scenes an ominous story was playing out.' Meanwhile, he continues, 'in a grim twist of fate, [Jackson's] untimely death has [resulted in] . . . sales of his albums and songs hav[ing] rocketed, putting him back on top of the music charts all over the world'.[3] The ferryman must be paid, after all.

As we reach the end of the first decade of the twenty-first century, we start to be able to reflect on the twentieth century as a historical period. As one would expect, despite the fact that the Gothic has enjoyed tremendous vibrancy throughout that century, it has equally relied upon texts written in the previous one for continued reinvigoration. Mary Shelley's *Frankenstein* (1818), Robert Louis Stevenson's *The Strange Case of Dr Jekyll and Mr Hyde* (1886), Bram Stoker's *Dracula* (1897) and, to a lesser extent, Oscar Wilde's *The Picture of Dorian Gray* (1890) and Charlotte Perkins Gilman's *The Yellow Wallpaper* (1892) are the key intertextual ancesters here. In this book I have also claimed, because of the sinister fascination with child abuse and paedophilia that dominates the end of the twentieth century and the start of the twenty-first, one can add to that list Henry James's *The Turn of the Screw* (1898). Of course, major world events of terrifying monstrosity occur in the twentieth century and it was at the end of the first of those, the First World War, that Sigmund Freud wrote his essay on 'The Uncanny' (1919), an essay that, though focused on the hidden dangers of the psyche is also, surely, prompted in part by 'outside' horrors. Those horrors preceded others, nevertheless, not least the global 'compulsion to repeat' that manifested itself as the Second World War, a conflict just prior to which Freud and his family were forced to flee Vienna for England because of the threat of Nazi persecution.

That Western culture never quite recovers from the Second World War seems apparent in the number of Gothic texts that continue to return to it as a central milieu. Waters's *The Little Stranger* is among them, set just after the war in 1947-8, but examining the ways in which the Second World War results in the wholesale dismantling of a family whose class (the aristocracy) no longer has a role to play in the 'new Britain'. The novel anticipates the introduction of the National Health Service in 1948 and therefore takes up precisely where the 1947 section of her previous novel, *The Night Watch* (2006), ends. While *The Night Watch* situates at its heart a community of single women, predominantly lesbian, *The Little Stranger* is told through the eyes of a first-person male narrator, Dr Faraday, to whom the reform of the health service is a matter for concern:

> I had only very recently begun to make a profit. Now . . . private doctoring seemed done for. On top of that, all my poorer patients would soon have the option of leaving my list and attaching them-selves to another man, thereby vastly reducing my income. I had had several bad nights over it.[4]

The novel is, then, primarily about changing class structures and the gradual democratisation of Britain and, though Jewish intellectuals such as Freud found England comparatively accepting of ethnic difference, Waters demonstrates how the lesbian remains edged out as 'peacetime' is restored, just as the old aristocratic family, the Ayreses, are edged out of their home, Hundreds Hall. Though the gradual 'downsizing' of the Ayreses' dominance begins prior to the narrative opening, it finds its most flagrant expression within it in the 'new build' council houses that spring up on part of their former estate, not as an act of philanthropy, but through economic necessity.

Just as twentieth-century Gothic looks back to important literary ancestors from the previous century, so *The Little Stranger* gestures towards Daphne Du Maurier's mid-century Gothic, not least in the fact that Hundreds, the country house the family inhabits, is described early on in ways resembling Manderley at the start of *Rebecca* (1938), sharing its preoccupation with memories, lost grandeur and family tragedy, not to mention the fact that what defines its dereliction is as much the garden as the house itself. Faraday tells us, 'I remembered a long approach to the house through neat rhododendron and laurel, but the park was now so overgrown and untended, my small car had to fight its way down the drive' (p. 5).[5] In this preoccupation with the garden, what is also established is the importance of land boundaries as affirmations of social boundaries. Faraday observes that, even in the house's heyday, 'The solid brown stone boundary wall, though not especially high, was high enough to seem forbidding' (p. 4) but, on the warm summer day when he first takes tea with the family, he contemplates the panoramic view through the French windows, down from the entrance to the south terrace, and what strikes him is the continual breaching of possible visual boundaries:

> An overgrown lawn ran away from the house for what looked like thirty or forty yards. It was bordered by flower beds, and ended at a wrought-iron fence. But the fence gave onto a meadow, which in turn gave onto the fields of the park; the fields stretched off into the distance for a good three-quarters of a mile. The Hundreds boundary wall was just about visible at the end of them, but since the land beyond the wall was pasture, giving way to tilth and cornfield, the prospect ran on, uninterrupted, finishing only where its paling colours bled away completely into the haze of the sky. (p. 25)

As if to point towards what Kenneth W. Graham identifies as Gothicism's tendency towards 'an ambiguity of relationship between prohibition and transgression', a tension is evident, even here, between the presence of boundary markers ('prohibition') and their breach ('transgression').[6] Verbs such as 'run away' convey nature's struggle to resist the family's elevation, an elevation that is implied to be topographical as much as social, for in order to be able to see this far into the distance one must be raised above one's surroundings. Furthermore, *The Little Stranger* is a novel about trespass: Faraday enters the house, in the fictive present, as the family doctor but he was previously here as a child of ten, on Empire Day, when the family were giving out commemorative medals to the village children. His mother had been in service to the family, a position that enabled her to gain access to the interior of the house for them both. As the boy wanders off to explore he is taken over by a sense of avarice – 'I wanted to possess a piece of [the house]' – an urge that results in him gouging from the wall a piece of a decorative plaster border, in the shape of an acorn (one is reminded of the economic maxim 'from little acorns do giant oak trees grow'), which he conceals in his pocket. Though he excuses his childhood vandalism as 'the work of a moment' (p. 3), the desire to possess never leaves him, a desire that finds expression, in part, in his decision to court Caroline, the daughter of the family and 'a "natural spinster"' (p. 9), who, when his advances are rebuffed, inspires in Faraday a rather sinister fantasy, as he lies in his own bed, contemplating 'nudg[ing] open the swollen front door . . . inch[ing] across the chequered marble; and then . . . creeping, creeping towards her, up the still and silent stairs' (p. 325).

Not a book just about trespass, *The Little Stranger* is primarily a book about *children* and trespass and, in that sense, reinforces our awareness of haunted childhood being the Gothic preoccupation par excellence for our society.[7] Hence, perhaps, Faraday's greatest reservation about the new council housing: 'the flimsy wire fences . . . would do nothing to keep the children of the twenty-four families out of the park' (p. 248). Despite this, by far the most intrusive of child trespassers belong to the upper classes, not the lower: Gillian Baker-Hyde (and who can overlook the Gothic implications of the word 'Hyde'?) and Susan, the dead daughter, whom Mrs Ayres longs to haunt the house. The Baker-Hydes are the rival nouveau riche family, recent incomers residing at Standish, the 'neighbouring' Elizabethan manor. Though disliking what the incomers represent, the Ayreses decide to throw a welcoming party, as if to prove to themselves they still can. Gillian is 'eight or nine' (p. 86) and her arrival startles everybody, being utterly unforeseen. The child is, undeniably, brattish, boasting that her parents 'regularly allowed her to drink brandy after her supper, and [she] had once smoked half a cigarette'; the other guests turn to Dr Faraday to prompt his disapproval, which, when forthcoming, is quickly augmented by Caroline's: 'It's bad enough the little wretches getting their hands on all the oranges' (p. 92).

When I interviewed Waters in 2006 she observed,

> I love London precisely because I have come to it from a small town in Pembrokeshire – which was a great place to grow up in, but London seemed to me to be the place to go to perhaps slightly re-invent your-self, or to find communities of people – in my case, gay people – that you couldn't find at home.[8]

At first sight, therefore, her decision to return to a rural setting in this novel seemed strange, until I realised that the rural Warwickshire setting enabled her to document how the lesbian becomes erased ('sent to Coventry', if you will) by the enforcement of a set of post-war governmental policies. Considering that Waters was born in 1966, twenty years after the setting of *The Little Stranger,* how much more difficult would it have been for a lesbian like Caroline Ayres to avoid negating her presence *as* a lesbian in the countryside. Caroline it is who first expresses the word 'queer' in the novel: 'Hundreds is quiet, but there's nothing queer about it' (p. 15), an assertion we initially take as a defence of the house, until we gradually realise she longs to leave it. As noted above, this is a moment when Britain is becoming more family-oriented than ever before, with its health reforms, its family housing policies and its emphasis upon women being impelled into marriage and motherhood as a means of re-plenishing the casualties of war. Perhaps here we have an explanation of her apparent rejection of those 'little wretches [who get] their hands on all the oranges', for they are, of course, the fruits of heterosexual reproduction, whose increasing numbers push the spinster more and more to the margins.

This book began with a consideration of the haunted child and the media storm surrounding paedophilia and child abuse. Countering that anxiety is another, that claims childhood and the unguarded stares of children as 'uncanny'. This aspect of childhood is one Waters explores here. Additionally, of course, Hundreds returns us to Alton Towers and Strawberry Hill, houses of former modest grandeur which fall into disrepair and must either be demolished or transformed:

> Hundreds Hall is still unsold. No one has the money or the inclination to take it on. For a while there was talk of the county council making a teacher-training centre of it. Then a Birmingham businessman apparently considered it for an hotel. But the rumours surface, and come to nothing; and recently they've begun to surface less often . . . children have chalked on the walls and thrown stones at the windows, and the house seems to sit in the chaos like some wounded, blighted beast. (p. 497)

Untenanted, the same kind of reversal between living and dead occu-pants that we encountered in *The Others* arrives. As Faraday assumes possession, his presence is enough to scare off the uncanny:

If Hundreds Hall is haunted . . . its ghost doesn't show itself to me. For I'll turn, and am disappointed – realising that what I am looking at is only a cracked window-pane, and that the face gazing distortedly from it, baffled and longing, is my own. (p. 499)

Towards the end of the twentieth century Fred Botting concluded his book *Gothic* by suggesting that the Gothic might have run its course. Writing of Coppola's film *Bram Stoker's Dracula* (1992), Botting identifies in it the 'mourn[ing of] an object that is too diffuse and un-certain to be recuperated . . . [and finds itself u]nable to do anything but half-heartedly tap the last nail in an old coffin'.[9] The contemporary Gothic does explore a paradox: though we may long to be haunted (and our appetite for the Gothic suggests we do), we can no longer believe in ghosts. So we respond by transforming them into meta-phors (the 'apparitional lesbian'), theme parks (Alton Towers or Jackson's Neverland ranch) or theme pubs (The Eerie Pub Co.). Alternatively, we clothe ourselves in Goth(ic) fashions and consume Goth(ic) music – and its artists, it seems. Ghosts may have died in the twentieth century, but our fascination with them in the twenty-first lives on.

Notes

Introduction

1   Eve Kosofsky Sedgwick, *The Coherence of Gothic Conventions, Revised Edition* (New York: Arno Press, 1980), pp. 1–2.

2   Judy Simons, 'Julia Briggs remembered', *The English Association Newsletter*, 187, Spring (2008), 1–3.

3   So influential was Punter's book that it was later revised and republished in two volumes: David Punter, *The Literature of Terror, Vol. 1: The Gothic Tradition* (Harlow: Longman, 1996) and *The Literature of Terror, Vol. 2: A History of Gothic Fictions from 1765 to the Present Day* (Harlow: Longman, 1996).

4   Chris Baldick and Robert Mighall, 'Gothic criticism', in David Punter (ed.), *A Companion to the Gothic* (Oxford: Basil Blackwell, 2000), pp. 209–28 (p. 210).

5   Allan Lloyd-Smith, *American Gothic Fiction: An Introduction* (New York: Continuum, 2004), p. 133.

6   According to Derrida, 'It is necessary to speak *of the* ghost, indeed *to the* ghost and *with* it, from the moment that no ethics, no politics, whether revolutionary or not, seems possible and thinkable'. Jacques Derrida, *Specters of Marx*, trans. Peggy Kamuf (New York: Routledge, 1994), p. xix (original emphasis). For Pearce, the metaphor of the ghostly reader enables her to construct a self-reflexive critique of her own reading practice, past and present, and between competing readerly 'selves' (the professionally motivated academic reading versus the 'off-duty' reading, for instance). Lynne Pearce, *Feminism and the Politics of Reading* (London: Arnold, 1997), p. 24.

7   Alfred Longueil, 'The word "Gothic" in eighteenth-century criticism', *Modern Language Notes*, 38 (1923), 453–6 (453, 454n).

8   *http://www.guidetorichmond.co.uk/strawberry.html* accessed 27/10/2008.

9   Horace Walpole, *A Description of the Villa of Mr. Horace Walpole, Youngest Son of Sir Robert Walpole Earl of Orford, at Strawberry-Hill near Twickenham, Middlesex.* (Strawberry Hill: Thomas Kirgate, 1784), p. 2.

10 Dianne S. Ames, 'Strawberry Hill: architecture of the "as if"', *Studies in Eighteenth-Century Culture*, 8 (1979), 351–63.

11 Walpole, *Description of the Villa*, p. i.

12 Ames, 'Strawberry Hill', p. 354.

13 Jerrold E. Hogle, 'The Gothic ghost of the counterfeit', in David Punter (ed.), *A Companion to the Gothic* (Oxford: Basil Blackwell, 2000), pp. 293–304 (p. 296).

14 Michael J. Fisher, *Alton Towers: A Gothic Wonderland* (Stafford: M. J. Fisher, 2004), pp. 147, 9.

15 Hogle, 'Ghost of the counterfeit', pp. 296–7.

16 Fisher, *Alton Towers*, p. 166.

17 Ibid., p. 98.

18 *http://www.warwick-castle.co.uk/misc/about_merlin.asp* accessed 27/10/2008.

19 *http://www.warwick-castle.co.uk/plan_your_day/explore_the_castle.asp* accessed 27/10/2008.

20 Longueil, 'The word "Gothic"', p. 453.

21 Lloyd-Smith, *American Gothic Fiction*, p. 35.

22 Mark Edmundson, *Nightmare on Main Street: Angels, Sadomasochism and the Culture of Gothic* (Cambridge, MA.: Harvard University Press, 1997), p. xii.

23 Mary Daly, *Gyn/Ecology: The Metaethics of Radical Feminism* (London: The Women's Press, 1979), p. 4.

24 Franco Moretti, 'Dialectic of fear', in *Signs Taken for Wonders: Essays in the Sociology of Literary Forms* (London: Verso, 1983) pp. 83–108 (pp. 107–8; my emphasis).

25 Edmundson, *Nightmare on Main Street*, pp. 20–1.

26 Ibid., pp. 31–2.

1   Gothic Pathologies: Haunted Children

1   Henry James, 'The Turn of the Screw', in *The Turn of the Screw and Other Stories* (1898; Oxford: Oxford University Press, 1992), p. 188.

2   Berthold Schoene-Harwood, *Writing Men: Literary Masculinities from Frankenstein to the New Man* (Edinburgh University Press, 2000), pp. 35, 39.

3   Eric Haralson, *Henry James and Queer Modernity* (Cambridge: Cambridge University Press, 2003), pp. 89–90.

4   Michael Bakewell, *Lewis Carroll: A Biography* (London: Heinemann, 1996), pp. 28–9; cited in Haralson, *Henry James and Queer Modernity*, p. 82; see also p. 100.

5   Lucie Armitt, *Fantasy Fiction: An Introduction* (New York: Continuum, 2005), p. 183.

6   'Sarah's Law' mirrors what, in the USA, is termed 'Megan's Law', which, as the BBC News website observes, is 'named after Megan Kanka, seven, who was killed by a convicted sex offender, the US law gives parents access to names

and addresses of known paedophiles'. *http://news.bbc.co.uk/1/hi/uk/654079.stm* (accessed 19/11/2008).

7   Sigmund Freud, 'The Uncanny', in *The Penguin Freud Library, Vol. 14, Art and Literature*, ed. Albert Dickson (Harmondsworth: Penguin, 1990), pp. 335–76 (p. 345).

8   *http://news.bbc.co.uk/1/hi/uk/6540749.stm* (accessed 19/11/2008).

9   Freud, 'The Uncanny', p. 368.

10 Graham Joyce, *The Tooth Fairy* (New York: Tom Docherty Associates, 1996), p. 55.

11 Amelia Hill, '"Stranger danger" drive harms kids', 23 May, 2004. *http://www.guardian.co.uk/politics/2004/may/23/uk.children* (accessed 11/11/2008). Michael Morpurgo also observes that the distance we permit our children to roam is now 'one ninth' of what it was in the Middle Ages (*The Invention of Childhood*, Hugh Cunningham and Michael Morpurgo (BBC Radio 4, 2006; episode 2).

12 'Views of London: Characters'. *http://www.adnax.com/views/viewsoflondoncharacters02.htm* (accessed 11/11/2008).

13 Angela Carter, 'Notes from the front line', in Michelene Wandor (ed.), *On Gender and Writing* (London: Pandora, 1983), pp. 69–77 (p. 69).

14 For a fuller critique of Bettelheim and the limitations of his consolationist reading of fairy tales, see Lucie Armitt, *Theorising the Fantastic* (London: Arnold, 1996), pp. 42–53 (p. 46).

15 See the BBC British History website. *http://www.bbc.co.uk/history/british/britain_wwtwo/evacuees_01.shtml* (accessed 11/6/2009).

16 *Household Stories by the Brothers Grimm*, trans. Lucy Crane, with pictures by Walter Crane (1886; New York: Dover, 1963), p. 89.

17 A. S. Byatt, 'The Thing in the Forest', in *The Little Black Book of Stories* (2003; London: Vintage, 2004), pp. 15–17. Subsequent quotations are referenced in the text.

18 On 12 February 1993, two-year-old James Bulger was abducted from a shopping centre in Bootle and later beaten and killed by two ten-year-old boys, Robert Thompson and Jon Venables.

19 According to Freud, 'To some people the idea of being buried alive by mistake is the most uncanny thing of all. And yet psychoanalysis has taught us that this terrifying phantasy is only a transformation of another phantasy which had originally nothing terrifying about it at all, but was qualified by a certain lasciviousness – the phantasy, I mean, of intra-uterine existence.' 'Uncanny', pp. 366–7.

20 Mark Edmundson, *Nightmare on Main Street: Angels, Sadomasochism, and the Culture of Gothic* (Cambridge, MA.: Harvard University Press, 1997), p. 36.

21 Janice Haaken, *Pillar of Salt: Gender, Memory, and the Perils of Looking Back* (London: Free Association Books, 1998), p. 1.

22 Joyce, *The Tooth Fairy*, p. 9. Subsequent quotations are referenced in the text.

23 *Household Stories by the Brothers Grimm*, pp. 118–19.

24 Lewis Spence, *The Fairy Tradition in Britain* (London: Rider and Company, 1948), p. 130.

25 Edwin Sidney Hartland, *The Science of Fairy Tales: An Inquiry into Fairy Mythology* (London: Walter Scott, 1891), pp. 6, 59.

26 Ibid., p. 73.

27 Freud, 'Uncanny', p. 352; '*lex talionis*' translates as 'the law of revenge or retaliation', *Collins English Dictionary* (3rd edn,1991).

28 Tzvetan Todorov, *The Fantastic: A Structural Approach to a Literary Genre*, trans. Richard Howard (Ithaca: Cornell University Press, 1975), p. 25.

29 Anthony Vidler, *The Architectural Uncanny: Essays in the Modern Unhomely* (Cambridge MA.: MIT Press, 1992), p. 7.

30 Steve Szilagyi, *Photographing Fairies* (London: Hodder and Stoughton, 1995), p. 43. Subsequent quotations are referenced in the text.

31 J. Sconce, *Haunted Media: Electronic Presence from Telegraphy to Television* (Durham: Duke University Press, 2000), p. 4; cited in Jo Collins and John Jervis, 'Introduction', in Collins and Jervis (eds), *Uncanny Modernity: Cultural Theories, Modern Anxieties* (Basingstoke: Palgrave Macmillan, 2008), pp. 1–9 (p. 5).

32 Ibid.

33 Nicola Bown, *Fairies in Nineteenth-Century Art and Literature* (Cambridge: Cambridge University Press, 2001), pp. 39, 68–9.

34 James R. Kincaid, *Child-Loving: The Erotic Child and Victorian Culture* (New York: Routledge, 1992), p. 4.

35 Edgar Allan Poe, 'The Pit and the Pendulum', in *The Fall of the House of Usher and Other Writings* (Harmondsworth: Penguin, 1986), p. 266.

36 Ibid., pp. 261–2.

37 J. M. Barrie, 'Peter Pan', in *The Plays of J. M. Barrie in One Volume* (London: Hodder and Stoughton, 1942), pp. 487–576 (p. 574).

38 Susan Stewart, *On Longing: Narratives of the Miniature, the Gigantic, the Souvenir, the Collection* (Baltimore: Johns Hopkins University Press, 1984), p. 61.

39 M. R. James, 'The Haunted Dolls' House', in *Ghost Stories* (Harmondsworth: Penguin, 1994), pp. 266–75 (p. 266). Subsequent quotations are referenced in the text.

40 Kincaid, *Child-Loving*, p. 5.

2   *Building Suspense: Architectural Gothic*

1 Daphne du Maurier, *Rebecca* (London: Arrow Books, 1992), p. 5.

2 Ann Radcliffe, *The Mysteries of Udolpho* (1794; Oxford: Oxford University Press, 1980), pp. 226–7; Bram Stoker, *Dracula* (1897; Ontario: Broadview, 1998), p. 44; Angela Carter, *The Bloody Chamber* (Harmondsworth: Penguin, 1979), p. 13.

3 Mark Madoff, 'Inside, outside, and the Gothic locked-room mystery', in Kenneth W. Graham (ed.), *Gothic Fictions: Prohibition / Transgression* (New York: AMS Press, 1989), pp. 49–62 (p. 49).

4 Anthony Vidler, *The Architectural Uncanny: Essays in the Modern Unhomely* (Cambridge, MA.: MIT Press, 1999), p. 38.

5 Eve Kosofsky Sedgwick, *The Coherence of Gothic Conventions* (1976; New York: Arno Press, 1980), pp. 28–9.

6   Mark Edmundson, *Nightmare on Main Street: Angels, Sadomasochism and the Culture of Gothic* (Cambridge, MA.: Harvard University Press, 1997), pp. 115–16.

7   Allan Lloyd-Smith, *American Gothic Fiction: An Introduction* (New York: Continuum, 2004), pp. 114–15.

8   The phrase 'Haunted geometries' is taken from and inspired by the article I co-authored with Sarah Gamble, 'The haunted geometries of Sarah Waters's *Affinity*', *Textual Practice*, 20, 1 (2006), 141–59.

9   See Tzvetan Todorov, *The Fantastic: A Structural Approach*, trans. Richard Howard (Ithaca: Cornell University Press, 1975).

10   Madoff, 'Locked-room mystery', p. 51.

11   Rudyard Kipling, 'Swept and Garnished', in *War Stories and Poems*, ed. Andrew Rutherford (Oxford: Oxford University Press, 1999), pp. 226–34 (p. 226). Subsequent quotations are referenced in the text.

12   Virginia Woolf, 'The Mark on the Wall', in *The Norton Anthology of English Literature, Sixth Edition, Vol. 2* (New York: W.W. Norton, 1993), pp. 1916–21 (pp. 1917, 1921).

13   Matthew 12: 43–5.

14   Umberto Eco, *The Name of the Rose*, trans. William Weaver (London: Vintage, 1998), p. 5. Subsequent quotations are referenced in the text.

15   Daniel 5: 26–8.

16   For a fuller discussion of this see Lucie Armitt, *Fantasy Fiction: An Introduction* (New York: Continuum, 2005), pp. 31–2.

17   Henry James, 'The Turn of the Screw', in *The Turn of the Screw and Other Stories* (1898; Oxford: Oxford University Press, 1992), p. 117; Jane Austen, *Northanger Abbey* (1818; Harmondsworth: Penguin, 1985): 'She now saw plainly that she must not expect a manuscript of equal length with the generality of what she had shuddered over in books, for the roll, seeming to consist entirely of small disjointed sheets, was altogether but of trifling size, and much less than she had supposed it to be at first' (p. 177).

18   Clive Barker, *The Hellbound Heart* (New York: HarperCollins, 1986), p. 21. Subsequent quotations are referenced in the text.

19   'In Xanadu did Kubla Khan / A stately pleasure dome decree: / Where Alph, the sacred river, ran / Through caverns measureless to man'.

20   Iain Banks, *The Wasp Factory* (London: Abacus, 1990), p. 44. Subsequent quotations are referenced in the text.

21   Peter Brooker, *New York Fictions: Modernity, Postmodernism, the New Modern* (London: Longman, 1996), pp. 3, 5.

22   Elizabeth Bowen, 'The Demon Lover', in *The Collected Stories of Elizabeth Bowen* (London: Vintage, 1999), pp. 661–6 (p. 662). Subsequent quotations are referenced in the text.

23   Charlotte Perkins Gilman, *The Yellow Wallpaper* (London: Virago, 1981), p. 9.

24   Eve Kosofky Sedgwick, *Between Men: English Literature and Male Homosocial Desire* (New York: Columbia University Press, 1985), p. 21.

25   Sarah Waters, *The Night Watch* (London: Virago, 2006), p. 7. Subsequent quotations are referenced in the text.

26 Elaine Showalter, *Hystories: Hysterical Epidemics and Modern Culture* (London: Picador, 1988), pp. 64, 49–50. Showalter's citation of Ward is from Lisa Tickner, *The Spectacle of Women* (Chicago: University of Chicago Press, 1988), p. 188.

27 Showalter, *Hystories*, pp. 14, 11.

28 Lloyd-Smith, *American Gothic Fiction*, pp. 26–7, 34.

29 *Halliwell's Film, Video and DVD Guide, 2005* (London: HarperCollins, 2004), p. 965.

30 Vidler, *Architectural Uncanny*, p. 63.

31 Steve Szilagyi, *Photographing Fairies* (London: Sceptre, 1995), p. 213.

32 Lynda Nead, *Victorian Babylon: People, Streets and Images in Nineteenth-Century London* (New Haven: Yale University Press, 2000), p. 9.

33 Lisa Hopkins, *Screening the Gothic* (Austin: University of Texas Press, 2005), p. 151.

34 '. . . it is easy to see that . . . it is only this factor of involuntary repetition which surrounds what would otherwise be innocent enough with an uncanny atmosphere, and forces upon us the idea of something fateful and inescapable when otherwise we should have spoken only of "chance".' Sigmund Freud, 'The Uncanny', in *The Penguin Freud Library, Vol. 14, Art and Literature*, ed. Albert Dickson (Harmondsworth: Penguin, 1990), pp. 335–76 (pp. 359–60); Henri Lefebvre, *The Production of Space*, trans. Donald Nicholson-Smith (Oxford: Basil Blackwell, 1991), p. 229.

3   Gothic Inhumanity

1 Jean-François Lyotard, *The Inhuman* (Cambridge: Polity, 1993), pp. 8–9.

2 Ibid., p. 184.

3 Howard Caygill, 'Surviving the inhuman', in Scott Brewster et al. (eds), *Inhuman Reflections: Thinking the Limits of the Human* (Manchester: Manchester University Press, 2000), pp. 217–29 (p. 217).

4 David Punter, 'Terrorism and the uncanny, or, the caves of Tora Bora' in Jo Collins and John Jervis (eds), *Uncanny Modernity: Cultural Theories, Modern Anxieties* (Basingstoke: Palgrave Macmillan, 2008), pp. 201–15 (pp. 202, 204).

5 E. M. Forster, *A Passage to India* (Harmondsworth: Penguin, 1979), p. 165.

6 Ibid., pp. 163–4.

7 Lyotard, *Inhuman*, p. 183.

8 Punter, 'Terrorism and the uncanny', pp. 205–6. Here, Punter is citing Hillman's *The Dream and the Underworld* (New York and London: Harper & Row, 1979), pp. 35–45.

9 Sir Arthur Conan Doyle, *The Hound of the Baskervilles* (Oxford: Oxford University Press, 1998), pp. 146, 38. Subsequent quotations are referenced in the text.

10 Edgar Allan Poe, 'The Fall of the House of Usher', in *The Fall of the House of Usher and Other Writings* (Harmondsworth: Penguin, 1986), pp. 138–57 (pp. 139, 138, 141–2).

11 Elisabeth Bronfen, *Over Her Dead Body: Death, Femininity and the Aesthetic* (Manchester: Manchester University Press, 1992), p. 294.

12 Ibid., p. 293.

13 Mary Shelley, *Frankenstein, Or, The Modern Prometheus* (1818; Harmondsworth: Penguin, 1985), p. 265.

14 Leonora Carrington, 'The Débutante', in Angela Carter (ed.), *Wayward Girls and Wicked Women* (London: Virago, 1986); pp. 22–4 (p. 23). Subsequent quotations are referenced in the text.

15 Leonora Carrington, 'As They Rode Along the Edge', in *The Seventh Horse and Other Tales* (London: Virago, 1989), p. 3. Subsequent quotations from this story, 'The Skeleton's Holiday' and 'The Sisters' are referenced in the text.

16 For a fuller discussion see Lucie Armitt, 'The fragile frames of The Bloody Chamber', in Joseph Bristow and Trev Broughton, *The Infernal Desires of Angela Carter: Fiction, Femininity, Feminism* (London: Longman 1997), pp. 88–99.

17 Umberto Eco, *The Name of the Rose*, trans. William Weaver (London: Vintage, 1998), p. 70.

18 Ibid., p. 104.

19 Angela Carter, 'The Lady of the House of Love', in *The Bloody Chamber* (Harmondsworth: Penguin, 1979), p. 104. Subsequent quotations are referenced in the text.

20 Clive Barker, *The Hellbound Heart* (New York: HarperCollins, 1986), p. 33. Subsequent quotations are referenced in the text.

21 J. K. Rowling, *Harry Potter and the Goblet of Fire* (London: Bloomsbury, 2000), pp. 555–6.

22 Ibid., p. 556.

23 Fred Botting, *Limits of Horror: Technology, Bodies, Gothic* (Manchester: Manchester University Press, 2008), p. 29.

24 'Documentary: All About *The Birds* – Making of', Alfred J. Hitchcock Productions, Inc., 1999.

25 Ibid.

26 Daphne Du Maurier, 'The Birds', in *The Birds and Other Stories* (London: Virago, 2004), p. 8. Subsequent quotations are referenced in the text.

27 Carol J. Clover, *Men, Women and Chainsaws: Gender in the Modern Horror Film* (London: BFI Publishing, 1992), p. 124.

28 Alfred Hitchcock, '*The Birds*, Final Draft'; 26 January, 1962 (London: Hollywood Scripts, Enterprise House, Cathles Road SW12), pp. 16–17, 18, 1.

29 Ibid., p. 63.

30 Sigmund Freud, 'The Uncanny', in *The Penguin Freud Library, Vol. 14, Art and Literature*, ed. Albert Dickson (Harmondsworth: Penguin, 1990), pp. 335–76 (p. 352).

31 According to Tippi Hedren, 'The ones that were taught individually basically could never be released, because they were taught to do *very bad things* ... like they'd be taught to dive bomb somebody or peck them, or really go after people.' 'Documentary ... *The Birds*'.

32 Ibid.

33 E. T. A. Hoffmann, 'The Sandman', *Tales of Hoffmann* trans. R. J. Hollingdale (Harmondsworth: Penguin, 1982), pp. 85–125 (p. 87).

34 Freud, 'Uncanny', p. 352.

[35] *Jekyll* (screenplay Steve Moffat, directors Douglas Mackinnon and Matt Lipsey, Hartswood Films in association with the BBC, 2007).

[36] For a fuller discussion of D.W.Winnicott's ideas and their application to Stevenson's *The Strange Case*, see Lucie Armitt, *Theorising the Fantastic* (London: Arnold, 1996), pp. 130–3 (p. 132).

4 Queering the Gothic

[1] Gordon Hirsch, '*Frankenstein*, detective fiction and *Jekyll and Hyde*', in William Veeder and Gordon Hirsch (eds), *Dr Jekyll and Mr Hyde After One Hundred Years* (Chicago: University of Chicago Press, 1988), pp. 223–41 (p. 241).

[2] *Jekyll* (screenplay Steve Moffat, directors Douglas Mackinnon and Matt Lipsey, Hartswood Films in association with the BBC, 2007).

[3] Robert Louis Stevenson, *The Strange Case of Dr Jekyll and Mr Hyde* (1886: Harmondsworth: Penguin, 1979), p. 69.

[4] Ibid., p. 70. For a fuller discussion of Stevenson's text and its homoerotic elements see Lucie Armitt, *Theorising the Fantastic* (London: Arnold, 1996), pp. 119–33 (p. 123).

[5] Stevenson, *Jekyll and Hyde*, pp. 40, 81; my emphasis.

[6] For a fuller discussion see Scott Brewster, 'Seeing things: Gothic and the madness of interpretation', in David Punter (ed.), *A Companion to the Gothic* (Oxford: Basil Blackwell, 2000), pp. 281–92.

[7] Eric Haralson, *Henry James and Queer Modernity* (Cambridge: Cambridge University Press, 2003), p. 1.

[8] Ibid., p. 7; citing Alfred Habegger, '"What Maisie Knew": Henry James's *Bildungsroman* of the artist as queer moralist', in Gert Buelens (ed.), *Enacting History in Henry James: Narrative, Power and Ethics* (Cambridge: Cambridge University Press, 1997), pp. 93–4.

[9] Haralson, *Henry James and Queer Modernity*, pp. 7–8. The comment on Wilde is from Hugh Stevens, *Henry James and Sexuality* (Cambridge: Cambridge University Press, 1998), p. 12.

[10] Stevenson, *Jekyll and Hyde*, pp. 29, 33.

[11] Daphne Du Maurier, 'The Birds', in *The Birds and Other Stories* (London: Virago, 2004), pp. 10, 27.

[12] Henry James, 'Preface' to *The Altar of the Dead and Other Tales*, cited in Edward Stone (ed.), *Henry James: Seven Stories and Studies* (New York: Appleton-Century-Crofts, Inc., 1961), p. 292.

[13] Henry James, 'The Jolly Corner', in Stone (ed.), *Henry James*, pp. 260–92 (pp. 260, 264, 284). Subsequent quotations are referenced in the text.

[14] Elizabeth Bowen, 'The Demon Lover', in *The Collected Stories of Elizabeth Bowen* (London: Vintage, 1999), pp. 661–6 (p. 665).

[15] Armitt, *Theorising the Fantastic*, pp. 146–7.

[16] Stevenson, *Jekyll and Hyde*, p. 94.

17 Allan Lloyd Smith, *American Gothic Fiction: An Introduction* (NewYork: Continuum, 2004), p. 106.

18 SarahWaters, *The Little Stranger* (London:Virago, 2009), pp. 9, 448.

19 Terry Castle, *The Apparitional Lesbian: Female Homosexuality and Modern Culture* (NewYork: Columbia University Press, 1993), p. 2.

20 Sarah Waters, *Tipping the Velvet* (London:Virago, 1999), pp. 416–17. Subsequent quotations are referenced in the text; Castle, *Apparitional Lesbian*, p. 2.

21 Ibid., p. 5.

22 SarahWaters, *Affinity* (London:Virago, 2000), pp. 336–340 *passim*; original italics.

23 Lucie Armitt, 'Interview with SarahWaters (CWWN conference, University of Wales, Bangor, 22nd April, 2006)', *Feminist Review*, 85 (2007), 116–27 (120).

24 Peter Brooker, *NewYork Fictions: Modernity, Postmodernism, the New Modern* (London: Longman, 1996), p. 3.

25 Sarah Waters, *The Night Watch* (London: Virago, 2006), p. 123. Subsequent quotations are from this edition and referenced in the text.

26 SarahWaters, *Fingersmith* (London:Virago, 2003), p. 32. Subsequent quotations are from this edition and referenced within the main text.

27 Kate Ferguson Ellis, *The Contested Castle: Gothic Novels and the Subversion of Domestic Ideology* (Urbana: University of Illinois Press, 1989), p. 3.

28 Charles Dickens, *Great Expectations* (Harmondsworth: Penguin, 1965), p. 87.

29 Waters, *Little Stranger*, p. 67.

30 Thomas Hardy, *Tess of the D'Urbervilles* (London: Macmillan, 1974), p. 433.

31 Mark Edmundson, *Nightmare on Main Street: Angels, Sadomasochism, and the Culture of Gothic* (Cambridge, MA.: Harvard University Press, 1997), p. 28.

32 Nina Auerbach, *Our Vampires, Ourselves* (Chicago: University of Chicago Press, 1995), p. 175.

33 Patrick McGrath, *The Grotesque* (Harmondsworth: Penguin, 1989), pp. 42, 186, 138–9.

34 Patrick McGrath, *Spider* (Harmondsworth: Penguin, 1992), p. 68. Elsewhere I have read *Spider* as a fictional exploration of the theories of cryptonomy, or transgenerational haunting. See Lucie Armitt, 'The magical realism of the contemporary Gothic', in Punter (ed.), *Companion to the Gothic*, pp. 305–16.

35 Patrick McGrath, *Doctor Haggard's Disease* (Harmondsworth: Penguin, 1994), p. 155. Subsequent quotations are referenced in the text.

36 Patrick McGrath, 'The Angel', in *Blood and Water* (Harmondsworth: Penguin, 1989), pp. 1–16 (p. 1). Subsequent quotations are referenced in the text.

37 OscarWilde, *The Picture of Dorian Gray* (Oxford: Oxford University Press, 1981), p. 15.

38 *http://www.nyc.gov/html/doh/html/ah/ah.shtml* accessed 28/5/09.

39 Jonathan Dollimore, *Death, Desire and Loss in Western Culture* (London: Allen Lane, 1998), pp. xi–xii.

40 Elisabeth Bronfen, *Over Her Dead Body: Death, Femininity and the Aesthetic* (Manchester: Manchester University Press, 1992), p. 294.

41 Castle, *Apparitional Lesbian*, p. 6.

5 Survey of Criticism

[1] Alfred Longueil, 'The word "Gothic" in eighteenth-century criticism', *Modern Language Notes*, 38 (1923), 453–6 (p. 453).
[2] Ibid., pp. 453–4.
[3] Catherine Spooner, *Contemporary Gothic* (London: Reaktion Books, 2006), p. 31.
[4] Ibid., p. 17 and p. 89.
[5] Longueil, 'Gothic', pp. 455–8 *passim*.
[6] Sigmund Freud, 'The Uncanny' in *The Penguin Freud Library, Vol. 14, Art and Literature*, ed. Albert Dickson (Harmondsworth: Penguin, 1990), pp. 335–76 (pp. 341–7, 359–60).
[7] Longueil, 'Gothic', pp. 460, 458.
[8] Nicholas Abraham, 'Notes on the phantom: a complement to Freud's meta-psychology', trans. Nicholas Rand, *Critical Inquiry*, 13, 2 (1987), 287–92 (p. 287).
[9] Ibid., pp. 288–90.
[10] 'Interview with Terry Castle', *Paradoxa: Studies in World Literary Genres*, 3, 3–4 (1997), 521–6 (p. 521).
[11] *Guardian*, 1 January 2000, p. 19; cited in Nicholas Royle, *The Uncanny* (Manchester: Manchester University Press, 2003), p. 3.
[12] Ibid., p. 23.
[13] Ibid., pp. 61–2, 107; original line formation.
[14] Freud, 'Uncanny', pp. 370–1; original italics; Royle, *Uncanny*, pp. 179–80.
[15] Ibid., p. 180.
[16] Ibid., p. 24, 67.
[17] Fred Botting, *Limits of Horror: Technology, Bodies, Gothic* (Manchester: Manchester University Press, 2008), pp. 47, 49.
[18] Ibid., p. 3.
[19] Jerrold E. Hogle, 'The Gothic ghost of the counterfeit and the progress of abjection', in David Punter (ed.), *A Companion to the Gothic* (Oxford: Basil Blackwell, 2000), pp. 293–304 (p. 295).
[20] Ibid.
[21] Ken Gelder, *Reading the Vampire* (London: Routledge, 1994), p. 5.
[22] Ibid., p. 87.
[23] Ibid., p.p 98, 87–8.
[24] Nina Auerbach, *Our Vampires, Ourselves* (Chicago: University of Chicago Press,1995), p. 3.
[25] Ibid., p. 126.
[26] Ibid., pp. 175,184.
[27] Julia Kristeva, *Powers of Horror: An Essay on Abjection* (New York: Columbia University Press, 1982), p. 7.
[28] Barbara Creed, *The Monstrous Feminine: Film, Feminism, Psychoanalysis* (London: Routledge, 1993), p. 1.
[29] Ibid., pp. 122, 105–7.
[30] Carol J. Clover, *Men, Women and Chainsaws: Gender in the Modern Horror Film* (London: BFI Press, 1992), p. 7.

31 Spooner, *Contemporary Gothic,* p. 96.
32 Clover, *Men, Women and Chainsaws,* p. 6.
33 Ibid., p. 19.
34 Ibid., p. 43.
35 Ibid., pp. 10, 30–31.
36 William Paul, *Laughing Screaming: Modern Hollywood Horror and Comedy* (New York: Columbia University Press, 1994), p. 67.
37 *Collins English Dictionary, Third Edition,* 1991.

6 *Conclusion:* Thriller *and* Stranger

1 Paul Theroux, 'My trip to Neverland . . . and the 4am call from Michael Jackson I'll never forget', *Sunday Telegraph,* 28 June 2009, 15–16 (p. 15).
2 Sean O'Hagan, 'Tragedy of the pop genius who never grew up', *The Observer Review,* 28 June 2009, 2–3 (p. 2).
3 Andrew Gumbel, 'Jackson used drugs to regain his lost crown', *Observer,* 28 June 2009, 4–5.
4 Sarah Waters, *The Little Stranger* (London: Virago, 2009), p. 36. Subsequent quotations are referenced in the main text.
5 Compare the opening description of Manderley in Daphne Du Maurier, *Rebecca* (1938; London: Arrow Books, 1992), p. 5. 'The drive wound away in front of me, twisting and turning as it had always done, but as I advanced I was aware that a change had come upon it . . . Nature had come into her own again and, little by little, in her stealthy, insidious way had encroached upon the drive with long, tenacious fingers.'
6 Kenneth W. Graham, 'Preface', in Kenneth W. Graham (ed.), *Gothic Fictions: Prohibition / Transgression* (New York: AMS Press, 1989), p. xiii.
7 Waters's title for the novel seems to have been taken from Simone de Beauvoir's *The Second Sex* (1949), in which she observes of the new mother and her baby: 'It is strangely miraculous to see and hold a living being formed within oneself . . . [and yet] she does not even recognize him because she does not know him. She has experienced her pregnancy without him: she has no past in common with this *little stranger.*' (Simone de Beauvoir, *The Second Sex,* trans. H. M. Parshley (London: Picador, 1988), pp. 522–3; italics mine).
8 Lucie Armitt, 'Interview with Sarah Waters (CWWN Conference, University of Wales, Bangor, 22nd April, 2006)', *Feminist Review,* 85 (2007), 117–27 (p. 119).
9 Fred Botting, *Gothic* (London: Routledge, 1996), p. 180.

Annotated Bibliography

Auerbach, Nina, *Our Vampires, Ourselves* (Chicago: University of Chicago Press, 1995).
Auerbach takes the figure of the vampire from Polidori's *The Vampyre* (1819) through to Brian Aldiss's *Dracula Unbound* (1991). Though some British work is considered, including Hammer Horror films of the 1960s and 1970s, the presiding sociocultural frame for this book is American party politics and gender theory.

Botting, Fred, *Gothic* (London: Routledge, 1996).
A student-centred book providing a clear and helpful introduction to the Gothic and the sublime. Botting spans the history of Gothic from Walpole's *The Castle of Otranto* through to twentieth-century Gothic, to which is dedicated his final chapter. Here the author considers 'post-punk' music, modern fiction and film. It is in this book that Botting first starts to lay down his interest in hybrid forms, such as the relationships between science fiction and the Gothic, and postmodernism and the Gothic.

Botting, Fred, *Limits of Horror: Technology, Bodies, Gothic* (Manchester: Manchester University Press, 2008).
Botting's work is always exciting, and this is a characteristically playful and creative monograph taking us from family narratives (in the chapter 'Daddy's Dead') to the surgical aesthetics of the avant-garde artist Orlan. This theoretically sophisticated study takes in Žižek, Freud, Merleau-Ponty, Marx, Derrida and beyond, but is as stimulating as it is challenging.

Brabon, Benjamin and Stéphanie Genz (eds), *Postfeminist Gothic: Critical Interventions in Contemporary Culture* (Basingstoke: Macmillan, 2007).
This essay collection takes a sustained gendered approach to both the Gothic and the contemporary and contains work on film, television and fiction, including *The Stepford Wives, Candyman, Star Trek* and *Buffy the Vampire Slayer* as well as the fiction of Nalo Hopkinson.

Brewster, Scott, John J. Joughin, David Owen and Richard J. Walker (eds), *Inhuman Reflections: Thinking the Limits of the Human* (Manchester: Manchester University Press, 2000).
This essay collection incorporates literary criticism, creative writing and film theory, though philosophy is perhaps most heavily represented here. As the volume interrogates (in)humanity, some essays are more conventionally 'Gothic' than others, but haunting and the ghostly feature centrally. Howard Caygill's 'Surviving the inhuman', discussed in detail in chapter 3 of this book, is published in this collection.

Briggs, Julia, *Night Visitors: The Rise and Fall of the English Ghost Story* (London: Faber, 1977).
A remarkably prescient study which, just prior to the wholesale explosion of interest in the Gothic, anticipates many of the key arguments that were to follow. Especially strong in this study are the analysis of the relationship between science and the supernatural as well as the sections on folklore in Scotland and on Indian mysticism.

Byron, Glennis and David Punter (eds), *Spectral Readings: Towards a Gothic Geography* (Basingstoke: Palgrave, 1999).
An important collection of essays looking primarily at nineteenth- and twentieth-century literature and culture. As well as incorporating work by Punter, Botting and Hogle, the collection includes two interesting essays on the Gothic city, by Alexandra Warwick and David Seed respectively, and a section of essays devoted to American Gothic. Readers of this book will also find of interest the essay by Eric Savoy on Henry James's 'The Jolly Corner', Avril Horner and Sue Zlosnik on Daphne Du Maurier's 'Don't Look Now' and Christine Ferguson on Patrick McGrath.

Castle, Terry, *The Apparitional Lesbian: Female Homosexuality and Modern Culture* (New York: Columbia University Press, 1993).
This highly influential study covers personal reminiscence, literary and

film criticism, an evaluation of the opera diva and historical analysis. The primary literary material stretches from Daniel Defoe's *The Apparition of Mrs. Veal* (1706) through to Henry James's *The Bostonians* (1886) and Sylvia Townsend Warner's *Summer Will Show* (1936).

Clover, Carol J., *Men, Women and Chainsaws: Gender in the Modern Horror Film* (London: British Film Institute Publishing, 1992). An important study informed by feminist theory and taking as its starting point the 1976 blockbuster movie, *Carrie*, but identifying as the antecedent of modern horror Hitchcock's *Psycho*. Clover goes on to discuss a series of 'canonical' horror movies such as *The Texas Chainsaw Massacre* (hence the title of the book), the *Halloween* movies, *Poltergeist*, *The Exorcist* and others. Her theory of 'the gaze' argues for a more complicated analysis of the relationship between male spectator and male predator, claiming that a cross-gendering of identification occurs, based around the Girl 'victim-hero', a character who flees from, but ultimately destroys, her assailant.

Collins, Jo and John Jervis (eds), *Uncanny Modernity: Cultural Theories, Modern Anxietie*s (Basingstoke: Palgrave Macmillan, 2008). A distinguished collection of essays on literature, film, television, medical, psychoanalytic and political discourses and including work by some highly significant names in the field. David Punter's 'Terrorism and the uncanny, or, the caves of Tora Bora', discussed in more detail in chapter 3, is published in this collection.

Creed, Barbara, *The Monstrous Feminine: Film, Feminism, Psychoanalysis* (London: Routledge, 1993). A highly influential post-Freudian psychoanalytic study of the female monster in horror cinema, framed theoretically by Julia Kristeva's *Powers of Horror* (1982). Though a wide range of films are discussed, particularly detailed readings are offered of *Alien, The Exorcist, The Brood, The Hunger, Carrie, I Spit on Your Grave* and *Psycho*.

Edmundson, Mark, *Nightmare on Main Street: Angels, Sadomasochism and the Culture of Gothic* (Cambridge, MA.: Harvard University Press, 1997). A short but accomplished monograph opening with a discussion of horror in relation to the O. J. Simpson case, American presidencies from Nixon to Bush Senr., and media culture more generally. It is the continuing emphasis on reading society through literature and film (rather than the other way around) that gives this book its sense of 'freshness'. See, especially, Edmundson's extended reading of *Forrest Gump* (dir. Zemeckis, 1994) as inverted Gothic.

Freud, Sigmund, 'The Uncanny', in *The Freud Penguin Library, Vol. 14, Art and Literature*, ed. Albert Dickson (Harmondsworth: Penguin, 1990).
This is the key source for any twentieth-century understanding of the Gothic. Freud's essay traces out the etymological root of the word '*unheimlich*'/ '*uncanny*' in relation to its antonym, '*heimlich*' (homely) before examining its manifestations in relation to automata (including a sustained reading of E. T. A. Hoffmann's 'The Sandman'), the double (drawing on the work of Otto Rank), the compulsion to repeat, the omnipotence of thoughts, the evil eye and what Freud describes as 'the distinction between imagination and reality [becoming] effaced, as when something that we have hitherto regarded as imaginary appears before us in reality' (p. 367).

Gelder, Ken, *Reading the Vampire* (London: Routledge, 1994).
An influential study of the vampire, from nineteenth-century political rhetoric through to contemporary fiction. *Dracula* is the pivotal text here, though a range of contemporary writers are discussed, Stephen King and Anne Rice being given particular attention. The book also contains a compelling chapter on vampire cinema (discussed in more detail in chapter 5).

Grixti, Joseph, *Terrors of Uncertainty: The Cultural Contexts of Horror Fiction* (London: Routledge, 1989).
A monograph focusing especially on the writings of James Herbert and Stephen King, but also looking at iconic figures such as Dracula and Jekyll and Hyde in relation to horror film and 'the beast within'. One section focuses upon the cultural impact of conservative voices, such as Margaret Thatcher, Mary Whitehouse and the *Daily Mail* newspaper, in relation to the broadcasting of horror content during the 1980s in Britain.

Halberstam, Judith, *Skin Shows: Gothic Horror and the Technology of Monsters* (Durham: Duke University Press, 1995).
This accomplished study of monster narratives incorporates work on key nineteenth-century texts, such as *Frankenstein*, *The Strange Case of Dr Jekyll and Mr Hyde*, *Dracula* and *The Picture of Dorian Gray*, but is framed primarily by a discussion of *The Silence of the Lambs* (dir. Jonathan Demme, 1991). Halberstam's reading of this film is especially compelling ('Murder is no

romance in *The Silence of the Lambs*, it is a lesson in home economics – eating and sewing' (p. 173)), but the whole book is authoritatively argued and particularly good on intertextuality. Other important films discussed in detail include *The Birds* and *The Texas Chainsaw Massacre*.

Hock-Soon Ng, Andrew *Dimensions of Monstrosity in Contemporary Narratives: Theory, Psychoanalysis, Postmodernism* (London: Palgrave Macmillan, 2004).
This book is particularly interesting in the emphasis it places upon the urban environment as a space of monstrosity, especially in relation to J. G. Ballard's novel *High-Rise* (1975) and, more generally, the serial killer. At times Hock-Soon Ng's use of psychoanalytic theory is densely theoretical, but many of his readings are clear and freshly articulated. Also of interest to readers of this book is his analysis of Iain Banks's *The Wasp Factory*.

Hopkins, Lisa, *Screening the Gothic* (Austin: University of Texas Press, 2005).
This monograph examines cinematic adaptations of a range of canonical literary texts, including *Hamlet, Clarissa, Sense and Sensibility* and *Jane Eyre*. Some of these are obvious candidates for the Gothic, such as *Mary Shelley's Frankenstein* and various adaptations of *Dracula*, others less so, such as *Clarissa*. Perhaps it is the final two chapters of the book that will hold most interest for readers of the twentieth-century Gothic. Here Hopkins offers Gothic-centred readings of *The Mummy, Harry Potter and the Philosopher's Stone* and *Lord of the Rings*, and also incorporates work on the *Indiana Jones* series.

Horner, Avril and Sue Zlosnik, *Gothic and the Comic Turn* (Basingstoke: Macmillan, 2005).
A scholarly but sedate survey of the humorous in Gothic literature, this book takes us from Austen's *Northanger Abbey* (1818) to the *Spitting Image* puppets of the 1980s, and is at its best when discussing *Nightwood* and *Trilby* in chapter 4.

Paul, William, *Laughing Screaming: Modern Hollywood Horror and Comedy* (New York: Columbia University Press, 1994).
A wide-ranging study of the relationship between fear and humour in the horror film, this book stresses the communal nature of the cinema experience and its innate 'youthfulness'. Audience reception is an important aspect of it.

Powell, Anna and Andrew Smith (eds), *Teaching the Gothic* (Basingstoke: Palgrave Macmillan, 2006).
This volume of essays prioritises the pedagogy of the Gothic rather than simply its content. From 'Romantic Gothic' to 'Postgraduate developments', this is a collection which reflects on teaching and course development as well as on how students read the Gothic.

Prawer, S. S., *Caligari's Children: The Film as Tale of Terror* (New York: Oxford University Press, 1980).
One of the first and still a highly respected book on Gothic film. This book focuses, in particular, on early classic Gothic cinema such as Mamoulian's *Jekyll and Hyde* (1932) and, as the title suggests, Wiene's *The Cabinet of Dr Caligari* (1920), though it also surveys a vast range of films of more recent vintage. This is a connoisseur's book: a highly impressive and utterly scholarly study.

Punter, David, *The Literature of Terror*, 2 vols (Harlow: Longman, 1996).
Initially published in a single volume in 1980, such was its impact that Punter revised and republished it in two volumes in 1996. The books span the history of Gothic literature from the late eighteenth century to the late twentieth century, but new in the revised edition is greater attention to the work of late twentieth-century women writers, such as Angela Carter and Emma Tennant, and to male writers of horror, such as Bret Easton Ellis and Iain Banks, and William Gibson's work on cyberpunk.

Punter, David, *Gothic Pathologies: The Text, the Body and the Law* (Basingstoke: Palgrave Macmillan, 1998).
A theoretically sophisticated study which looks at the relationship between the Gothic, the law and sociocultural forms. Spanning the history of narrative from Richardson and Defoe through to postmodern writers such as William Gibson and Don DeLillo, Punter's overall framework is psychoanalysis, but always rooted in a social consciousness.

Punter, David (ed.), *A Companion to the Gothic* (Oxford: Basil Blackwell, 2000).
A definitive essay collection bringing together work by a number of the key critics in the field, including Fred Botting, Victor Sage, Allan Lloyd-Smith, Julia Briggs, Jerrold E. Hogle and, of course, Punter himself. The scope of the book takes us from the origins of the Gothic to what Punter calls 'The continuing debate' and it is in this final section that one finds Hogle's essay

on 'The Gothic ghost of the counterfeit . . .' (discussed in more detail in chapter 5).

Royle, Nicholas, *The Uncanny* (Manchester: Manchester University Press, 2003).
This playful monograph makes for compelling, if occasionally quizzical, reading. Wide-ranging in focus and philosophical scope, Royle takes us on an eclectic intellectual journey, commencing with the more traditional end of the Gothic spectrum in his reading of 'The Sandman', through to debates around national university research and teaching agendas, or questions set by a more 'personalist' theoretical agenda, such as the doppelganger effect of his relationship with his writerly double, the 'other' Nicholas Royle.

Sage, Victor and Allan Lloyd Smith (eds), *Modern Gothic: A Reader* (Manchester: Manchester University Press, 1996).
Though this is a collection of essays looking at twentieth-century film and fiction, a number of these return to the traditional Romantic period to contextualise their contemporary critiques. Of especial interest in this very good essay collection are Laura Mulvey's reading of *Blue Velvet*, David Punter's essay on Stephen King and Victor Sage's essay on Iain Banks and John Banville.

Sedgwick, Eve Kosofsky, *The Coherence of Gothic Conventions* (London, 1986).
An important and influential study containing an especially informative reading of Thomas de Quincey and the work of the eighteenth-century Venetian artist, Giovanni Battista Piranesi (as discussed in chapter 2 of this book). Live burial is a concept rooted at the heart of Kosofsky Sedgwick's monograph, a concept she explores in a number of contexts, literal and metaphorical.

Smith, Andrew, *Gothic Literature* (Edinburgh: Edinburgh University Press, 2007).
A 'student-facing' book tracing the history of Gothic literature from what Smith calls its 'Heyday, 1760–1820' to *The Silence of the Lambs* (1988). Emphasis is placed, throughout, on clear and detailed explications of texts and associated theoretical and critical arguments. A pedagogic section at the end is aimed directly at the student, offering a list of resources and a sample student essay (with commentary).

Smith, Andrew and Jeff Wallace (eds), *Gothic Modernisms* (Basingstoke: Palgrave Macmillan, 2001).
An imaginative collection of essays focusing on literary modernism and the Gothic elements that arise within texts more commonly associated with the literary mainstream. This results in an unusual selection of primary material for a volume on the Gothic, including Virginia Woolf's *Mrs Dalloway* and *To the Lighthouse*, James Joyce's *Dubliners* and D. H. Lawrence's *Sons and Lovers*.

Spooner, Catherine, *Contemporary Gothic* (London: Reaktion Books, 2006).
A wide-ranging book looking at the prominence of the Gothic in popular culture (including film and fiction), visual art and fashion. Highlights include her discussions of the Eerie Pub Co. and Gunther von Hagen's 'Body Worlds' exhibition (2002).

Twitchell, James B., *Dreadful Pleasures: An Anatomy of Modern Horror* (Oxford: Oxford University Press, 1985).
A scholarly monograph tracing the history of horror from cave paintings through to late twentieth-century film and taking in psychological and mythological influences on modern horror. Particularly influential is Twitchell's painstaking analysis of the many cinematic remakes of classic narratives such as *Dracula, Jekyll and Hyde* and *Frankenstein*, to which he dedicates three of the six chapters. In 'Jekyll and the Wolfman', as the chapter heading implies, he connects Stevenson's transformation narrative and its various film versions with other horror metamorphoses, including the Hammer horror movie *Dr Jekyll and Sister Hyde* (1971) and its role as 'adult' horror.

Vidler, Anthony, *Architectural Uncanny: Essays in the Modern Unhomely* (Cambridge, MA: MIT Press, 1992).
A first-class monograph taking its readers from the Burkeian sublime through to virtual reality. The book is subdivided into three sections, 'Houses', 'Bodies' and 'Spaces', but that apparently simple structure is replete with scholarship of extraordinary breadth and depth. Whether discussing Piranesi or the Office of Metropolitan Architecture in New York, Vidler's work is inspirational and educational in equal measure.

Wheatley, Helen, *Gothic Television* (Manchester: Manchester University Press, 2006).
This is an interesting study examining all aspects of television, from the

implications and attitudes expressed in memoranda by BBC executives to the use of camera-work and special effects. Wheatley convincingly outlines the difficulties of using the word 'Gothic' in the context of a medium in which neither audiences nor producers employ the term, and continues by examining a wide range of British and American television programmes, from *The Addams Family* and *The Munsters* to *Dr Who* and *Twin Peaks*.

Index

꩜